Perfect English Salon
普斐特英语慢阅读

ENGLISH SALON ABOUT BEAUTIFUL FAIRY TALES

寻找你心中的童话

成应翠 杨金鑫 主编

全国首套英语“慢阅读”，倾情打造，超值奉献，本套书**演讲、电影、童话、人物**全包括。

近**100**篇原汁原味的美丽英语文章、**300**多段地道英语、**400**多句名家肺腑之言、

近**300**个文化词详尽破解、近**100**篇“名人背后的故事”。

天天慢阅读，帮你将头脑中的“中文系统”转换为“英文系统”，

加强你的**“英文思考力”**！

哈爾濱工業大學出版社
HARBIN INSTITUTE OF TECHNOLOGY PRESS

图书编委会

图书在版编目(CIP)数据

寻找你心中的童话/成应翠等主编.—哈尔滨:哈尔滨工业大学出版社,2010.12
（普斐特英语慢阅读）
ISBN 978-7-5603-3146-1

Ⅰ.①寻…　Ⅱ.①成…　Ⅲ.①英语-汉语-对照读物②童话-作品集-世界　Ⅳ.①H319.4:Ⅰ

中国版本图书馆CIP数据核字(2010)第265301号

策划编辑　孙　杰　田　秋
责任编辑　孙　杰　田　秋
封面设计　嘉美和·设计
出版发行　哈尔滨工业大学出版社
社　　址　哈尔滨市南岗区复华四道街10号　邮编150006
传　　真　0451-86414749
网　　址　http://hitpress.hit.edu.cn
印　　刷　哈尔滨市石桥印务有限公司
开　　本　787mm×960mm　1/16　印张14　字数306千字
版　　次　2011年2月第1版　2011年2月第1次印刷
书　　号　ISBN 978-7-5603-3146-1
定　　价　28.00元

序
FOREWORD

在那个静谧的时代，人们茶余饭后吟诵勃朗宁夫人的十四行诗，那样的日子是爱书人最向往的读书日子；在冬季的深夜，放下窗帘，封了炉火，在沉静的灯光下，靠在椅上翻着白天买来的新书，那是读书大家叶灵凤读书的情景；在一个雪夜，坐在炉前，炉上的水壶铿铿作响，拿了数十本哲学、经济学、诗歌、传记的书，堆在长椅上，然后闲逸地拿起几本翻翻，找到一本爱读的书时，便细细品酌起来，那是文学大师林语堂的阅读生活……

我们怀念那个闲暇幽静、倾心"慢读"的年代，怀念那些曾让我们沉醉、让我们着迷的醇厚书香。然而，在当今这个"速读"时代，"慢读"已与我们渐行渐远，人们用吃快餐的方式对待阅读，希望用尽量少的时间把尽量多的信息储存到大脑里。针对这一现象，美国新罕布什尔大学的一位教授提出了**"慢阅读"**的概念，他希望通过"慢阅读"来帮助人们重新"琢磨"和"品味"文字。

"慢阅读"，光听听这个理念，就能让我们的心灵减减压；"慢阅读"，让我们缅怀那些闲散飘逸的时光；"慢阅读"，多么美妙的阅读方式……尽管我们的生活节奏越来越快，可是我们心中依旧在追寻"慢"时光。为了找到释放"慢"的情怀，传达"慢"的诉求，于是，我们怀揣一份美好的愿景，尝试将"慢阅读"理念引用到英语阅读上来，倾力打造并推出**《普斐特英语慢阅读系列》**。本套图书精选近百篇精粹文章，从励志、童话、电影、演讲等角度，很好地将"慢阅读"理念渗透到英语阅读中，其间或感人、或美好、或激情、或励志的篇章，值得你慢慢品读。

当英语遇到"慢阅读"，定能收获一份美妙的喜悦。

这里，有缤纷的西方文化，有优美的英文表达，有不屈的心灵，有引人深思的故事，有感人的经典瞬间，有催人奋进的语言……

《失败100次也坚决不倒》——读书一定要读那些最经典的东西，读励志故事也要读励志中的经典：脱口秀女王奥普拉·温芙瑞、坚强不屈的"超人"克里斯托弗·里夫、逆境中蜕变的爵士天后比莉·哈乐黛……让这些励志人物、励志话语冲刷我们疲惫且浮躁的心灵。微启书页，有他们伴你左右。

《寻找你心中的童话》——让5岁的孩子倾听童话；让15岁的少年阅读童话；让25岁的青年人品味童话；让35岁的成年人理解童话；让45～99岁的人思索和回味

童话……童话带给我们的不仅仅是温馨、欢乐和启迪，更多的是思考和品味。每一个童话都是一个美丽的梦：穿靴子的猫、丑小鸭的企盼、顽皮的匹诺曹、彼得兔的故事、世上唯一的玫瑰、糖果屋历险记……童话犹如一盏盏温暖的灯，照亮的不仅仅是我们的童年！

《当幸福来敲门》——穿越时空的隧道，重温《当幸福来敲门》的感人瞬间、《心灵捕手》的哲思睿语、《勇敢的心》中传奇人物的非凡魅力、《辛德勒的名单》中人性光辉的悲悯温情……每一部电影都是一场美妙绝伦的视听盛宴，一座文化的桥梁，英语电影从多角度展示了英语民族的文化。随书赠送的原声光盘，让你感受英语的永恒魅力。

《像他们那样激情演讲》——演讲是一种机智幽默激励人心的艺术，它把语言的美与生活的真完美地结合起来。在本书中你可以欣赏到美国著名演讲家鲁塞·康维尔的《钻石就在你家后院》、苹果公司创始人乔布斯的《我生命中的三个故事》、微软前总裁比尔·盖茨的《改变不公平》……这些演讲引经据典、古朴雄辩、机敏睿智、发人深思。

在“慢阅读”中品味生活，用英语了解世界，本套书将带你进入一个从容的慢读书状态：

1. 天天慢阅读，帮你寻回阅读的乐趣！本套书将引领你“工作再忙心不忙、生活再累心不累”的境界。

2. 激荡心灵的文字，启发你的“英文创造力”。本套书从你“最感兴趣”的话题出发，如充满智慧的小语、带给你希望的童话、蕴含文化积淀的故事……都是你可以任意拈来用于英文写作的素材。

3. 原汁原味的英文练习摹本，锻炼你的“英文组织力”。每一篇文章都是你最好的练习摹本，原汁原味的英文表达定会让你爱不释手。且每篇文章还有对文化点的解析，让你轻松学习无障碍。

4. 用英文品读精彩文字，加强你的“英文思考力”。彻底将头脑中的“中文系统”转换为“英文系统”，使你在不知不觉中学会了用英文思考问题！

编者

2010年圣诞于北京

目录

CONTENTS

Tale 1

Puss in Boots

穿靴子的猫

还记得那只在《怪物史莱克》系列第2集中的靴子猫吗？它可是人气最高的配角了，追溯起这只靴子猫的来历，还要从法国作家夏尔·佩罗的童话说起。《穿靴子的猫》中那只勇敢的猫就是这个高人气配角的原型。在佩罗的童话中，这只聪明的猫要帮助它穷困潦倒的主人翻身。于是它向主人要了一双靴子和一个布袋，穿过荆棘到森林里打猎。它把每次获得的猎物都献给了国王，它用机智和勇敢打败了富有的食人妖魔，最终帮助主人得到了国王的青睐和公主的爱慕。这只靴子猫的造型已经成为经典，下面，就让我们一起走近这只靴子猫的精彩吧！

慢阅读小语

细细品位字里行间流淌出的语言美和思想美，你就会感受到“Jump and get an apple”的喜悦，不知不觉间自身修养得到了提升……

1 **Do not look so sad, master. Just give me a bag and a pair of boots, and I will show you that you did not receive such a poor inheritance in me.**

我的主人，你用不着垂头丧气，只要你给我一个口袋，再让人给我做一双能穿着它在树丛中走动的靴子就行了。你会发现，你分得的这份财产并不是那么糟糕。

2 **The Cat's master had often seen him play a great many cunning tricks to catch rats and mice, as when he used to hang by the heels, or hide himself in the grain, and pretend to be dead; Thinking this over, he thought that it wasn't impossible that the cat could help him after all.**

猫的主人经常能看到这只猫在捉老鼠时总会想出很多狡猾的计策，比如，它总有办法藏在面粉里或是倒挂着装死。这位主人仔细想了想，说不定这只猫真的能帮到他呢。

3 **If you will follow my advice your fortune is made.**

如果你能照着我说的话做，你的好运气就会来了。

4 **If you do not tell the King that the meadow you mow belongs to my Lord Marquis of Carabas, those soldiers will chop you up like herbs for the pot.**

如果你们不对国王说这片草地属于卡拉巴司侯爵的话，士兵就会把你们像草一样剁碎，然后放入罐子里。

5 **Puss became a great lord, and never ran after mice any more, except for pleasure.**

从此以后，穿靴子的猫也成了大人物，它已经不再去捕捉老鼠了，即便见到它在捉老鼠，也不过是在消遣。

童话慢讲述：靴子猫的伟大计划

磨坊主的遗产

从前，有一个磨房主，死的时候给他的三个儿子留下的唯一财产仅仅是一个磨坊，一头驴和一只猫。老大拿走了磨坊，老二带走了那头驴，最后只有那只猫留给了老三。老三自然觉得委屈。可不管怎么说，这只猫还确实有点表演的天赋和狡猾的心眼。它要用行动向主人证明，他的这份财产可没想象得那么糟。

Once upon a time there was a poor miller who had three sons. The years went by and the miller died, leaving nothing but his mill, his donkey, and a cat. The eldest son took the mill, the second-born son rode off on the donkey, and the youngest son inherited the cat.

“Oh, well,” said the youngest son, “I'll eat this cat, and make some mittens out of his fur. Then I will have nothing left in the world and shall die of hunger.”

The Cat was listening to his master complain like this, but he pretended not to have heard anything. Instead, he put on a serious face and said:

“Do not look so sad, master. Just give me a bag and a pair of boots, and I will show you that you did not receive such a poor inheritance (遗产) in me.”

The Cat's master had often seen him play a great many cunning (狡猾的) tricks to catch rats and mice, as when he used to hang by the heels, or hide himself in the grain, and pretend to be dead; Thinking this over, he thought that it wasn't impossible that the cat could help him after all. And so he gave the cat his bag and spent his last pennies on ordering a fine pair of boots to be made especially for the cat.

靴子猫狩猎记

这只机灵的猫向主人要了一个口袋和靴子后，就踏上了它的神奇之旅。看这只猫多神气，它背着口袋、戴着帅气的帽子、穿着靴子，胸有成竹地和主人道别。这只穿靴子的猫有什么伟大的计划呢？秘密就在前方……

The cat looked very gallant（英勇的）in his boots, and putting his bag around his neck, he held the strings of it in his two forepaws and lay by a rabbit warren which was home to a great many rabbits.

He put bran（糠、麸）and corn into his bag, and stretching as if he were dead, he waited for some young rabbits, still not acquainted with the deceits of the world, to come and rummage（到处翻寻）in his bag for the bran and corn.

Not long after he lay down, he had what he wanted. A rash and foolish young rabbit jumped into his bag, and Monsieur Puss, immediately drew close the strings and caught him.

Proud of his prey, he went with it to the palace and asked to speak with his majesty. He was shown upstairs into the King's apartment, and, making a low bow, said to him: "I have brought you, sir, a rabbit of the warren, which my noble lord the **Marquis**（侯爵）of Carabas" (for that was the title which puss was pleased to give his master) "has commanded me to present to your majesty from him."

"Tell your master," said the king, "that I thank him and that he does me a great deal of pleasure."

Another time he went and hid himself among a corn field, holding still his bag open, and when a brace of partridges ran into it he drew the strings and so caught them both. He went and made a present of these to the king, as he had done before of the rabbit. The king, in like manner, received the partridges with great pleasure, and ordered him some money for drink.

Marquis 侯爵。侯爵是英国贵族爵位中的一种，在英国，除了英国王室以外，贵族分为五等，即公爵（duke）、侯爵（marquis）、伯爵（earl）、子爵（viscount）与男爵（baron）。侯爵这级爵号最初不被认可，到了15世纪，才被贵族们所看重，与其他4个等级的贵族相比，侯爵的数目一向最少。

安排主人与国王见面

3个月来，这只穿靴子的猫一直为国王送礼物，而且都以它主人的名义，这让国王对它的主人很好奇，很想认识一下这位有礼貌的主人。这对它的主人可不是什么好消息，主人的秘密会被揭穿吗？这次穿靴子的猫又要如何是好呢？

In this way, the Cat continued for two or three months to bring presents to the king, always saying that they were from his master, the Marquis of Carabas. One day in particular, he heard at the palace that the King was planning to drive in his carriage along the river-bank, taking with him his daughter, the most beautiful princess in the world. Puss in Boots said to his master.

"If you will follow my advice your fortune is made. You have nothing else to do but go and wash yourself in the river, in the place that I shall show you, and leave the rest to me."

The miller's son did what the Cat advised him to, without knowing why or wherefore. While he was washing the King passed by, and the Cat began to cry out:

"Help! Help! My Lord Marquis of Carabas is going to be drowned."

At this noise the King put his head out of the coach-window, and, finding it was the Cat who had so often brought him such good game, he commanded his guards to run immediately to the assistance of his Lordship the Marquis of Carabas. While they were drawing the poor Marquis out of the river, the Cat came up to the coach and told the King that, while his master was washing, there came by some rogues, who went off with his clothes, though he had cried out: "Thieves! Thieves!" several times, as loud as he could.

This cunning Cat had hidden the clothes under a great stone. The King immediately commanded the officers of his wardrobe to run and fetch one of his best suits for the Lord Marquis of Carabas.

靴子猫的聪明才智

不能不佩服这只穿靴子的猫，可是这些小伎俩能让国王和公主相信它的主人是富有的卡拉巴司侯爵吗？不用替它担心，穿靴子的猫总会有无穷的好点子，就连凶恶的吃人魔鬼都败在它的手下。

The King was very pleased to meet the Marquis of Carabas, and the fine clothes he had given him suited him extremely well, for although poor, he was a handsome and well built fellow. The King's daughter took a secret inclination to him, and the Marquis of Carabas had no sooner cast two or three respectful and somewhat tender glances but she fell in love with him to distraction. The King invited him to sit in the coach and ride along with them, with the lifeguards in glittering uniform trotting along side. The Cat, quite overjoyed to see his project begin to succeed, marched on before, and, meeting with some countrymen, who were mowing a meadow, he said to them:

"Good people, you who are mowing, if you do not tell the King that the meadow you mow belongs to my Lord Marquis of Carabas, those soldiers will chop you up like herbs for the pot."

The King did not fail asking of the mowers to whom the meadow they were mowing belonged.

"To my Lord Marquis of Carabas," answered they altogether, for the Cat's threats had made them terribly afraid.

"You see, sir," said the Marquis, "this is a meadow which never fails to yield a plentiful harvest every year."

The Master Cat, who went still on before, met with some reapers, and said to them: "Good people, you who are reaping, if you do not tell the King that all this corn belongs to

the Marquis of Carabas, you shall be chopped up like herbs for the pot."

The King, who passed by a moment after, wished to know to whom all that corn, which he then saw, did belong.

"To my Lord Marquis of Carabas," replied the reapers, and the King was very well pleased with it, as well as the Marquis, whom he congratulated.

Then the King said, "Let us now go to your **castle**."

The miller's son, not knowing what to reply, looked at puss who said: "If your Majesty will but wait an hour, I will go on before and order the castle to be made ready for you."

With that she jumped away and went to the castle of a great **ogre**（食人魔鬼）and asked to see him saying he could not pass so near his home without having the honor of paying his respects to him.

The ogre received him as civilly as an ogre could do, and made him sit down.

"I have been assured," said the Cat, "that you have the gift of being able to change yourself into all sorts of creatures as you wish; you can, for example, transform yourself into a lion, or elephant, and the like."

"That is true," answered the ogre very briskly; "and to convince you, you shall see me now become a lion."

Puss was so terrified at the sight of a lion so near him that he immediately climbed up the curtains, not without difficulty, because his

castle 城堡。城堡是欧洲中世纪的产物，欧洲贵族为争夺土地、粮食、牲畜、人口而不断爆发战争，密集的战争导致贵族们修建越来越多、越来越大的城堡，来守卫自己的领地。欧洲有十大著名城堡，英格兰的“利兹城堡”（Leeds Castle）、英格兰的“林肯城堡”（Lincoln Castle）、捷克共和国的“布拉格城堡”（Prague Castle）、葡萄牙的“圣乔治城堡”（Castelo de Sao Jorge）、西班牙的“阿尔卡萨尔城堡”（El Alcazar）、德国的“新天鹅堡”（Neuschwanstein Castle）、德国的“弗兰肯斯坦城堡”（Frankenstein Castle）、法国的“圣米歇尔山城堡”（Mont Saint-Michel）、法国的“尚博城堡”（Chateau de Chambord）、苏格兰的“格拉姆斯城堡”（Glamis Castle）。

ogre 食人魔鬼。食人魔鬼是欧洲神怪传说中的一个种族。传说食人魔鬼是巨大、丑恶、贪婪的生物，他们与其他怪物一起捕食弱者，总是靠暴力来解决问题。在英语中，“恶魔”的英语是devil，这个词很有趣，倒过来就是lived，所以有一句冷幽默的话就是“把“生活”倒着过，就是恶魔”。

boots were no use to him for climbing. A little while after, when Puss saw that the ogre had resumed his natural form, he came down, and admitted he had been very much frightened.

"However," said the cat, "I fear that you will not be able to save yourself even in the form of a lion, for the king is coming with his army and means to destroy you."

The ogre looked out of the window and saw the king waiting outside with his soldiers, and said, "What shall I do? How shall I save myself?"

Puss replied: "If you can also change yourself into something very small, then you can hide".

And in an instant, the ogre himself into a mouse, and began to run about the floor. Puss no sooner saw this but he fell upon him and ate him up.

梦想成真

能拥有如此聪明、忠诚的猫是每个主人梦寐以求的梦想，它的大智慧可一点都不比加菲猫少，甚至还多了几分潇洒。穿靴子的猫用自己的智慧和勇敢不仅为主人赢得了国王的赏识，也为主人赢得了美好的爱情。

Puss, who heard the noise of his Majesty's coach running over the draw-bridge, ran out, and said to the King:

"Your Majesty is welcome to this castle of my Lord Marquis of Carabas."

"What! My Lord Marquis," cried the King, "and does this castle also belong to you? There can be nothing finer than this court and all the stately buildings which surround it; let us go into it, if you please."

The Marquis gave his hand to the Princess, and followed the King, who went first. They passed into a spacious hall, where they found a magnificent rum punch, which the ogre had prepared for his friends, who were that very day to visit him. The friends, however dared not to enter, knowing that the King was there. His Majesty was perfectly charmed with the good qualities of my

Lord Marquis of Carabas, as was his daughter, who had fallen violently in love with him, and, seeing the vast estate he possessed, said to him, after having drunk five or six glasses:

"If you do not, my Lord Marquis, become my son in law, it will be of your own choosing."

The Marquis, making several low bows, accepted the honor which his Majesty conferred upon him, and forthwith, that very same day, married the Princess.

Puss became a great lord, and never ran after mice any more, except for pleasure.

背后的故事

《穿靴子的猫》传奇的延续

"穿靴子的猫"是《怪物史莱克》系列从第2集开始出现的人气很高的配角。梦工厂宣布将开拍以它为主角的动画片《穿靴子的猫》，并将于2012年3月20日上映。

其实和《怪物史莱克》中很多角色一样，"穿靴子的猫"也是来自经典童话里的著名角色，只不过在《怪物史莱克》中被小小的无厘头恶搞了一下。

"穿靴子的猫"原来的童话故事说的是一个磨坊主的小儿子从父亲那里继承了一只聪明的猫，这只猫穿上靴子帮助磨坊主的儿子得到了国王的赏识，并促成了他和公主的婚姻。不过在梦工厂版本的《穿靴子的猫》里，原来的童话可能会变得面目全非。为"穿靴子的猫"配音的安东尼奥·班德拉斯说他看过剧本了，他很喜欢这个剧本，而且他透露整个故事是原创的，将从"靴子猫"小时候讲起。观众会看到他为什么要当杀手、他是如何成为杀手的以及他又为什么放弃了这个行当。影片和《怪物史莱克》充满对流行文化的恶搞不同，将走另一条路，有点像史诗，有时还会非常感人。安东尼奥·班德拉斯还透露《穿靴子的猫》的剧本前后一共创作了3年，他相信观众看到影片会大吃一惊的，因为这和观众期待的会完全不同。

Tale 2

The Selfish Giant

自私的巨人

王尔德的每一个故事都是一首诗。有一次，王尔德给儿子讲故事，讲着讲着他流下了眼泪。儿子问他为什么要哭，他说："真正美丽的事物总会使人流下眼泪。"王尔德讲述的正是本文中的故事，有春天的地方是美好的，可为什么在巨人的花园里春天来得那么迟？是春天抛弃了巨人，还是巨人拒绝了春天？只要有爱的地方，就会有春天，只有懂得分享的人，才能拥有春天。

慢阅读小语

细细品位字里行间流淌出的语言美和思想美，你就会感受到“Jump and get an apple”的喜悦，不知不觉间自身修养得到了提升……

1 **Snow covered up the grass, and ice covered all the trees with silver.**

雪把草地盖得严严实实，霜也让所有的树木披上银装。

2 **The giant was lying in bed one morning when he heard some beautiful music. It was a little bird singing outside his window. It was so long since he had heard the song of a bird that it seemed to him the most beautiful music in the world.**

一日清晨，巨人躺在床上，这时耳边传来阵阵美妙的音乐。原来窗外唱歌的不过是一只小鸟，只因巨人好长时间没听到鸟儿在花园中歌唱，所以此刻感到它妙不可言。

3 **Now I know why the spring would not come here. I'll put the little boy on the top of the tree. Then I'll pull down the wall and my garden shall be a children's playground forever.**

现在我明白为什么春天不肯到我这儿来了。我要把那可怜的孩子抱上树，然后再把围墙都推倒，让我的花园永远成为孩子们的游戏场所。

4 **I have many beautiful flowers, but the children are the most beautiful flowers of all.**

我有好多美丽的鲜花，但孩子们才是最美的花朵。

5 **These are the wounds of love.**

这些都是爱的烙印。

巨人的美丽花园

巨人拥有一个很可爱的大花园，长满了绿茸茸的青草，美丽的鲜花随处可见，多得像天上的星星。在花园里还有12棵果树，一到春天，花儿香香，栖息在树枝上的鸟儿会唱出欢乐的曲子。

Every afternoon, as the children were coming back from school, they used to go and play in the **giant**'s **garden**.

It was a beautiful large garden. Beautiful flowers grew in the grass. There were twelve fruit trees. In the spring the fruit trees were covered with red and white flowers, and later in the year they bore rich fruit. The birds sang in the trees so sweetly that sometimes the children stopped their games and listened to them. "How happy we are here!" they cried to each other.

One day the giant came back. He had been away for seven years. When he arrived, he saw the children playing in his garden. "What are you doing here?" he cried in a very loud voice. The children ran away.

"My own garden is my own

giant 巨人。在古希腊神话中曾有过关于泰坦巨人的描述，他们一共6男6女，是天神乌拉诺斯和母亲大地女神的孩子。和巨人相对的人就是小矮人dwarf，著名的动画片《白雪公主和七个小矮人》Snow White and the Seven Dwarfs中七个小矮人的名字分别是：万事通（Doc）、害羞鬼（Bashful）、瞌睡虫（Sleepy）、喷嚏精（Sneezy）、开心果（Happy）、迷糊鬼（Dopey）、小生气（Grumpy）。

garden 花园。一般在欧洲，每家都有自己的私人花园，这些花园精巧别致，仿佛童话一样。除了欧洲拥有得天独厚的气候条件外，美丽的花园最终还得靠主人们的精心打造。在整理花园时，会用到一些工具，比如剪枝剪（pruning shears）、整篱剪（hedge shears）、伐木剪（tree shears）、高枝剪（long arm tree pruner）、扫地机（sweeper）、松土机（scarifier）、打草机（grass brusher/cutter）等。

garden," said the giant. "I will allow no one to play in it but myself." So he built a high wall round it and put up a notice: Keep out. He was a very selfish giant.

So the children had nowhere to play. They tried to play on the road, but the road was dusty（积满灰尘的）and full of hard stone, and they did not like it. They wandered（徘徊）round the high walls when their lessons were finished and talked about the beautiful garden inside. "How happy we were there!" they said to each other.

春天在哪里

春天来了，到处是一片春意盎然的景象，鲜花遍地，莺歌燕舞，可是在巨人的花园里却仍是一派残冬的景象。自私的巨人想不明白这是为什么，为什么他的花园没有春天？为什么他的花园失去了笑声？为什么他如此失落？

The spring came, and there were flowers and little birds all over the country. But in the garden of the Selfish Giant it was till winter the birds did not like to sing in it because there were no children, and the trees forgot to bear flowers. Snow covered up the grass, and ice covered all the trees with silver. The north wind came, and driving rain.

"I can't understand why the spring is so late in coming," said the Selfish Giant as he sat at the window of his house and looked out at his cold white garden. "I hope that there will be a change in the weather."

But the spring never came, nor the summer. When there was golden fruit in every other garden, there was no fruit in the giant's garden. It was always winter there with the north wind, and snow, and ice, and driving rain.

The giant was lying in bed one morning when he heard some beautiful music. It was a little bird singing outside his window. It was so long since he had heard the song of a bird that it seemed to him the most beautiful music in the world. Then the north wind and the rain stopped.

"I believe that spring has come at last!" said the giant. He jumped out of bed and looked out.

What did he see?

He saw a most wonderful sight. The children had come in through a hole in the wall and were sitting in the branches of the trees. There was a little child in every tree that he could see. The trees were so glad to have the children back that they had covered themselves with flowers: the birds were flying about and singing with joy, and flowers were looking up through the green grass.

A little boy was standing in the farthest corner of the garden. He was so small that he could not reach up to the branches（树枝）of the tree, but was wandering round it and weeping（哭泣）. That tree was still covered with ice and snow.

"How selfish I have been!" said the giant. "Now I know why the spring would not come here. I'll put the little boy on the top of the tree. Then I'll pull down the wall and my garden shall be a children's playground forever." He was really sorry for what he had done.

巨人找回了春天

因为有爱，所以不会惧怕寒冷；因为有爱，所以巨人的花园又充满了欢笑。孩子们又可以到巨人的花园里玩耍了，春天也随着孩子们一起回到了花园。美丽的故事也应有美丽的结尾，巨人也找到了美丽的春天。

So he went down: he opened the door very quietly, and went out into the garden. But, when the children saw him, they were afraid and ran away. Only the little boy did not run: his eyes were so full of tears that he did not see the giant coming. The giant came quietly behind him. He took the little boy gently in his hand and put him up into the tree. Then the tree was suddenly covered with flowers, and the birds came and sang in it, and the little boy put his arms round the giant's neck and kissed him.

The other children saw that giant was not bad and selfish now, so they came running back.

"It's your garden now, little

children," said the giant, and he pulled down the wall.

When the people were going along the road to the town, they found the giant playing with the children in the most beautiful garden they had ever seen.

The children played all day, and in the evening they came to the giant to say goodbye to him.

"But where is your little friend?" he said. "Where is the little boy I put in the tree?" The giant loved him best because the little boy had kissed him.

"We don't know," answered the children. " He has gone away."

"You must tell him to come tomorrow, he must come tomorrow."

"We don't know where he lives. We had never seen him before." The giant felt very sad.

Every afternoon when school ended, the children came and played with the giant. But the little boy whom the giant loved was never seen again. The giant was very kind to all the children, but he did want to see his first little friend. "How much I would like to see him!" he said.

许多年过去了，巨人变得年迈而体弱。他已无力再与孩子们一起嬉戏，只能坐在一把巨大的扶手椅上，一边观看孩子们玩游戏，一边欣赏着自己的花园。在他心中，无论花园中的花朵多么赏心悦目，都无法代替孩子们的欢声笑语，孩子们才是他心中最美丽的花朵。

Years went by, and the giant became very old and weak（虚弱）. He could not play in the garden now; so he sat in a big chair and watched the children at their games and looked at his beautiful garden. "I have many beautiful flowers," he said, "but the children are the most beautiful flowers of all."

One morning, when he was dressing himself, he looked out of the window. He did not hate the winter now, because he knew that the spring was sleeping and the flowers were resting: he knew that they would come again.

Suddenly he rubbed（擦、搓）his eyes; he looked again at the wonderful sight! In the farthest corner of the garden there was a tree quite covered with beautiful white flowers. Its branches were golden, and silver fruit hung down from them. And the little boy whom he loved was standing under the tree.

He ran out into the garden: he hurried across the grass and came near the child. When he came quite close, his face became red with anger and he said, "Who has dared to wound you?" There were marks on the child's hands, and on the little feet.

"Who had dared to wound you?" cried the giant. "Tell me and I will take my sword and kill him!"

"No," said the child, "These are the wounds（伤口）of love."

"Who are you?" said the giant. He was afraid, and knelt before the little child.

"You once let me play in your garden," said the child. "Today you'll come with me into my garden in **heaven**."

When the children came into the garden on that afternoon, they found the giant lying dead under the tree, covered with white flowers.

heaven 天堂。天堂的定义：根据基督教传统，这是唯一神祇与众天使、圣人居住的地方。一般，如果怀有敬虔的信仰并且一生无罪的人就有可能进入天堂。圣经中有关天堂的称呼很多，如，主的圣所——天堂、圣徒的国度、圣徒的家乡、圣徒安息日之处、圣徒的城邑。在英语中也可以用不同的词表示天堂，如City of God、land of the leal、paradise、pie in the sky、the upper regions。

背后的故事

王尔德的童话王国

奥斯卡·王尔德是19世纪英国最伟大的艺术家之一，他的剧作、诗歌、童话和小说有很多都很著名。在他那颓废唯美、猖狂放浪的表面姿态下，是一颗纯美纯善、永难泯灭的童心。而这可贵童心一经与卓绝才智结合，便诞生了《王尔德童话》。这部作品不仅证明了王尔德在文学界不可撼动的地位，更成为世界文学宝库中的传世佳作。王尔德的语言纯正优美堪称典范，而且他写的童话意境高洁悠远、益人心智，值得每一个童稚未凿的孩子阅读，也值得每一位童心未泯的成人赏阅。

王尔德的童话可以有不同的解读领悟，所以受到孩童和大人的双重喜爱：孩子们可以从节选的段落中看出天真、纯洁和美好，而成年人为真善美而感动的同时，更会因为体会到美丽童话背后那真正凄婉唯美的实质而落泪。“真正美的东西都是让人忧伤的。”这是作者在给自己的儿子讲《自私的巨人》时说的话，这也可以看作是对王尔德创作理念的一种诠释。

Tale 3

A Beautiful Mind

美丽心灵

—An Episode from The Happy Prince

——节选自《快乐王子》

快乐王子是美的化身。他的真诚、善良让我们油然而生敬意，而他悲惨的结局更是震撼着每一个人的心灵。每每读到此刻，每一位读者的心再也无法平静！小燕子跌倒在地的声音更是撞击着每一位读者的心灵。快乐王子那颗破裂成两半的铅心让人心痛不已，他为了别人的幸福而牺牲了自己。这种崇高，这种伟大，无法用言语来描绘，只能让我们心底的爱意慢慢升腾起来，内心的感动一点点弥漫开去……

慢阅读小语

细细品位字里行间流淌出的语言美和思想美，你就会感受到“Jump and get an apple”的喜悦，不知不觉间自身修养得到了提升……

1 **And now that I am dead they have set me up here so high that I can see all the ugliness and all the misery of my city, and though my heart is made of lead yet I cannot choose but weep.**

而眼下我死了，他们把我这么高高地立在这儿，使我能看见自己城市中所有的丑恶和贫苦，尽管我的心是铅做的，可我还是忍不住要哭。

2 **Dear Prince, I must leave you, but I will never forget you, and next spring I will bring you back two beautiful jewels in place of those you have given away. The ruby shall be redder than a red rose, and the sapphire shall be as blue as the great sea.**

亲爱的王子，我不得不离你而去了，只是我永远也不会忘记你的，明年春天我要给你带回两颗美丽的宝石，弥补你因送给别人而失掉的那两颗，红宝石会比一朵红玫瑰还红，蓝宝石也会比大海更蓝。

3 **Leaf after leaf of the fine gold the Swallow picked off, till the Happy Prince looked quite dull and grey. Leaf after leaf of the fine gold he brought to the poor...**

小燕子将足赤的黄金叶子一片一片地啄了下来，直到快乐王子变得灰暗无光。小燕子又把这些纯金叶片——送给了穷人……

4 **At that moment a curious crack sounded inside the statue, as if something had broken. The fact is that the leaden heart had snapped right in two. It certainly was a dreadfully hard frost.**

就在此刻，雕像体内发出一声奇怪的爆裂声，好像有什么东西破碎了。其实是王子的那颗铅做的心裂成了两半。这的确是一个可怕的寒冷冬日。

与快乐王子的美丽邂逅

快乐王子的雕像高高地耸立在城市上空，他潇洒地站在一根高大的石柱上面。他浑身上下镶满了薄薄的黄金叶片，他的双眼是由明亮的蓝宝石做成的，他的剑柄上还嵌着一颗硕大的红色宝石，红宝石在阳光下熠熠发光。城市的每一位市民都羡慕快乐王子的快乐，也被他的美丽所倾倒。

High above the city, on a tall column, stood the statue of the Happy Prince. He was gilded all over with thin leaves of fine gold, for eyes he had two bright sapphires（蓝宝石）, and a large red ruby glowed on his sword-hilt.

He was very much admired indeed. "He is as beautiful as a weathercock（风标）," remarked one of the Town Councillors who wished to gain a reputation for having artistic tastes; "only not quite so useful," he added, fearing lest people should think him unpractical, which he really was not.

"Why can't you be like the Happy Prince?" asked a sensible mother of her little boy who was crying for the moon. "The Happy Prince never dreams of crying for anything."

"I am glad there is someone in the world that is quite happy," muttered a disappointed man as he gazed at the wonderful statue.

"He looks just like an **angel**," said the Charity Children as they came out of the **cathedral** in their bright scarlet

angel 天使。原意是神的使者，在中世纪的天使学中，天使分为九个级别，按等级从最高到最低依次是：炽爱天使，普智天使，宝座天使，统治天使，美德天使，制权天使，天使长，大天使和天使。由于天使的形象多为带翅膀的少女或小孩子，于是现在常用“天使”来比喻天真可爱的人。与angel有关的谚语有两个，一个是rush in where angels fear to tread，指“胆大妄为，愚蠢而自负地去冒险”；还有一个是Speak of angels, and you will hear their wings. 指“说到某人，某人就到。”与汉语中的“说曹操，曹操就到。”相似，另外，在这个谚语中speak也可以换成talk。

cathedral 教堂。教堂是进行宗教仪式的场所，一般特指西方宗教，包括天主教、东正教、新教等。教堂建筑分四个等级：小堂/礼拜堂、圣堂/礼拜堂、座堂、大殿/圣殿，其中座堂为cathedral，为教区的主教所在地。我们熟悉的church是泛指基督教的教堂，而“小礼拜堂”用chapel。

cloaks and their clean white pinafores.

"How do you know?" said the Mathematical Master, "you have never seen one."

"Ah! But we have, in our dreams," answered the children; and the Mathematical Master frowned and looked very severe, for he did not approve of children dreaming.

天使物语

一只燕子飞到了这座城市，来到了快乐王子的身边。前世500次的回眸才换得今生的擦肩而过，燕子和快乐王子将是一种怎样的相遇、相知？冥冥中的安排，让他们有了爱，这只燕子是天使派来的使者吗？还是天使落入了人间？

One night there flew over the city a little Swallow. His friends had gone away to Egypt six weeks before. "Where shall I put up?" he said; "I hope the town has made preparations."

Then he saw the statue on the tall column.

"I will put up there," he cried; "it is a fine position, with plenty of fresh air." So he alighted just between the feet of the Happy Prince.

"I have a golden bedroom," he said softly to himself as he looked round, and he prepared to go to sleep; but just as he was putting his head under his wing a large drop of water fell on him. "What a curious thing!" he cried; "there is not a single cloud in the sky, the stars are quite clear and bright, and yet it is raining. The climate in the north of Europe is really dreadful. The Reed used to like the rain, but that was merely her selfishness."

Then another drop fell.

"What is the use of a statue if it cannot keep the rain off?" he said; "I must look for a good chimney-pot," and he determined to fly away.

But before he had opened his wings, a third drop fell, and he looked up, and saw – Ah! What did he see?

The eyes of the Happy Prince were filled with tears, and tears were running down his golden cheeks. His face was so beautiful in the moonlight that the little Swallow was filled with pity.

"Who are you?" he said.

"I am the Happy Prince."

"Why are you weeping then?"

asked the Swallow; "you have quite drenched me."

"When I was alive and had a human heart," answered the statue, "I did not know what tears were, for I lived in the Palace of Sans-Souci（无忧宫）, where sorrow is not allowed to enter. In the daytime I played with my companions in the garden, and in the evening I led the dance in the Great Hall. Round the garden ran a very lofty wall, but I never cared to ask what lay beyond it, everything about me was so beautiful. My courtiers called me the Happy Prince, and happy indeed I was, if pleasure be happiness. So I lived, and so I died. And now that I am dead they have set me up here so high that I can see all the ugliness and all the misery of my city, and though my heart is made of lead yet I cannot choose but weep."

"What! Is he not solid gold?" said the Swallow to himself. He was too polite to make any personal remarks out loud.

快乐王子继续用低缓而悦耳的声音继续讲述着："远处的一条小街上住着一户穷人。一扇窗户开着，透过窗户我能看见一个女人坐在桌旁。她那瘦削的脸上布满了倦意，一双粗糙发红的手上到处是针眼，因为她是一个裁缝。在房间角落里的一张床上躺着她生病的孩子。孩子在发烧，嚷着要吃桔子。可是他的妈妈除了给他喂几口河水外什么也没有……"善良的快乐王子对这对贫穷的母子是不会置之不理的，于是他向小燕子提出了他的第一个请求"你不肯陪我过一夜，做我的信使吗？"

"Far away," continued the statue in a low musical voice, "far away in a little street there is a poor house. One of the windows is open, and through it I can see a woman seated at a table. Her face is thin and worn, and she has coarse, red hands, all pricked by the needle, for she is a seamstress. She is embroidering passion-flowers（西番莲）on a satin gown for the loveliest of the Queen's maids-of- honour to wear at the next Court-**ball**. In a bed in the corner of the room her little boy

She is embroidering passion-flowers on a satin gown for the loveliest of the Queen's maids-of-honour to wear at the next Court-ball. 这句的意思是"她正在给缎子衣服上绣西番莲花，这件衣服是为皇后最喜欢的宫女准备的，宫女要在下一次宫廷舞会上穿这件衣服。"

ball 舞会。舞会是西方一种正式的跳舞的集会，参加者要穿着晚礼服等正装，整场舞会中很大的一部分由交际舞构成。在美国一般用prom表示舞会，英国用dance party，而ball是通用的舞会称呼。说起ball，就不能不说ball的一个习语：have a ball at one's feet，意思是对某人看好，深信某人有机会成功。

is lying ill. He has a fever, and is asking for oranges. His mother has nothing to give him but river water, so he is crying. Swallow, Swallow, little Swallow, will you not bring her the ruby out of my sword-hilt? My feet are fastened to this pedestal and I cannot move."

"I am waited for in Egypt," said the Swallow. "My friends are flying up and down the Nile, and talking to the large lotus-flowers. Soon they will go to sleep in the tomb of the great King. The King is there himself in his painted coffin. He is wrapped in yellow linen, and embalmed with spices. Round his neck is a chain of pale green jade, and his hands are like withered leaves."

"Swallow, Swallow, little Swallow," said the Prince, "will you not stay with me for one night, and be my messenger? The boy is so thirsty, and the mother so sad."

"I don't think I like boys," answered the Swallow. "Last summer, when I was staying on the river, there were two rude boys, the miller's sons, who were always throwing stones at me. They never hit me, of course; we swallows fly far too well for that, and besides, I come of a family famous for its agility; but still, it was a mark of disrespect."

But the Happy Prince looked so sad that the little Swallow was sorry. "It is very cold here," the little swalllow said; "but I will stay with you for one night, and be your messenger."

"Thank you, little Swallow," said the Prince.

So the Swallow picked out the great ruby from the Prince's sword, and flew away with it in his beak over the roofs of the town.

He passed by the cathedral tower, where the white marble angels were sculptured. He passed by the palace and heard the sound of dancing. A beautiful girl came out on the balcony with her lover. "How wonderful the stars are," he said to her, "and how wonderful is the power of love!"

"I hope my dress will be ready in time for the State-ball," she answered; "I have ordered passion-flowers to be embroidered on it; but the seamstresses are so lazy."

He passed over the river, and saw the lanterns hanging to the masts of the ships. He passed over the Ghetto（犹太人区）, and saw the old Jews bargaining with each other, and weighing out money in copper scales. At last he came to the poor house and looked in. The boy was tossing feverishly on his bed, and the mother had fallen asleep, she was so tired. In he hopped, and laid the great ruby on the table beside the woman's thimble（顶针）. Then he flew gently round the bed, fanning the boy's forehead with his wings. "How cool I feel," said the boy, "I must be getting better"; and he sank into a delicious slumber.

Then the Swallow flew back to the Happy Prince, and told him what he had done. "It is curious," he remarked, "but I feel quite warm now, although it is so cold."

"That is because you have done a good action," said the Prince. And the little Swallow began to think, and then he fell asleep. Thinking always made him sleepy.

爱的陪伴

小燕子被快乐王子的善良感动了，他决定再陪王子一夜。他又会遇到怎样的感动呢？快乐王子变得不再英俊，但是他那颗铅做的心却越来越温暖。快乐王子失去了眼睛，但是他的心就是他的眼睛。

When day broke he flew down to the river and had a bath. "What a remarkable phenomenon," said the Professor of Ornithology as he was passing over the bridge. "A swallow in winter!" And he wrote a long letter about it to the local newspaper. Every one quoted it, it was full of so many words that they could not understand.

"To-night I go to Egypt," said the Swallow, and he was in high spirits at the prospect. He visited all the public monuments, and sat a long time on top of the church steeple. Wherever he went the Sparrows chirruped, and said to each other, "What a distinguished stranger!" so he enjoyed himself very much.

When the moon rose he flew back to the Happy Prince. "Have you any commissions for Egypt?" he cried; "I am just starting."

"Swallow, Swallow, little Swallow," said the Prince, "will you not stay with me one night longer?"

"I am waited for in Egypt," answered the Swallow. "To-morrow my friends will fly up to the Second Cataract. The river-horse couches there among the bulrushes, and on a great granite throne sits the God Memnon. All night long he watches the stars, and when the morning star shines he utters one cry of joy, and then he is silent. At noon the yellow lions come down to the water's edge to drink. They have eyes like green beryls, and their roar is louder than the roar of the cataract.

"Swallow, Swallow, little Swallow," said the Prince, "far away across the city I see a young man in a garret. He is leaning over a desk covered with papers, and in a tumbler by his side there is a bunch of withered violets. His hair is brown and crisp, and his lips are red as a pomegranate, and he has large and dreamy eyes. He is trying to finish a play for the Director of the Theatre, but he is too cold to write any more. There is no fire in the grate, and hunger has made him faint."

"I will wait with you one night longer," said the Swallow, who really had a good heart. "Shall I take him another ruby?"

"Alas! I have no ruby now," said the Prince; "my eyes are all that I have left. They are made of rare sapphires, which were brought out of India a thousand years ago. Pluck out one of them and take it to him. He will sell it to the jeweller, and buy food and firewood, and finish his play."

"Dear Prince," said the Swallow, "I cannot do that"; and he began to weep.

"Swallow, Swallow, little Swallow," said the Prince, "do as I command you."

So the Swallow plucked out the Prince's eye, and flew away to the student's garret. It was easy enough to get in, as there was a hole in the roof. Through this he darted, and came

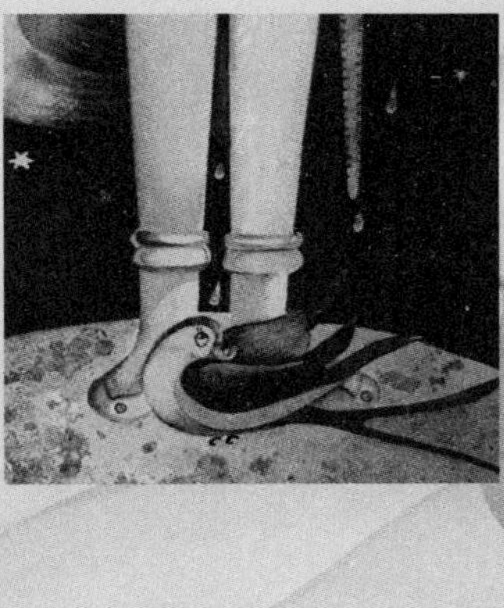

into the room. The young man had his head buried in his hands, so he did not hear the flutter of the bird's wings, and when he looked up he found the beautiful sapphire lying on the withered violets.

"I am beginning to be appreciated," he cried; "this is from some great admirer. Now I can finish my play," and he looked quite happy.

小燕子的每次道别都不成功，因为他无法拒绝快乐王子的请求。他自己也慢慢地爱上了快乐王子的请求，甚至冥冥中似乎有什么力量牵动着他，让他无法离开快乐王子。其实，那种让小燕子弄不明白的力量是爱，只有那些拥有爱心的人才懂得如何去爱别人。

The next day the Swallow flew down to the harbour. He sat on the mast of a large vessel and watched the sailors hauling big chests out of the hold with ropes. "Heave a-hoy!" they shouted as each chest came up. "I am going to Egypt!" cried the Swallow, but nobody minded, and when the moon rose he flew back to the Happy Prince.

"I am come to bid you good-bye," he cried.

"Swallow, Swallow, little Swallow," said the Prince, "will you not stay with me one night longer?"

"It is winter," answered the Swallow, "and the chill snow will soon be here. In Egypt the sun is warm on the green palm-trees, and the crocodiles lie in the mud and look lazily about them. My companions are building a nest in the Temple of Baalbec, and the pink and white doves are watching them, and cooing to each other. Dear Prince, I must leave you, but I will never forget you, and next spring I will bring you back two beautiful jewels in place of those you have given away. The ruby shall be redder than a red rose, and the sapphire shall be as blue as the great sea."

"In the square below," said the Happy Prince, "there stands a little match-girl. She has let her matches fall in the gutter, and they are all spoiled. Her father will beat her if she does not bring home some money, and she is crying. She has no shoes or stockings, and her little head is bare. Pluck out my other eye, and give it to her, and her father will not beat her."

"I will stay with you one night longer," said the Swallow, "but I cannot pluck out your eye. You would be quite blind then."

"Swallow, Swallow, little Swallow," said the Prince, "do as I command you."

So he plucked out the Prince's other eye, and darted down with it. He swooped past the match-girl, and slipped the jewel into the palm of her hand. "What a lovely bit of glass," cried the little girl; and she ran home, laughing.

Then the Swallow came back to the Prince. "You are blind now," he said, "so I will stay with you always."

"No, little Swallow," said the poor Prince, "you must go away to Egypt."

"I will stay with you always," said the Swallow, and he slept at the Prince's feet.

在寒冷的冬日，小燕子坐在快乐王子的肩头，为快乐王子讲述着他所看到的一切。"请把我身上的金片取下，送给那些穷人。"这是快乐王子对小燕子的最后请求。小燕子会接受快乐王子的请求吗？生活在冬日的小燕子又将有怎样的归宿呢?

All the next day he sat on the Prince's shoulder, and told him stories of what he had seen in strange lands. He told him of the red ibises, who stand in long rows on the banks of the Nile, and catch gold-fish in their beaks; of the Sphinx, who is as old as the world itself, and lives in the desert, and knows everything; of the merchants, who walk slowly by the side of their camels, and carry amber beads in their hands; of the King of the Mountains of the Moon, who is as black as ebony, and worships a large crystal; of the great green snake that sleeps in a palm-tree, and has twenty priests to feed it with honey-cakes; and of the pygmies who sail over a big lake on large flat leaves, and are always at war with the butterflies.

"Dear little Swallow," said the Prince, "you tell me of marvellous things, but more marvellous than anything is the suffering of men and of women. There is no Mystery so great as Misery. Fly over my city, little Swallow, and tell me what you see there."

So the Swallow flew over the great city, and saw the rich making merry in their beautiful houses, while the beggars were sitting at the gates. He flew into dark lanes, and saw the white faces of starving children looking out listlessly at the black streets. Under the archway（拱道）of a bridge two little boys were lying in one another's arms to try and keep themselves warm. "How hungry we are!" they said. "You must not lie here," shouted the Watchman, and

they wandered out into the rain.

Then he flew back and told the Prince what he had seen.

"I am covered with fine gold," said the Prince, "you must take it off, leaf by leaf, and give it to my poor; the living always think that gold can make them happy."

Leaf after leaf of the fine gold the Swallow picked off, till the Happy Prince looked quite dull and grey. Leaf after leaf of the fine gold he brought to the poor, and the children's faces grew rosier, and they laughed and played games in the street. "We have bread now!" they cried.

Then the snow came, and after the snow came the frost. The streets looked as if they were made of silver, they were so bright and glistening; long icicles like crystal daggers hung down from the eaves of the houses, everybody went about in furs, and the little boys wore scarlet caps and skated on the ice.

The poor little Swallow grew colder and colder, but he would not leave the Prince, he loved him too well. He picked up crumbs outside the baker's door when the baker was not looking and tried to keep himself warm by flapping his wings.

But at last he knew that he was going to die. He had just strength to fly up to the Prince's shoulder once more. "Good-bye, dear Prince!" he murmured, "will you let me kiss your hand?"

"I am glad that you are going to Egypt at last, little Swallow," said the Prince, "you have stayed too long here; but you must kiss me on the lips, for I love you."

"It is not to Egypt that I am going," said the Swallow. "I am going to the House of Death. Death is the brother of Sleep, is he not?"

And he kissed the Happy Prince on the lips, and fell down dead at his feet.

At that moment a curious crack sounded inside the statue, as if something had broken. The fact is that the leaden heart had snapped right in two. It certainly was a dreadfully hard frost.

背后的故事

真实的痛苦好过虚假的快乐——《快乐王子》

《快乐王子》中讲述了生之欢愉死后悲悯世人的王子，絮絮叨叨真诚善良的小燕子，俗不可耐趋炎附势的大小官员，日夜挣扎难见光明的穷苦人们，共同构成的一段故事，就像快乐王子身上的一片金叶子或一粒蓝宝石，长久地闪闪发光。

快乐王子穷其一生都在追寻快乐、享受快乐，人生对他来说不过是一场由自己做主的盛宴。他不去希望，因为从来不会失望；他不去索求，因为从来不必付出。如果思考不能使他感到快乐，他一定拒绝行使这份权利。因此，他快乐时，世界都为他快乐，他死后，他的快乐便只能成为供人景仰的标本，凄美地立在城市上方，任何人无法复制。快乐王子在死后改变了自己的高度，也断然否定了过去的自己。他不再快乐，他很痛苦，因为他发觉原来世界并不是逍遥自在的王宫，原来自己过去的快乐是那样没心没肺。世界观的颠覆是可怕的，王子付出的代价是粉身碎骨。但也许对他来说，真实的痛苦好过虚假的快乐。

在生活中，可能有许多快乐是因为无知，因为懵懂。就如人生中永不能复来的童年，让人一生留恋的不就是那份茫然无知、所以无畏的快乐吗？可是渐渐长大了，就必须勇敢地接受生活中的种种痛，宁愿选择清醒的痛楚，也不要在自己或别人的围墙内麻痹了自己真实的感觉。接受，然后面对；改变，或许被改变。如果你的快乐是真实的，请珍惜它，呵护它，哪怕它像入口即化的冰淇淋，甜在舌尖也只一瞬；如果有份痛苦是真实的，是成长必须经历的挣扎与痛，那也请珍惜它，呵护它，哪怕它会像一把锯着心灵的钝刀，痛在心里绵长而细密。都是好的，五味俱全才是生活，只要你拥有自己真实的感受，就是好的。

Tale 4

The Ugly Ducking's Dream

丑小鸭的企盼

—An Episode from The Ugly Duckling

——节选自《丑小鸭》

丑小鸭历经千辛万苦、重重磨难之后变成了白天鹅。是金子早晚会发光。命运其实没有轨迹，关键在于对美好境界、美好理想的追求。人生中的挫折和痛苦是不可避免的，要学会把它们踩在脚下，每个人都会有一份属于自己的梦想，只要学会树立生活目标，在自信、拼搏中，人们会真正的认识到自己原来也可以变成“白天鹅”，也可以像丑小鸭一样实现心中的梦想。

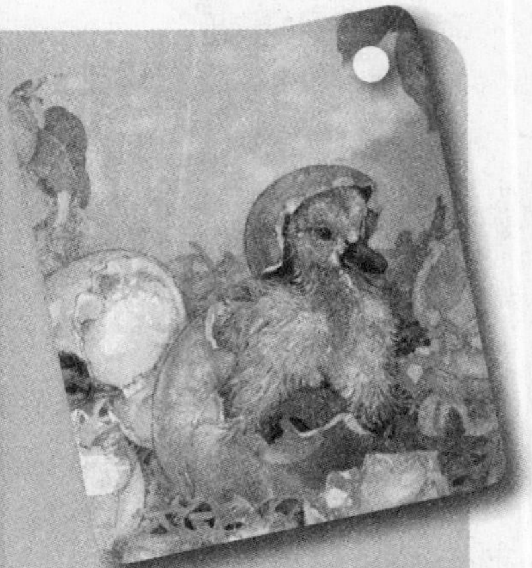

慢阅读小语

细细品位字里行间流淌出的语言美和思想美，你就会感受到“Jump and get an apple”的喜悦，不知不觉间自身修养得到了提升……

1 **The duckling had never seen birds so beautiful. They were dazzling white, with long graceful necks. They were swans.**
小鸭从来没有看到过这样美丽的东西，他们白得发亮，颈项又长又柔软。这就是天鹅。

2 **He could not forget them–those splendid, happy birds. When he could no longer see them he dived to the very bottom. And when he came up again he was quite beside himself. He did not know what birds they were or whither they were bound, yet he loved them more than anything he had ever loved before.**
他再也忘记不了这些美丽的鸟儿，这些幸福的鸟儿。当他看不见他们的时候，就沉入水底；但是当他再冒到水面上来的时候，却感到非常空虚。他不知道这些鸟儿的名字，也不知道他们要向什么地方飞去。不过他爱他们，好像他从来还没有爱过什么东西似的。

3 **Being born in a duck yard does not matter, if only you are hatched from a swan's egg.**
只要你曾经在一只天鹅蛋里呆过，就算你是生在养鸭厂里也没有什么关系。

4 **He felt quite glad that he had come through so much trouble and misfortune, for now he had a fuller understanding of his own good fortune, and of beauty when he met with it.**
对于过去所受的不幸和苦恼，他现在感到非常高兴。他清楚地认识到幸福和美好正在向他招手。

5 **He felt so very happy, but he wasn't at all proud, for a good heart never grows proud.**
他感到太幸福了，但他一点也不骄傲，因为拥有一颗美好心灵的人是永远都不会骄傲的。

丑小鸭出生了

乡下真是非常美丽。这正是夏天！小麦是金黄的，燕麦是绿油油的，干草在绿色的牧场上堆成垛。鸭妈妈正忙着孵小鸭，每一个未知的小生命都是她的希望。她的孩子似乎听到了妈妈的呼唤，争先恐后地来到这个世上，可是有一个小生命似乎和鸭妈妈捉迷藏，迟迟不肯从蛋壳里爬出来。

It was so beautiful out on the country, it was summer—the wheat fields were golden, the oats were green, and down among the green meadows the hay was stacked. There the stork minced about on his red legs, clacking away in **Egyptian**, which was the language his mother had taught him. Round about the field and meadow lands rose vast forests, in which deep lakes lay hidden. Yes, it was indeed lovely out there in the country.

In the midst of the sunshine there stood an old manor house that had a deep moat around it. From the walls of the manor（庄园）right down to the water's edge great **burdock**（牛蒡）leaves grew, and there were some so tall that little children could stand upright beneath the biggest of them. In this wilderness of leaves, which was as dense as the forests itself, a duck sat on her nest, hatching her ducklings. She was becoming somewhat weary, because sitting is such a dull business and scarcely anyone came to see her.

At last the eggshells began to crack, one after another. "Peep, peep!" said the little things, as they

Egyptian 埃及人。埃及人又称"埃及阿拉伯人"，是古埃及人的直接后裔。古埃及人是非洲大陆最古老的民族，曾创造了光辉灿烂的文化，其发祥地为尼罗河中游。埃及人也是非洲最大的民族，属欧罗巴人种地中海类型，使用阿拉伯语，属闪含语系闪米特语族。埃及人是典型的阿拉伯文化继承者，他们的风俗习惯多渊源于阿拉伯文化的影响。

burdock 牛蒡。牛蒡原产于中国，有"东洋参"的美誉。牛蒡全身是宝，富含菊糖、纤维素、蛋白质、钙、磷、铁等人体所需的各种矿物质、氨基酸等，牛蒡所含的胡萝卜素比胡萝卜高280倍，堪称蔬菜之王。

came to life and poked out their heads. But the biggest egg still lies here. The mother duck was really rather tired of it all. At last the big egg did crack. "Peep," said the young one, and out he tumbled, but he was so big and ugly.

备受欺辱的丑小鸭

迟到的小家伙终于从蛋壳里探出了脑袋，但是他又大又丑。只因为他"丑"，便"处处挨啄，被排挤，被讪笑"，遭遇"一天比一天更糟"。在鸭场，其他鸭子会无缘无故就啄他的头，就连被公认为最有声望的人也和鸭妈妈说"希望能把他再孵一次"。丑小鸭默默地忍受着一切……

The mother duck took a look at him. "That's a frightfully big duckling," she said. "He doesn't look the least like the others. Can he really be a turkey baby? Well, well! I'll soon find out. Into the water he shall go, even if I have to shove him in myself."

Next day the weather was perfectly splendid, and the sun shone down on all the green burdock leaves. The mother duck led her whole family down to the moat. Splash! She took to the water. "Quack, quack," said she, and one duckling after another plunged in. The water went over their heads, but they came up in a flash, and floated to perfection. Their legs worked automatically, and they were all there in the water. Even the big, ugly gray one was swimming along.

"Why, that's no turkey," she said. "See how nicely he uses his legs, and how straight he holds himself. He's my very own son after all, and quite good-looking if you look at him properly. Quack! Quack! Come with me. I'll lead you out into the world and introduce you to the duck yard. But keep close to me so that you won't get stepped on, and watch out for the cat!"

Thus they sallied into the duck yard, where all was in an uproar because two families were fighting over the head of an eel. But the cat got it, after all.

"You see, that's the way of the world." The mother duck licked her bill because she wanted the eel's（鳗鱼）head for herself. "Stir your legs. Bustle about（忙碌）, and mind that you bend your necks to that old duck over there. She's the noblest of us all, and has Spanish blood in her. That's why she's so fat. See that red rag around her leg? That's a wonderful thing, and the highest distinction a duck can get. It shows that they don't want to lose her, and that she's to have special attention from man and beast. Shake yourselves! Don't turn your toes in. A well-bred duckling turns his toes way out, just as his father and mother do–this way. So then! Now duck your necks and say quack!"

They did as she told them, but the other ducks around them looked on and said right out loud, "See here! Must we have this brood too, just as if there weren't enough of us already? And–fie! what an ugly-looking fellow that duckling is! We won't stand for him." One duck charged up and bit his neck.

"Let him alone," his mother said. "He isn't doing any harm."

"Possibly not," said the duck who bit him, "but he's too big and strange, and therefore he needs a good whacking."

"What nice-looking children you have, Mother," said the old duck with the rag around her leg. "They are all pretty except that one. He didn't come out so well. It's a pity you can't hatch him again."

"That can't be managed, your ladyship," said the mother. "He isn't so handsome, but he's as good as can be, and he swims just as well as the rest, or, I should say, even a little better than they do. I hope his looks will improve with age, and after a while he won't seem so big. He took too long in the egg, and that's why his figure isn't all that it should be." She pinched his neck and preened his feathers. "Moreover, he's a drake, so it won't matter so much. I think he will be quite strong, and I'm sure he will amount to something."

离家出走的丑小鸭

可怜的丑小鸭受尽大家的欺负，妈妈对她的爱是他唯一留恋的东西，也是他不愿离开的理由。但是，他有自己的梦想。当他妈妈也不再爱他的时候，他选择了离家出走，去追求自由。于是他飞过篱笆，一口气跑到野鸭住的沼泽地，在那里度过了孤独的一夜。

On the duck yard, the poor duckling who had been the last one out of his egg, and who looked so ugly, was pecked and pushed about and made fun of by the ducks, and the chickens as well. "He's too big," said they all. The turkey gobbler, who thought himself an emperor because he was born wearing spurs, puffed up like a ship under full sail and bore down upon him, gobbling and gobbling until he was red in the face. The poor duckling did not know where he dared stand or where he dared walk. He was so sad because he was so desperately ugly, and because he was the laughing stock of the whole barnyard.

So it went on the first day, and after that things went from bad to worse. The poor duckling was chased and buffeted about by everyone. Even his own brothers and sisters abused him. "Oh," they would always say, "how we wish the cat would catch you, you ugly thing." And his mother said, "How I do wish you were miles away." The ducks nipped him, and the hens pecked him, and the girl who fed them kicked him with her foot.

So he ran away; and he flew over the fence. The little birds in the bushes darted up in a fright. "That's because I'm so ugly," he thought, and closed his eyes, but he ran on just the same until he reached the great marsh where the wild ducks lived. There he lay all night long, weary and disheartened.

丑小鸭“走到广大的世界里去”、享受自由生活的理想始终坚定不移。一天，丑小鸭看到一群美丽的鸟，丑小鸭看到这些鸟儿就莫名地兴奋，更让他吃惊的是他竟然也能发出和美丽鸟儿一样的叫声。从那以后，丑小鸭再也忘不了这些鸟儿了。斗转星移，四季轮回，丑小鸭经受了“严冬”的“困苦和灾难”，他能否迎来“一个美丽的春天”呢？

Autumn came on. The leaves in

the forest turned yellow and brown. The wind took them and whirled them about. The heavens looked cold as the low clouds hung heavy with snow and hail. Perched（栖息）on the fence, the raven screamed, "Caw, caw!" and trembled with cold. It made one shiver to think of it. Pity the poor little duckling!

One evening, just as the sun was setting in splendor, a great flock of large, handsome birds appeared out of the reeds. The duckling had never seen birds so beautiful. They were dazzling white, with long graceful necks. They were **swans**. They uttered a very strange cry as they unfurled their magnificent wings to fly from this cold land, away to warmer countries and to open waters. They went up so high, so very high, that the ugly little duckling felt a strange uneasiness come over him as he watched them. He went around and round in the water, like a wheel. He craned his neck to follow their course, and gave a cry so shrill and strange that he frightened himself. Oh! He could not forget them–those splendid, happy birds. When he could no longer see them he dived to the very bottom. And when he came up again he was quite beside himself. He did not know what birds they were or whither they were bound, yet he loved them more than anything he had ever loved before. It was not that he envied them, for how could he ever dare dream of wanting their marvelous beauty for himself? He would have been grateful if only the ducks would have tolerated him–the poor ugly creature.

The winter grew cold—so bitterly cold that the duckling had to swim to and fro in the water to keep it from freezing over. But every night the hole in which he swam kept getting smaller

swans 天鹅。东方文化和西方文化不约而同地把白色的天鹅作为纯洁、忠诚、高贵的象征。天鹅一词最早出现于唐朝李商隐的诗句"拨弦警火凤，交扇拂天鹅"。和swan相关的习惯用语有两个，一个是All your swans are geese.意思是"语言全落空，希望成泡影。"另一个是as graceful as a swan，字面意思是"像天鹅一样优雅"，引申为"姿态优美，举止端庄"。

and smaller. Then it froze so hard that the duckling had to paddle（划水）continuously to keep the crackling ice from closing in upon him. At last, too tired to move, he was frozen fast in the ice.

But it would be too sad to tell of all the hardships and wretchedness he had to endure during this cruel winter. When the warm sun shone once more, the duckling was still alive among the reeds of the marsh. The larks began to sing again. It was beautiful springtime.

丑小鸭的华丽转身

百灵鸟唱起了春天的歌，春天又回到了大地怀抱。春天会给任何人带来希望和幸福，对于丑小鸭也不例外。丑小鸭已经不是那只又丑又令人讨厌的小鸭子了，清澈的湖水映出他的俊美。丑小鸭的春天充满了无限的美好，正如丑小鸭说的"我做梦都没有想到会有这么多的幸福。"

Then, quite suddenly, he lifted his wings. They swept through the air much more strongly than before, and their powerful strokes carried him far. Before he quite knew what was happening, he found himself in a great garden where apple trees bloomed. The lilacs filled the air with sweet scent and hung in clusters from long, green branches that bent over a winding stream. Oh, but it was lovely here in the freshness of spring!

From the thicket before him came three lovely white swans. They ruffled their feathers and swam lightly in the stream. The duckling recognized these noble creatures, and a strange feeling of sadness came upon him.

"I shall fly near these royal birds, and they will peck me to bits because I, who am so very ugly, dare to go near them. But I don't care. Better be killed by them than to be nipped by the ducks, pecked（啄）by the hens, kicked about by the hen-yard girl, or suffer such misery in winter."

So he flew into the water and swam toward the splendid swans. They saw him, and swept down upon him with their rustling feathers raised. "Kill me!" said the poor creature, and he bowed his head down over the water to wait for death. But what did he see there, mirrored in the clear stream? He beheld his own image, and it was no longer the reflection of a clumsy, dirty, gray bird, ugly and offensive. He himself was a swan! Being born in a duck yard does not matter, if only you are hatched from a swan's egg.

He felt quite glad that he had come through so much trouble and misfortune, for now he had a fuller understanding of his own good fortune, and of beauty when he met with it. The great swans swam all around him and stroked him with their bills.

Several little children came into the garden to throw grain and bits of bread upon the water. The smallest child cried, "Here's a new one," and the others rejoiced, "Yes, a new one has come." They clapped their hands, danced around, and ran to bring their father and mother.

And they threw bread and cake upon the water, while they all agreed, "The new one is the most handsome of all. He's so young and so good-looking." The old swans bowed in his honor.

Then he felt very bashful, and tucked his head under his wing. He did not know what this was all about. He felt so very happy, but he wasn't at all proud, for a good heart never grows proud. He thought about how he had been persecuted and scorned, and now he heard them all call him the most beautiful of all beautiful birds. The lilacs dipped their clusters into the stream before him, and the sun shone so warm and so heartening. He rustled his feathers and held his slender neck high, as he cried out with full heart: "I never dreamed there could be so much happiness, when I was the ugly duckling."

背后的故事

安徒生与丑小鸭

“丑小鸭”的遭遇和作者安徒生有类似之处。世俗的偏见已经把它推到社会之外，使他成为化外之民。他正视生活，在四面八方的压力纷至沓来的时候，他也没有放弃生的意愿和对美的追求。世俗的偏见和习惯势力在他心灵上所造成的压抑和忧郁不能摧毁他对美的追求和向往。终于他攀上了他所向往的美的高峰，他感到幸福，感到生活的真实意义。这篇故事不仅概括地描写出了安徒生青少年时代的苦难和斗争，也表达出了他在面临困境的时候所坚持的信念。

“丑小鸭”终于实现了他所追求的理想。安徒生也是一样，他终于成了一个伟大的童话作家，创作出了那么多充满了爱和鼓舞人们向真、善、美追求的美丽的故事，给人们带来快乐、希望和幸福。在他年老的时候，他的故乡奥登塞市的居民赠他以“奥登塞市荣誉公民”的称号。在授予这个光荣称号的那天晚上，他们举行了火炬游行，庆祝他们饱经沧桑的儿子安徒生归来。面对着故乡的人们，安徒生这样描述他当时的感情：我觉得我自己很卑微、无力和渺小。我好像是站在我的上帝面前一样。我在思想、言语和行为各方面的弱点，现在都在我面前展开。这一切都在我的灵魂里突出地直立着，好像这个纪念日就是我的审判日似的。当人们这样称赞和尊重我的时候，上帝一定会知道我是感到多么卑微。(安徒生：《我的一生的童话》)

这就是安徒生的本色，也是“丑小鸭”的本色。他虽然通过一生的努力在工作中取得了巨大的成就，得到世人的尊敬，但“在上帝面前”却感到非常卑微。这里的“上帝”，对安徒生来说就是人民；对丑小鸭说来，就是那些美丽的天鹅。只有在这个“上帝”面前，只有得到这个“上帝”的承认，我们的成就才能表现出它所具有的真正的价值和意义。

Tale 5

The Eternal Soul

永恒的灵魂

—An Episode from The Little Sea Maid

——节选自《海的女儿》

《海的女儿》是一个美丽而忧伤的童话。童话中的小美人鱼是意志坚强、善良而美丽的姑娘，她为了追求人的高洁、纯真的爱情和不死的灵魂，放弃了华贵的生活和三百年的寿命，甘受种种的痛苦，最终在希望幻灭之时，不惜抛弃生命，去诠释何为真正的人。虽然最终小美人鱼变成了海上的泡沫，但是安徒生没有让读者们失望，他用一个不灭的灵魂，承载了美人鱼超越世俗的存在。

慢阅读小语

细细品位字里行间流淌出的语言美和思想美，你就会感受到“Jump and get an apple”的喜悦，不知不觉间自身修养得到了提升……

1 **We have not an immortal soul; we never receive another life; we are like the green sea-weed, which, when once cut through, can never bloom again.**

我们没有一个不灭的灵魂。我们从来得不到一个死后的生命。我们像那绿色的海草一样，只要被割断了，就再也绿不起来！

2 **Men, on the contrary, have a soul which lives forever, which lives on after the body has become dust; it mounts up through the clear air, up to all the shining stars!**

相反地，人类有一个灵魂；它永远活着，即使身体化为尘土，它仍是活着的。它升向晴朗的天空，一直升向那些闪耀着的星星！

3 **Only if a man were to love you so that you should be more to him than father or mother; if he should cling to you with his every thought and with all his love, and let the priest lay his right hand in yours with a promise of faithfulness here and in all eternity, then his soul would be imparted to your body, and you would receive a share of the happiness of mankind.**

只有当一个人爱你、把你当做比他父母还要亲切的人的时候；只有当他把他全部的思想和爱情都放在你身上的时候；只有当他让牧师把他的右手放在你的手里、答应现在和将来永远对你忠诚的时候，他的灵魂才会转移到你的身上去，而你就会得到一份人类的快乐。

4 **A sea-maid has no immortal soul, and can never gain one, except she win the love of a mortal. Her eternal existence depends upon the power of another.**

人鱼是没有不灭的灵魂的，而且永远也不会有这样的灵魂，除非她获得了一个凡人的爱情。她的永恒的存在要依靠外来的力量。

小美人鱼的身世

在海的深处，水是那么蓝，像最美丽的矢车菊花瓣；水是那么清澈，像最纯净的水晶。在如此美丽的海底，住着6位美丽的人鱼公主，她们长着美丽的鱼尾，而不是双脚。

Far out in the sea the water is as blue as the petals of the most beautiful corn-flower（矢车菊）, and as clear as the purest glass. But it is very deep, deeper than any cable will sound; many steeples must be placed one above the other to reach from the ground to the surface of the water. And down there live the sea-people.

Now, you must not believe there is nothing down there but the naked sand; no,—the strangest trees and plants grow there, so pliable in their stalks and leaves that at the least motion of the water they move just as if they had life. All fishes, great and small, glide among the twigs, just as here the birds do in the trees. In the deepest spot of all lies the Sea-king's castle: the walls are of coral, and the tall, Gothic windows of the clearest amber; shells form the roof, and they open and shut according as the water flows. It looks lovely, for in each shell lie gleaming pearls, a single one of which would have great value in a queen's diadem.

The Sea-king below there had been a widower for many years, while his old mother kept house for him. She was a clever woman, but proud of her rank, so she wore twelve oysters on her tail, while the other great people were only allowed to wear six. Beyond this she was deserving of great praise, especially because she was very fond of her grand-daughters, the little Sea-princesses. These were six pretty children; but the youngest was the most beautiful of all. Her skin was as clear and as fine as a rose leaf; her eyes were as blue as the deepest sea; but, like all the rest, she had no feet, for her body ended in a fish-tail.

There was no greater pleasure for the youngest princess than to hear of the world of men above them. The old grandmother had to tell all she knew of ships and towns, of men and animals. It seemed particularly beautiful to her that up on the earth the flowers shed fragrance, for they had none down at the bottom of the sea, and that the trees were green, and that the fishes which one saw there among the trees could sing so loud and clear that it was a pleasure to hear them. What the grandmother called fishes were the little birds; the Princess could not understand them in any other way, for she had never seen a bird.

"When you have reached your fifteenth year," said the grandmother, "you shall have leave to rise up out of the sea, to sit on the rocks in the moonlight, and to see the great ships as they sail by. Then you will see forests and towns!"

梦想成真

小美人鱼终于等到自己的15岁，她也可以像姐姐们一样去海面上探寻另一个世界。她对海面上的世界充满了好奇，她会遇到人类吗？她激动的心情无法用言语来表达，她不知道的是等待她的是一个妙不可言的奇缘。

At last she was really fifteen years old.

"Now, you see, you are grown up," said the grandmother, the old dowager. "Come, let me adorn you like your sisters."

And she put a wreath of white lilies in the little maid's hair, but each flower was half a pearl; and the old lady let eight great oysters attach themselves to the Princess' tail, in token of her high rank.

"But that hurts so!" said the little Sea-maid.

"Yes, pride must suffer pain," replied the old lady.

O! How glad she would have been to shake off all the tokens of rank and lay aside the heavy wreath! Her red flowers in the garden suited her better; but she could not help

it. "Farewell!" she said, and then she rose, light and clear as a water-bubble, up through the sea.

The sun had just set when she lifted her head above the sea, but all the clouds still shone like roses and gold, and in the pale red sky the evening-stars gleamed bright and beautiful. The air was mild and fresh, and the sea quite calm. There lay a great ship with three masts（桅杆）; one single sail only was set, for not a breeze stirred, and around in the shrouds（船的横桅索）and on the yards sat the sailors.

There was music and singing, and as the evening closed in, hundreds of colored lanterns were lighted up, and looked as if the flags of every nation were waving in the air. The little Sea-maid swam straight to the cabin window, and each time the sea lifted her up she could look through the panes, which were clear as crystal, and see many people standing within dressed in their best. But the handsomest of all was the young Prince with the great black eyes: he was certainly not much more than sixteen years old; it was his birthday, and that was the cause of all this feasting.

王子的船遇到了暴风雨，善良的小美人鱼怎能不出手相救？更何况她已经被王子深深吸引。勇敢的小美人鱼救上了遇难的王子，可是王子并不知道是小美人鱼救了他。小美人鱼在远处望着王子，一丝丝忧伤荡在心间。

It became late; but the little Sea-maid could not turn her eyes from the ship and from the beautiful Prince. The colored lanterns were extinguished, rockets ceased to fly into the air, and no more cannons were fired; but there was a murmuring and a buzzing deep down in the sea; and she sat on the water, swaying up and down, so that she could look into the cabin. But as the ship got more way, one sail after another was spread. And now the waves rose higher, great clouds came up, and in the distance there was lightning. O! It was going to be fearful weather, therefore the sailors furled the sails. The great ship flew in swift career over the wild sea: the waters rose up like great black mountains, which wanted to roll over the masts; but like a swan the ship dived into the valleys between these high waves, and then let itself be lifted on high again. To the little Sea-maid this seemed merry sport, but to the sailors it appeared very differently. The ship groaned and creaked; the thick planks were bent by the heavy blows; the sea broke into the ship; the mainmast snapped（突然折断）in two like a thin reed（芦苇）, and the ship lay over on her side, while the water rushed into the hold. Now the little Sea-maid saw that the people were in peril; she herself was obliged to take care to avoid the beams and fragments of the ship which were floating about on the waters.

No, he must not die: so she swam about among the beams and planks that strewed the surface, quite forgetting that one of them might have crushed her. Diving down deep under the water, she again rose high up among the waves, and in this way she at last came to the Prince, who could scarcely swim longer in that stormy sea. His arms and legs began to fail him, his beautiful eyes closed, and he would have died had the little Sea-maid not come. She held his head up over the water, and then allowed the waves to carry her and him whither they listed.

When the morning came the storm had passed by. Of the ship not a fragment was to be seen. The sun came up red and shining out of the water; it was as if its beams brought back the hue of life to the cheeks of the Prince, but his eyes remained closed. The Sea-maid kissed his high, fair forehead and put back his wet hair, and he seemed to her to be like the marble statue in her little garden: she kissed him again and hoped that he might live.

The Sea-maid perceived that the Prince came back to life. But he did not cast a smile at her: he did not know that she had saved him. And she felt very sorrowful; and when he was led away into the great building, she dived mournfully under the water and returned to her father's **palace**.

palace 宫殿。最初是君主所用的建筑物的专称，一般称举行礼仪和办公用的主体建筑物为“殿”，而称生活起居的部分为“宫”，后用来泛指君主或重要公众人物所居住的房屋。宫殿的象征意义引申为政治或宗教的代号，如克里姆林宫和白宫。在中国有著名的“故宫”（Forbidden City），也称“故宫博物院”（the Palace Museum），还有与宫殿有关的“颐和园”（Summer Palace）。再如西藏的“布达拉宫”，就译成Potala Palace。

一个永恒的灵魂

小美人鱼爱上了人类，但是她是人鱼，是没有灵魂的。这让小美人鱼困惑，她渴望像人类一样生活，渴望能和王子幸福地在一起。但是祖母的话让她的梦破了，她引以自豪的鱼尾真的是很难看吗？从她悲哀的眼神中，我们读到了心痛。

She had always been gentle and melancholy（忧郁）, but now she became much more so. Her sisters asked her what she had seen the first time she rose up to the surface, but she would tell them nothing.

More and more she began to love mankind, and more and more she wished to be able to wander about among those whose world seemed far larger than her own. For they could fly over the sea in ships, and mount up the high hills far above the clouds, and the lands they possessed stretched out in woods and fields farther than her eyes could reach. There was much she wished to know, but her sisters could not answer all her questions; therefore she applied to the old grandmother; and the old lady knew the upper world, which she rightly called "the countries above the sea," very well.

"If people are not drowned," asked the little Sea-maid, "can they live forever? Do they not die as we die down here in the sea?"

"Yes," replied the old lady. "They too must die, and their life is even shorter than ours. We can live to be three hundred years old, but when we cease to exist here, we are turned into foam on the surface of the water, and have not even a grave down here among those we love. We have not an immortal soul; we never receive another life; we are like the green sea-weed, which, when once cut through, can never bloom again. Men, on the contrary, have a soul which lives forever, which lives on after the body has become dust; it mounts up through the clear air, up to all the shining stars! As we rise up out of the waters and behold all the lands of the earth, so they rise up to unknown glorious places which we can never see."

"Why did we not receive an immortal soul?" asked the little Sea-maid, sorrowfully. "I would gladly give all the hundreds of years I have to live to be a human being only for one day, and to have a hope of partaking the heavenly kingdom."

"You must not think of that," replied the old lady. "We feel ourselves far more happy and far better than mankind yonder."

"Then I am to die and be cast as foam upon the sea, not hearing the music of the waves, nor seeing the pretty flowers and the red sun? Can I not do anything to win an immortal soul?

"No!" answered the grandmother. "Only if a man were to love you so that you should be more to him than father or mother; if he should cling to you with his every thought and with all his love, and let the **priest** lay his right hand in yours with a promise of faithfulness here and in all eternity, then his soul would be imparted to your body, and you would receive a share of the happiness of mankind. He would give a soul to you and yet retain his own. But that can never come to pass. What is considered beautiful here in the sea—the fish-tail—they would consider ugly on the earth: they don't understand it; there one must have the clumsy supports which they call legs, to be called beautiful."

Then the little Sea-maid sighed and looked mournfully upon her fish—tail.

小美人鱼从海底巫师那里求得了一双人类的腿，但是同时她也失去了她的声音。她每走一步都是钻心的剧痛，但是她不怕，她依然来到了王子的身边，为的是得到王子的爱，为了能与王子一起拥有不灭的灵魂。可是王子没有办法读到小美人鱼的心，王子的新娘不是小美人鱼。在王子新婚的那一刻，等待小美人鱼的是变成海上那虚无缥缈的泡沫。

Once more the little **mermaid** looked with half-extinguished eyes upon the Prince; then she threw

priest 牧师。牧师是在一般基督新教的教会中，专职负责带领及照顾其他基督徒的人。在俚语中，也经常用priest of the blue bag来表示“律师”。而且，在英国方言中，还会用the priest's Crown来表示“蒲公英”。最有趣的是还有一个与priest相关的谚语，Like priest, like people. 意思是“有怎样的牧师，就有怎样的教徒”。这与汉语中的“有其父必有其子”有异曲同工之妙。

mermaid 美人鱼。美人鱼经常出现于各地传说与童话中，而且它们的形象都很相似。在某些文化当中，“美人鱼”可以同时指塞壬（海妖）和女性的人鱼。因为安徒生的童话《海的女儿》而使美人鱼的传说广泛流传，所以在丹麦的哥本哈根有一座美人鱼的铜像，mermaid不仅指美人鱼，因为鱼在水里游泳很快，所以mermaid也引申为“女性游泳健将”。

herself from the ship into the sea, and felt her frame dissolving into foam.

Now the sun rose up out of the sea. The rays fell mild and warm upon the cold sea-foam, and the little Sea-maid felt nothing of death. She saw the bright sun, and over her head sailed hundreds of glorious ethereal（天上的）beings—she could see them through the white sails of the ship and the red clouds of the sky; their speech was melody, but of such a spiritual kind that no human ear could hear it, just as no human eye could see them; without wings they floated through the air. The little Sea-maid found that she had a frame like these, and was rising more and more out of the foam.

"Whither am I going?" she asked; and her voice sounded like that of other beings, so spiritual, that no earthly music could be compared to it.

"To the daughters of the air!"

replied the others. "A sea-maid has no immortal soul, and can never gain one, except she win the love of a mortal. Her eternal existence depends upon the power of another. The daughters of the air have likewise no immortal soul, but they can make themselves one through good deeds. We fly to the hot countries, where the close, pestilent air kills men, and there we bring coolness. We disperse the fragrance of the flowers through the air, and spread refreshment and health. After we have striven for three hundred years to accomplish all the good we can bring about, we receive an immortal soul, and take part in the eternal happiness of men. You, poor little Sea-maid, have striven with your whole heart after the goal we pursue; you have suffered and endured; you have by good works raised yourself to the world of spirits, and can gain an immortal soul after three hundred years."

And the little Sea-maid lifted her glorified eyes toward God's sun, and for the first time she felt them fill with tears. On the ship there was again life and noise. She saw the Prince and his bride searching for her; then they looked mournfully at the pearly foam, as if they knew that she had thrown herself into the waves. Invisible, she kissed the forehead of the bride, fanned the Prince, and mounted with the other children of the air on the rosy cloud which floated through the ether.

背后的故事

人鱼的经典传说

在哥本哈根海港有一座著名的雕像——人鱼公主，她默默无语地坐在大海中央，低垂的头，默默地凝望着湛蓝的海水深处，沉浸在无边的忧伤遐想之中。她是一座铜像，是人们对童话的演绎与怀念，她又是一座爱情纪念碑，默默唤起和分享所有人心里旧日的伤痛。

《海的女儿》是安徒生所有的故事中最著名的一篇，也是一个堪称经典的爱情故事。《海的女儿》写于1837年，是安徒生童话创作初期的作品，也是安徒生最具自我象征意义的作品。那时，安徒生历尽坎坷，已从贫困、饥饿和世俗的歧视中奋争出来，并在文坛上崭露头角，在社会上有了一定的立足之地，人生的理想和信念已经基本确立。他不仅体验到人世的艰难、辛酸和痛苦，而且感受到爱、同情和人道是多么宝贵；不仅理解了人类生命的意义，而且选定了生活和事业的道路。总之，他在趋向自我实现。这一切，都较为完整而真实地融汇在他精心制作的童话《海的女儿》里，渗透到作品的幻想形象——小美人鱼身上。

Tale 6

The Tale of Peter Rabbit

彼得兔的故事

堪称绘本鼻祖的彼得兔系列，在西方被称为经典中的经典，百年来长销不衰，赢得了几代人的心。作者毕翠克丝·波特也因此让全世界的读者为她着迷。人们不仅仅喜欢她的精妙幽默的文字，还同样热爱她手绘的精彩、绚丽、生动的图画。

有一年，毕翠克丝·波特家庭教师的孩子生病，为了安慰这个5岁的小孩，毕翠克丝给他写了一封带图画的信，信里讲了一只调皮的兔子彼得的故事。由此，彼得兔诞生了。

慢阅读小语

细细品位字里行间流淌出的语言美和思想美，你就会感受到“Jump and get an apple”的喜悦，不知不觉间自身修养得到了提升……

1 **You may go into the fields or down the lane, but don't go into Mr. McGregor's garden: your Father had an accident there; he was put in a pie by Mrs. McGregor.**

现在你们可以到田野上去玩了，不过要记得走小路，千万别跑到蛮哥古里古先生的菜园里去，你们的爸爸就是在那儿出的事——他被蛮哥古里古的夫人，放进一个大馅饼里面去了。

2 **First he ate some lettuces and some French beans; and then he ate some radishes; and then, feeling rather sick, he went to look for some parsley.**

他先是尝了尝那儿的莴苣和四季豆，接着又啃起了小红萝卜。不过，吃了太多的萝卜让他觉得有点不舒服，他又想找一些芹菜来换换胃口。

3 **Peter was most dreadfully frightened; he rushed all over the garden, for he had forgotten the way back to the gate.**

彼得从来没受过这样的惊吓，他一路飞奔着逃跑，跑遍了整个菜园，因为他已经忘记了大门是开在哪边。

4 **Peter scuttered underneath the bushes. But presently, as nothing happened, he came out, and climbed upon a wheel-barrow and peeped over.**

彼得吓得一头钻进了灌木丛，可过了一会儿，因为什么可怕的东西都没出现，所以他又大着胆子从藏身处爬了出来，爬上了一辆独轮手推车，从那上面向下窥望。

5 **Peter never stopped running or looked behind him till he got home to the big fir-tree.**

彼得这时在不停地奔跑，一边跑，一边惊魂未定地往后瞧，直到他跑回了无花果大树底下的家里。

兔子妈妈的叮咛

从前，有这么四只小兔子，他们的大名是：跳跳、蹬蹬、短尾巴还有彼得。他们和兔子妈妈一起，住在一棵高大的无花果树脚下的一个小土包后面。一天早上，兔子妈妈让她的孩子们去田野上玩，不过她一再嘱咐孩子们，千万不能去蛮哥古里古先生家的菜园，这是为什么呢？

Once upon a time there were four little Rabbits, and their names were Flopsy, Mopsy, Cotton-tail, and Peter.

They lived with their Mother in a sand-bank, underneath the root of a very big fir-tree.

"Now, my dears," said old Mrs. Rabbit one morning, "you may go into the fields or down the lane, but don't go into Mr. McGregor's garden: your Father had an accident there; he was put in a pie by Mrs. McGregor."

"Now run along, and don't get into mischief. I am going out."

Then old Mrs. Rabbit took a basket and her umbrella, and went through the wood to the baker's. She bought a loaf of **brown bread** and five currant（葡萄干）**buns.**

brown bread 黑面包。黑面包科学的叫法应该称为麸皮面包或者全麦面包。由于其制作的原料并不全是精面粉，而是混合了小麦在磨粉过程中被碾下来的皮层、胚芽、糊粉层及少量胚乳等麸皮，因此比精面粉面包更具有营养价值。几种生活中常见的粗粮面包有：燕麦黑面包（brash bread）、粗全麦粉面包（chiselly bread）、粗磨面粉面包（coarse bread）、黑麦面包（rye bread），除了粗粮面包，超市里常卖的还有三种面包，分别是玉米面包（corn bread）、葡萄干面包（raisin bread）、奶油面包（butter bread）。

bun 圆面包。面包在西方就像米饭在中国一样，虽然他们不一定每餐都吃面包，但是吃的次数还是很多的，任何一个类似的圆面包，不论它的大小如何，都可以叫做圆面包（bun）。西方的面包有很多种，如，大面包（loaf）；用来做汉堡的那种小圆面包（Hamburg bun）；这是新月形的面包（croissant），或者叫做牛角面包；长棍面包（bread stick）；切片面包（slice）。

菜园历险记

跳跳、蹬蹬和短尾巴，都是很乖的小兔子，他们就沿着小路走到田野上，去采摘黑莓浆果了。可是，彼得这个淘气包，却立刻就朝着蛮哥古里古先生的菜园跑去，他从关着的大门下面挤了进去！

Flopsy, Mopsy, and Cotton-tail, who were good little bunnies, went down the lane to gather blackberries:

But Peter, who was very naughty, ran straight to Mr. McGregor's garden, and squeezed under the gate!

First he ate some lettuces and some French beans（四季豆）; and then he ate some radishes（萝卜）; And then, feeling rather sick, he went to look for some parsley（欧芹）.

But round the end of a cucumber frame, whom should he meet but Mr. McGregor!

Mr. McGregor was on his hands and knees planting out young cabbages, but he jumped up and ran after Peter, waving a rake and calling out, "Stop thief!"

Peter was most dreadfully frightened; he rushed all over the garden, for he had forgotten the way back to the gate.

He lost one of his shoes among the cabbages, and the other shoe amongst the potatoes.

彼得真是不幸，他竟然在菜园里碰到了蛮哥古里古先生！他一路飞奔着逃跑，跑遍了整个菜园，因为他已经忘记了大门是开在哪边。他在卷心菜的旁边跑丢了一只鞋，另一只鞋也被甩进了土豆地里。不过，丢了鞋子以后，他甩开四条腿，反而跑得更快了，淘气的彼得能逃过蛮哥古里古先生的追赶吗？

After losing them, he ran on four legs and went faster, so that I think he might have got away altogether if he had not unfortunately run into a gooseberry net, and got caught by the large buttons on his jacket. It was a blue jacket with brass buttons, quite new.

Peter gave himself up for lost, and shed big tears; but his sobs were overheard by some friendly sparrows, who flew to him in great excitement, and implored him to exert himself.

Mr. McGregor came up with a sieve（滤网）, which he intended to pop upon the top of Peter; but Peter wriggled（扭动）out just in time, leaving his jacket behind him.

And rushed into the tool-shed, and jumped into a can. It would have been a beautiful thing to hide in, if it had not so much water in it.

Mr. McGregor was quite sure that Peter was somewhere in the tool-shed, perhaps hidden underneath a flower-pot. He began to turn them over carefully, looking under each.

Presently Peter sneezed – "Kertyschoo!" Mr. McGregor was after him in no time.

And tried to put a foot upon Peter, who jumped out of a window, upsetting three plants. The window was too small for Mr. McGregor, and he was tired of running after Peter. He went back to his work.

菜园逃生记

机灵聪明的彼得终于运用智慧躲过了蛮哥古里古先生的追赶，彼得终于可以坐下来歇一会儿啦。他还在为刚才的惊吓瑟瑟发抖，气喘吁吁，而且也不知道现在究竟该往哪儿走才好。又过了一会儿，他才渐渐缓过神来，开始慢慢地、慢慢地向前移动了几步，同时东看看、西望望。他的小脑袋里又打着自己的小主意：该怎么回家呢？

Peter sat down to rest; he was out of breath and trembling with fright, and he had not the least idea which way to go. Also he was very damp with sitting in that can.

After a time he began to wander about, going lippity—lippity—not very fast, and looking all around.

He found a door in a wall; but

it was locked, and there was no room for a fat little rabbit to squeeze underneath.

An old mouse was running in and out over the stone doorstep, carrying peas and beans to her family in the wood. Peter asked her the way to the gate, but she had such a large pea in her mouth that she could not answer. She only shook her head at him. Peter began to cry.

Then he tried to find his way straight across the garden, but he became more and more puzzled. Presently, he came to a pond where Mr. McGregor filled his water-cans. A white cat was staring at some gold-fish, she sat very, very still, but now and then the tip of her tail twitched as if it were alive. Peter thought it best to go away without speaking to her; he had heard about cats from his cousin, little Benjamin Bunny.

He went back towards the tool-shed, but suddenly, quite close to him, he heard the noise of a hoe – scr-r-ritch, scratch, scratch, scritch. Peter scuttered underneath the bushes. But presently, as nothing happened, he came out, and climbed upon a wheel-barrow and peeped over. The first thing he saw was Mr. McGregor hoeing（挖掘）onions. His back was turned towards Peter, and beyond him was the gate!

Peter got down very quietly off the wheel-barrow, and started running as fast as he could go, along a straight walk behind some black-currant bushes.

Mr. McGregor caught sight of him at the corner but Peter did not care. He slipped underneath the gate, and was safe at last in the wood outside the garden.

温暖的家

蛮哥古里古先生最终也没有追上淘气的彼得兔，他把彼得在逃跑中落下的小夹克衫和鞋子挂在了竹竿上，权且充当一个稻草人，用来吓唬那些过路的山雀。彼得这时却在不停地奔跑，他跑得精疲力尽，一回到兔子洞，就一头栽倒在柔软的沙土地板上，闭上了双眼。兔子妈妈看着狼狈的彼得真是很无奈，因为这已经是两个星期来，彼得丢掉的第二件夹克衫和第二双小鞋子了！不得不遗憾地告诉读者，彼得那天晚上还是病了。而跳跳、蹬蹬和短尾巴却吃了一顿面包、牛奶加黑莓浆果的香喷喷的晚饭。

Mr. McGregor hung up the little jacket and the shoes for a scare-crow to frighten the blackbirds.

Peter never stopped running or looked behind him till he got home to the big fir-tree.

He was so tired that he flopped down upon the nice soft sand on the floor of the rabbit-hole, and shut his eyes. His mother was busy cooking; she wondered what he had done with his clothes. It was the second little jacket and pair of shoes that Peter had lost in a fortnight.

I am sorry to say that Peter was not very well during the evening.

His mother put him to bed, and made some **camomile tea**（甘菊茶）; and she gave a dose of it to Peter!

"One tablespoon to be taken at bed-time."

But Flopsy, Mopsy, and Cotton-tail had bread and milk and blackberries, for supper.

camomile tea 甘菊茶。甘菊茶能镇定精神、舒缓情绪、提升睡眠质量，还可改善过敏皮肤。生活中常喝的茶有红茶（dark tea）、绿茶（green tea）、花茶（scented tea）、滋补茶（nutritious tea）、醒酒茶（sober-up tea）、水果茶（fruit tea）、花果茶（flower tea）。本文中的甘菊茶就属于花果茶，而“柠檬果茶”lemon tea就属于水果茶。

背后的故事

彼得兔的“妈妈”

彼得兔的名字，是来自于作者波特小姐童年时所饲养的一只兔子。最早的彼得兔故事原形，是来自于1893年，波特小姐写给她家庭教师的儿子的信件。这位家庭老师的儿子长期卧病在床，所以波特小姐以说故事的方式，作为这位小男孩的娱乐，并且在故事当中鼓励他。一次毕翠克丝写信的时候写道，不知道该说些什么，那就讲个故事吧：“从前有四只小兔子，他们的名字叫跳跳、蹬蹬、短尾巴和彼得。”《彼得兔》的故事就这样开始了。

波特小姐1866年7月28日出生在维多利亚时代一个富裕的家庭，她在伦敦长大，从小就受到良好的美术以及写作教育。波特小姐的父母对子女的保护意识非常强，不喜欢他们和其他小孩子接触，于是没有玩伴的姐弟俩从小就养了各种小动物——青蛙，蜥蜴，小蛇，乌龟，当然还有兔子。这些小动物几乎都在波特小姐后来的童话故事中出现过。彼得兔其实就是她自己的宠物兔子的名字。

Tale 7

The Naughty Pinocchio

顽皮的匹诺曹

—An Episode from The Adventures of Pinocchio

——节选自《木偶奇遇记》

当仁慈的木匠皮帕诺睡觉的时候，梦见一位蓝色的天使赋予他最心爱的木偶匹诺曹生命，于是小木偶开始了他的冒险。如果他要成为真正的男孩，他必须通过勇气、忠心以及诚实的考验。在历险中，他因说谎而鼻子变长，因贪玩而逃学，因贪心而受骗，还因此变成了驴子。最后，他掉进一只大鲸鱼的腹中，意外与皮帕诺相逢……经过这次历险，匹诺曹终于长大了，他变得诚实、勤劳、善良，成为了一个真真正正的男孩。这部童话向我们演绎了一个人由不完美走向完美、由不幸福走向幸福的曲折历程。

慢阅读小语

细细品位字里行间流淌出的语言美和思想美，你就会感受到“Jump and get an apple”的喜悦，不知不觉间自身修养得到了提升……

1 **As far as I'm concerned, I think that when the dead weep, it means they do not want to die.**

依我看，死人会哭，就表明他不想死。

2 **I'm a boy, you see, and all boys hate medicine more than they do sickness.**

你知道的，我是个男孩，所有的男孩比怕生病更怕喝药水。

3 **Lies, my boy, are known in a moment. There are two kinds of lies, lies with short legs and lies with long noses. Yours, just now, happen to have long noses.**

我的孩子，谎话一下子就可以看出来，因为说了谎话有两种变化，一种是腿变短，一种是鼻子变长，你正是鼻子变长的一种。

4 **He was dressed in court livery. A tricorn trimmed with gold lace was set at a rakish angle over a wig of white curls that dropped down to his waist. He wore a jaunty coat of chocolate-colored velvet, with diamond buttons, and with two huge pockets which were always filled with bones, dropped there at dinner by his loving mistress. Breeches of crimson velvet, silk stockings, and low, silver-buckled slippers completed his costume. His tail was encased in a blue silk covering, which was to protect it from the rain.**

这只卷毛狗身穿车夫的礼服，头戴金边小三角帽，白色假卷发垂到脖子上。巧克力色的上衣上钉着宝石钮扣，两边有两个大口袋，放主人吃饭时赏它的肉骨头。下身穿一条大红天鹅绒裤子、一双丝袜、一双开口软鞋。后面还有一样东西，很像雨伞套，蓝绸子做的。下雨的时候用来藏它的尾巴。

童话慢讲述：说谎的代价

匹诺曹得救了

匹诺曹虽然一直想做个好孩子，可是又经不起诱惑。他逃学、撒谎、结交坏朋友，几次上当可还是屡教不改，他受狐狸的欺骗,差点被海盗吊死，多亏天蓝色头发的仙女救了他，仙女让老鹰去解开匹诺曹的绳子，而且仙女还让卷毛狗去请医生来为他治病。

The **Assassins** chase Pinocchio, catch him, and hang him to the branch of a giant oak tree. The Lovely Maiden with Azure（天蓝色）Hair sends for the poor **Marionette**（牵线木偶）, puts him to bed, and calls three Doctors to tell her if Pinocchio is dead or alive.

If the poor Marionette had dangled there much longer, all hope would have been lost. Luckily for him, the Lovely Maiden with Azure Hair once again looked out of her window. Filled with pity at the sight of the poor little fellow being knocked helplessly about by the wind, she clapped her hands sharply together three times.

At the signal, a loud whirr of wings in quick flight was heard and a large Falcon（猎鹰）came and settled itself on the window ledge.

"What do you command, my charming **Fairy**?" asked the Falcon, bending his beak in deep reverence

assassins 刺客。assassins一词源于古阿拉伯语，该职业在西方最早于12世纪以刺杀十字军为目标的伊斯兰密教组织。如今此词通常指出于政治原因，负责对目标实施谋杀或者暗杀的人，比如特工队伍或恐怖组织中负责刺杀敌方人员、重要人物的高级间谍，许多国家的安全局都有刺客，例如美国的中央情报局（CIA）、苏联的克格勃（KGB）等。

marionette 牵线木偶。木偶泛指戏剧表演用的人偶，即傀儡。我国和西方的木偶剧有很大不同，国内制作的木偶剧大都是“歌舞升平”，而且几乎100%都是孩子们的专利。但是在国外，木偶剧是一门严肃的表演艺术，它的表现手法多种多样，对人物的刻画也十分成熟，并且木偶剧在国外拥有着相当广泛的成人群体，他们观看木偶剧的态度和观看话剧、芭蕾等演出没有任何差别。

fairy 仙女。fairy原指西方文化里的一种传说生物。其体型娇小，外型状似少女，但长有翅膀。英文词汇fairy，有时也能作为对精灵、矮人、地精和哥布林等各种外形接近人或具有超自然力量的生物总称。在这样的情况下，fairy就会被翻译成精灵或妖精。

(尊敬)(for it must be known that, after all, the Lovely Maiden with Azure Hair was none other than a very kind Fairy who had lived, for more than a thousand years, in the vicinity of the forest).

"Do you see that Marionette hanging from the limb of that giant oak tree?"

"I see him."

"Very well. Fly immediately to him. With your strong beak, break the knot which holds him tied, take him down, and lay him softly on the grass at the foot of the oak."

The Falcon flew away and after two minutes returned, saying, "I have done what you have commanded."

"How did you find him? Alive or dead?"

"At first glance, I thought he was dead. But I found I was wrong, for as soon as I loosened the knot around his neck, he gave a long sigh and mumbled with a faint voice, "Now I feel better!" "

The Fairy clapped her hands twice. A magnificent Poodle appeared, walking on his hind legs just like a man. He was dressed in court livery. A tricorn(三角帽)trimmed with gold lace was set at a rakish angle over a wig of white curls that dropped down to his waist. He wore a jaunty coat of chocolate-colored velvet, with diamond buttons, and with two huge pockets which were always filled with bones, dropped there at dinner by his loving mistress. Breeches of crimson velvet, silk stockings, and low, silver-buckled slippers completed his costume. His tail was encased in a blue silk covering, which was to protect it from the rain.

"Come, Medoro," said the Fairy to him. "Get my best coach ready and set out toward the forest. On reaching the oak tree, you will find a poor, half-dead Marionette stretched out on the grass. Lift him up tenderly, place him on the silken cushions of the coach, and bring him here to me."

The Poodle, to show that he understood, wagged his silk-covered tail two or three times and set off at a quick pace.

In a few minutes, a lovely little coach, made of glass, with lining as

soft as whipped cream and chocolate pudding, and stuffed with canary feathers, pulled out of the stable. It was drawn by one hundred pairs of white mice, and the Poodle sat on the coachman's seat and snapped his whip gayly in the air, as if he were a real coachman in a hurry to get to his destination.

In a quarter of an hour the coach was back. The Fairy, who was waiting at the door of the house, lifted the poor little Marionette in her arms, took him to a dainty room with mother-of-pearl walls, put him to bed, and sent immediately for the most famous doctors of the neighborhood to come to her.

三位医生的诊治

仙女请附近最有名的三位大夫来为匹诺曹诊治，匹诺曹还活着吗？听听三位大夫有趣的诊断吧：乌鸦说“我认为木偶完全死了，但万一他没有死，那就有可靠的迹像表明，他完全活着！”，但是猫头鹰却说“我认为，木偶完全活着，但万一他不幸没有活着，那就有可靠的迹像表明，他的确死了！”，剩下的蟋蟀会给出什么样的结论呢？在你捧腹大笑同时也有些许人生道理待你细细体会。看似无聊的废话，如果慢慢品味，会嚼出不一样的味道来。

One after another the doctors came, a Crow, and Owl, and a Talking Cricket.

"I should like to know, signori," said the Fairy, turning to the three doctors gathered about Pinocchio's bed, "I should like to know if this poor Marionette is dead or alive."

At this invitation, the Crow stepped out and felt Pinocchio's pulse, his nose, his little toe.

Then he solemnly pronounced the following words:

"To my mind this Marionette is dead and gone; but if, by any evil chance, he were not, then that would be a sure sign that he is still alive!"

"I am sorry," said the Owl, "to have to contradict the Crow, my famous friend and colleague. To my mind this Marionette is alive; but if, by any evil chance, he were not, then that would be a sure sign that he is wholly dead!"

"And do you hold any opinion?" the Fairy asked the Talking Cricket.

"I say that a wise doctor, when he does not know what he is talking about, should know enough to keep his mouth shut. However, that Marionette is not a stranger to me. I have known him a long time!"

Pinocchio, who until then had been very quiet, shuddered so hard that the bed shook.

"That Marionette," continued the Talking Cricket, "is a rascal of the worst kind."

Pinocchio opened his eyes and closed them again.

"He is rude, lazy, a runaway."

Pinocchio hid his face under the sheets.

"That Marionette is a disobedient son who is breaking his father's heart!"

Long shuddering sobs were heard, cries, and deep sighs.

Think how surprised everyone was when, on raising the sheets, they discovered Pinocchio half melted in tears!

"When the dead weep, they are beginning to recover," said the Crow solemnly.

"I am sorry to contradict my famous friend and colleague," said the Owl, "but as far as I'm concerned, I think that when the dead weep, it means they do not want to die."

不爱吃药的匹诺曹

吃药对小孩子真的那么难吗？看看匹诺曹的表现就知道了，他对着药水大叫“这该死的药水是苦的，我不要喝，不喝，不喝，不喝……”生病很痛苦的，如果吃药病就会好起来，为什么小孩还那么不喜欢吃药呢？匹诺曹为我们解开了这个疑惑，“我们孩子都这样！我们比怕生病更怕喝药水。”

As soon as the three doctors had left the room, the Fairy went to Pinocchio's bed and, touching him on the forehead, noticed that he was burning with fever.

She took a glass of water, put a white powder into it, and, handing it to the Marionette, said lovingly to him:

"Drink this, and in a few days you'll be up and well."

Pinocchio looked at the glass, made a wry（歪曲的）face, and asked in a whining voice: "Is it sweet or bitter?"

"It is bitter, but it is good for you."

"If it is bitter, I don't want it."

"Drink it!"

"I don't like anything bitter."

"Drink it and I'll give you a lump of sugar to take the bitter taste from your mouth."

"Where's the sugar?"

"Here it is," said the Fairy, taking a lump from a golden sugar bowl.

"I want the sugar first, then I'll drink the bitter water."

"Do you promise?"

"Yes."

The Fairy gave him the sugar and Pinocchio, after chewing and swallowing it in a twinkling, said, smacking his lips:

"If only sugar were medicine! I should take it every day."

"Now keep your promise and drink these few drops of water. They'll be good for you."

Pinocchio took the glass in both hands and stuck his nose into it. He lifted it to his mouth and once more stuck his nose into it.

"It is too bitter, much too bitter! I can't drink it."

"How do you know, when you haven't even tasted it?"

"I can imagine it. I smell it. I want another lump of sugar, then I'll drink it."

The Fairy, with all the patience of a good mother, gave him more sugar and again handed him the glass.

"I can't drink it like that," the Marionette said, making more wry faces.

"Why?"

"Because that feather pillow on my feet bothers me."

The Fairy took away the pillow.

"It's no use. I can't drink it even now."

"What's the matter now?"

"I don't like the way that door looks. It's half open."

The Fairy closed the door.

"I won't drink it," cried Pinocchio, bursting out crying.

"I won't drink this awful water. I won't. I won't! No, no, no, no!"

"My boy, you'll be sorry."

"I don't care."

"You are very sick."

"I don't care."

"In a few hours the fever will take you far away to another world."

"I don't care."

"Aren't you afraid of death?"

"Not a bit. I'd rather die than drink that awful medicine."

最终匹诺曹还是把药吃了，虽然匹

诺曹说“宁愿死也不吃药”。可是当他看到兔子把棺材抬到他跟前时，匹诺曹一定被吓到了，竟然嚷着要吃药。吃完药，匹诺曹又活跃起来，满屋子又跑又跳，“活像一只刚会啼的小公鸡”。看来对付顽皮的孩子，“吓唬”这招很管用。

At that moment, the door of the room flew open and in came four Rabbits as black as ink, carrying a small black coffin on their shoulders.

"What do you want from me?" asked Pinocchio.

"We have come for you," said the largest Rabbit.

"For me? But I'm not dead yet!"

"No, not dead yet; but you will be in a few moments since you have refused to take the medicine which would have made you well."

"Oh, Fairy, my Fairy," the Marionette cried out, "give me that glass! Quick, please! I don't want to die! No, no, not yet—not yet!"

And holding the glass with his two hands, he swallowed the medicine at one gulp.

"Well," said the four Rabbits, "this time we have made the trip for nothing."

And turning on their heels, they marched solemnly out of the room, carrying their little black coffin and muttering and grumbling between their teeth.

In a twinkling, Pinocchio felt fine. With one leap he was out of bed and into his clothes.

The Fairy, seeing him run and jump around the room gay as a bird on wing, said to him:

"My medicine was good for you, after all, wasn't it?"

"Good indeed! It has given me new life."

"Why, then, did I have to beg you so hard to make you drink it?"

"I'm a boy, you see, and all boys hate medicine more than they do sickness."

"What a shame! Boys ought to know, after all, that medicine, taken in time, can save them from much pain and even from death."

"Next time I won't have to be begged so hard. I'll remember those black Rabbits with the black coffin on their shoulders and I'll take the glass and pouf!—down it will go!"

撒谎的孩子鼻子会变长

仙女教育匹诺曹不能说谎，可是顽皮的匹诺曹如果不得到教训的话是不会听话的。所以仙女给他施了魔法，每当他说一次慌他的鼻子就长一截。当匹诺曹连说三次慌后,鼻子长得连在屋子里转身都不能了。这时匹诺曹才开始醒悟，做一个诚实的孩子真是太重要了。

"Come here now and tell me how it came about that you found yourself in the hands of the Assassins."

"It happened that Fire Eater gave me five gold pieces to give to my Father, but on the way, I met a Fox and a Cat, who asked me, "Do you want the five pieces to become two thousand?" And I said, "Yes." And they said, "Come with us to the Field of Wonders." And I said, "Let's go." Then they said, "Let us stop at the Inn of the Red Lobster for dinner and after midnight we'll set out again." We ate and went to sleep. When I awoke they were gone and I started out in the darkness all alone. On the road I met two Assassins dressed in black coal sacks, who said to me, "Your money or your life!" and I said, "I haven't any money"; for, you see, I had put the money under my tongue. One of them tried to put his hand in my mouth and I bit it off and spat it out; but it wasn't a hand, it was a cat's paw. And they ran after me and I ran and ran, till at last they caught me and tied my neck with a rope and hanged me to a tree, saying, "Tomorrow we'll come back for you and you'll be dead and your mouth will be open, and then we'll take the gold pieces that you have hidden under your tongue."

"Where are the gold pieces now?" the Fairy asked.

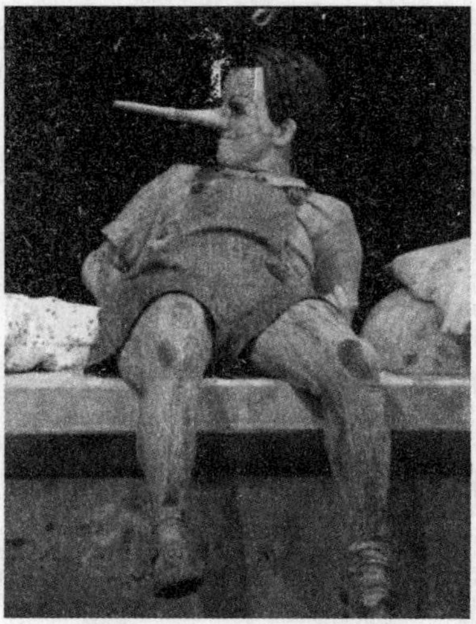

"I lost them," answered Pinocchio, but he told a lie, for he had them in his pocket.

As he spoke, his nose, long though it was, became at least two inches longer.

"And where did you lose them?"

"In the wood near by."

At this second lie, his nose grew a few more inches.

"If you lost them in the near-by wood," said the Fairy,

"We'll look for them and find them, for everything that is lost there is always found."

"Ah, now I remember," replied the Marionette, becoming more and more confused. "I did not lose the gold pieces, but I swallowed them when I drank the medicine."

At this third lie, his nose became longer than ever, so long that he could not even turn around. If he turned to the right, he knocked it against the bed or into the windowpanes (窗框内的玻璃); if he turned to the left, he struck the walls or the door; if he raised it a bit, he almost put the Fairy's eyes out. The Fairy sat looking at him and laughing.

"Why do you laugh?" the Marionette asked her, worried now at the sight of his growing nose.

"I am laughing at your lies."

"How do you know I am lying?"

"Lies, my boy, are known in a moment. There are two kinds of lies, lies with short legs and lies with long noses. Yours, just now, happen to have long noses."

Pinocchio, not knowing where to hide his shame, tried to escape from the room, but his nose had become so long that he could not get it out of the door.

背后的故事

心中永远的匹诺曹

木偶奇遇记的作者科洛迪(1826—1890年)是意大利儿童文学作家，很早就投身于民族复兴运动，后从事新闻工作，撰写社会新闻和戏剧评论。19世纪70年代开始发表童话《贾涅蒂诺漫游意大利》和《米努佐洛》，用生动有趣的故事和对话，向小读者介绍各方面的科学知识。1880年，在《儿童日报》上连载其代表作《木偶奇遇记》，1883年出版单行本。作品想象丰富，情节曲折有趣，语言生动幽默，寓教于生动风趣的故事之中。

《木偶奇遇记》出版后，被译成多种文字，成为世界著名的儿童文学作品，深得各国小读者的喜爱。改编的同名迪士尼经典动画片荣获两项奥斯卡金像奖，包括最佳歌曲When You Wish Upon A Star及最佳配乐。在迪士尼乐园里也有“木偶奇遇记”的游乐设施。而片中的小蟋蟀、小黑猫、金鱼等角色后来都曾在迪士尼其他动画作品中再度出现。

Tale 8

The Neverland

梦幻岛

—An Episode from Peter Pan

——节选自《彼得·潘》

这是一个小女孩的冒险故事。在一个黑暗的夜晚，一个会飞的男孩彼得·潘飞到了她的窗前，说要教会她和弟弟们飞翔，并带他们去一个充满冒险的地方——梦幻岛。每个孩子都想飞翔，都幻想着自己的“梦幻岛”。小女孩一飞到梦幻岛，立刻被这个美丽而神秘的海岛吸引住了，那里有茂密的丛林、高大的树木，还有野蛮的印第安人以及横行附近海面的坏蛋海盗。不巧，他们被彼得的死敌海盗胡克船长发现，为躲避攻击，温迪三人不幸从空中掉下。小女孩和其他男孩死里逃生，彼得带着他们找到了六、七个隐蔽的树洞，这就是他们在梦幻岛上的秘密基地，平时他们在海岛的深处探险，晚上累了就回到树洞休息游戏。

慢阅读小语

细细品位字里行间流淌出的语言美和思想美，你就会感受到“Jump and get an apple”的喜悦，不知不觉间自身修养得到了提升……

1 **Peter measures you for your tree as carefully as for a suit of clothes: the only difference being that the clothes are made to fit you, while you have to be made to fit the tree.**

彼得为寻找适合你的树洞而量你的身材时，就像给你量一身衣裳一样仔细。唯一不同的地方是，衣裳是按照你的身材剪裁的；而树呢，必须用你的身体去适应。

2 **The bed was tilted against the wall by day, and let down at 6:30, when it filled nearly half the room; and all the boys slept in it, except Michael, lying like sardines in a tin. There was a strict rule against turning round until one gave the signal, when all turned at once.**

床铺白天就靠墙斜立着，到晚上六点半钟时才放下来，这时候，床铺几乎占去了半间屋子。除迈克尔外，所有的孩子都睡在这张床上，一个挨一个躺着，像罐头里的沙丁鱼一样。翻身有严格的规定，由一个人发号令，大家一齐翻身。

3 **The couch, as she always called it, was a genuine Queen Mab, with club legs; and she varied the bedspreads according to what fruit-blossom was in season. Her mirror was a Puss-in-Boots, of which there are now only three, unchipped, known to fairy dealers; the washstand was Pie-crust and reversible, the chest of drawers an authentic Charming the Sixth, and the carpet and rugs the best (the early) period of Margery and Robin.**

她的床——她总是管它叫卧榻，真正是麦布女王式的，有三叶草形的床脚。床罩随着不同季节的果树花更换。她的镜子是穿长筒靴的猫用的那种镜子，在仙子商贩的货架上，如今只剩下三面还没有被打碎的。洗脸盆是馅饼壳式的，可以翻过来；抽屉柜是货真价实的迷人六世时代的，地毯是马杰里和罗宾极盛时代（早期）的产品。

初到梦幻岛

到了梦幻岛，彼得为温迪他们做的头一件事就是给他们量身材？这是为什么呢？因为在梦幻岛有一个传统，大家都是住在空心树里的，下去时，你只消吸一口气，就能不快不慢地往下滑；上来时，你只消交替着一呼一吸，就能蠕动着爬上来。光是听着就很有趣，这一上一下，还有助于大家锻炼身体呢。

One of the first things Peter did next day was to measure Wendy and John and Michael for hollow trees. Hook, you remember, had sneered at the boys for thinking they needed a tree apiece（每人）, but this was ignorance, for unless your tree fitted you it was difficult to go up and down, and no two of the boys were quite the same size. Once you fitted, you drew in [let out] your breath at the top, and down you went at exactly the right speed, while to ascend you drew in and let out alternately, and so wriggled up. Of course, when you have mastered the action you are able to do these things without thinking of them, and nothing can be more graceful.

But you simply must fit, and Peter measures you for your tree as carefully as for a suit of clothes: the only difference being that the clothes are made to fit you, while you have to be made to fit the tree. Usually it is done quite easily, as by your wearing too many garments or too few, but if you are bumpy in awkward places or the only available tree is an odd shape, Peter does some things to you, and after that you fit. Once you fit, great care must be taken to go on fitting, and this, as Wendy was to discover to her delight, keeps a whole family in perfect condition.

Wendy and Michael fitted their trees at the first try, but John had to

be altered a little.

练了几天以后，温迪他们就能像井里的水桶一样上下自如了。而且他们渐渐地都热烈地爱上了这个地下的家，特别是温迪。这个家像所有的家一样，有着温暖的感觉，但是这个家也是很简陋的，和小熊在地下安的家没差多少。重要的一点是，这是孩子们自己动手建成的家，所以对这个家有着特别的情愫。

After a few days' practice they could go up and down as gaily as buckets in a well. And how ardently they grew to love their home under the ground; especially Wendy. It consisted of one large room, as all houses should do, with a floor in which you could dig [for worms] if you wanted to go fishing, and in this floor grew stout mushrooms of a charming colour, which were used as stools. A Never tree tried hard to grow in the centre of the room, but every morning they sawed the trunk through, level with the floor. By **tea-time** it was always about two feet high, and then they put a door on top of it, the whole thus becoming a table; as soon as they cleared away, they sawed off the trunk again, and thus there was more room to play. There was an enourmous **fireplace** which was in almost any part of the room where you cared to light it, and across this Wendy stretched strings, made of fibre, from which she suspended her washing. The bed was tilted against the wall by day, and let down at 6:30, when it filled nearly half the room; and all the boys slept in it, except Michael, lying like sardines in a tin. There was a strict rule against turning round until one gave the signal,

tea-time 下午吃茶点的时间。下午茶的英文是afternoon tea，一般在下午3点到5点之间。下午茶这个概念大约形成在公元18世纪中叶的英国，刚开始的时候只是一种晚餐之前的止饥方法。英国贵族的晚餐吃得晚，通常都要到晚上八点之后，所以在中餐与晚餐之间，受不了饥饿的人，就开始找些东西来果腹，香浓的温热“红茶”（dark tea）加上糖，或者牛奶（这就成了奶茶），再配上可口的茶点，久而久之，便成了一种惯例，tea-time就是下午茶时间。

fireplace 壁炉。壁炉原本用于西方国家，有装饰作用和实用价值。在西方，壁炉与各种节日有着密切的关系。在万圣节，最重要的仪式就是点燃炉火。在圣诞节的早上，孩子们要做的第一件事情就是飞奔到壁炉旁寻找圣诞老人带给他们的礼物。记忆词尾是“ace”的单词有一个顺口溜，非常有意思：西游记有一段preface（序言），刻在无花果的surface（表面），说天空好大的space（空间），猴王翻筋斗好grace（优美），誓把玉皇大帝replace（取代），被捉后关进了fireplace（壁炉）。

when all turned at once. Michael should have used it also, but Wendy would have [desired] a baby, and he was the littlest, and you know what women are, and the short and long of it is that he was hung up in a basket.

It was rough and simple, and not unlike what baby bears would have made of an underground house in the same circumstances. But there was one recess in the wall, no larger than a bird-cage, which was the private apartment of Tinker Bell. It could be shut off from the rest of the house by a tiny curtain, which Tink, who was most fastidious [particular], always kept drawn when dressing or undressing. No woman, however large, could have had a more exquisite boudoir [dressing room] and bed-chamber combined. The couch, as she always called it, was a genuine **Queen Mab**, with club legs; and she varied the bedspreads according to what fruit-blossom was in season. Her mirror was a Puss-in-Boots, of which there are now only three, unchipped, known to fairy dealers; the washstand was Pie-crust and reversible, the chest of drawers an authentic Charming the Sixth, and the carpet and rugs the best (the early) period of Margery and Robin. There was a chandelier（树枝型的装饰灯）from Tiddlywinks for the look of the thing, but of course she lit the residence herself. Tink was very contemptuous of the rest of the house, as indeed was perhaps inevitable, and her chamber, though beautiful, looked rather conceited, having the appearance of a nose permanently turned up.

Queen Mab 麦布女王。《麦布女王》为英国浪漫主义诗人雪莱（1792-1822）所作的诗。麦布女王是其最早长诗。这部长诗富于哲理，以梦幻的方式，表达了年轻的诗人对于人类最终摆脱愚昧和专制统治，走向光明未来的憧憬和信念。

忙碌的温迪

对温迪来说，梦幻岛的一切都是那么让她着迷，这些喧闹的孩子让她一刻都闲不下来。真的，除了有时候在晚上带一只袜子到地面上来补，整整一个礼拜，她都没有到地面上过。就说做饭吧，她的鼻子就老是离不开那口锅。不过温迪是快乐的，她享受着忙碌的乐趣。

I suppose it was all especially entrancing to Wendy, because those rampagious（喧闹的）boys of hers gave her so much to do. Really there were whole weeks when, except perhaps with a stocking in the evening, she was never above ground. The cooking, I can tell you, kept her nose to the pot, and even if there was nothing in it, even if there was no pot, she had to keep watching that it came aboil just the same. You never exactly knew whether there would be a real meal or just a make-believe, it all depended upon Peter's whim: he

could eat, really eat, if it was part of a game, but he could not stodge [cram down the food] just to feel stodgy [stuffed with food], which is what most children like better than anything else; the next best thing being to talk about it. Make-believe was so real to him that during a meal of it you could see him getting rounder. Of course it was trying, but you simply had to follow his lead, and if you could prove to him that you were getting loose for your tree he let you stodge.

Wendy's favourite time for sewing and darning was after they had all gone to bed. Then, as she expressed it, she had a breathing time for herself; and she occupied it in making new things for them, and putting double pieces on the knees, for they were all most frightfully hard on their knees.

When she sat down to a basketful of their stockings, every heel with a hole in it, she would fling up her arms and exclaim, "Oh dear, I am sure I sometimes think spinsters are to be envied!"

Her face beamed when she exclaimed this.

You remember about her pet wolf.

Well, it very soon discovered that she had come to the island and it found her out, and they just ran into each other's arms. After that it followed her about everywhere.

忙里偷闲，为了不忘记爸爸妈妈和世间的生活，她用考试的方式来留住旧日的回忆。别的孩子觉得这有趣极了，硬是要参加考试。他们自备了石板，围坐在桌旁。温迪用另一块石板写下问题，给他们传看。他们看了问题，都用心想，用心写。不过有一个人例外，那就是彼得，他没有参加考试。一来除了温迪，所有的母亲他都瞧不起，二来他是岛上唯一一个不会读写的孩子，连最短的字也不会。

As time wore on did she think much about the beloved parents she had left behind her? This is a difficult question, because it is quite impossible to say how time does wear on in the Neverland, where it is calculated by moons and suns, and there are ever so many more of them than on the mainland. But I am afraid that Wendy did not really worry about her father and mother; she was absolutely confident that they would always keep the window open for her to fly back by, and this gave her complete ease of mind. What did disturb her at times was that John remembered his parents vaguely only, as people he had once known, while Michael was quite willing to believe that she was really his mother. These things scared her a little, and nobly anxious to do her duty, she tried to fix the old life in their minds by setting them examination papers on it, as like as possible to the ones she used to do at school. The other boys thought this awfully interesting, and insisted on joining, and they made slates for themselves, and sat round the table, writing and thinking hard about the questions she had written on another slate and passed round. They were the most ordinary questions—

"What was the colour of Mother's eyes? Which was taller, Father or Mother? Was Mother blonde（白皙皮肤的）or brunette（浅黑肤色的）? Answer all three questions if possible." "(A) Write an essay of not less than 40 words on How I spent my last Holidays, or The Characters of Father and Mother compared. Only one of these to be attempted." Or "(1) Describe Mother's laugh; (2) Describe Father's laugh; (3) Describe Mother's Party Dress; (4) Describe the Kennel and its Inmate."

They were just everyday questions like these, and when you could not answer them you were told to make a cross; and it was really dreadful what a number of crosses even John made. Of course the only boy who replied to every question was Slightly, and no one could have been more hopeful of coming out first, but his answers were perfectly ridiculous, and he really came out last: a melancholy (郁闷) thing.

Peter did not compete. For one thing he despised all mothers except Wendy, and for another he was the only boy on the island who could neither write nor spell; not the smallest word. He was above all that sort of thing.

By the way, the questions were all written in the past tense. What was the colour of Mother's eyes, and so on. Wendy, you see, had been forgetting, too.

梦幻岛上的冒险故事

在梦幻岛上，冒险的事天天有。因为这里住着一位冒险家，彼得可是个不折不扣的冒险大王。不过彼得是个爱忘事的孩子，有时候他也记不起来自己的冒险事。我们就姑且认为他说的冒险经历都是真的吧，哪有孩子不喜欢听故事呢？尤其是冒险故事。

Adventures, of course, as we shall see, were of daily occurrence; but about this time Peter invented, with Wendy's help, a new game that fascinated him enormously, until he suddenly had no more interest in it, which, as you have been told, was what always happened with his games. It consisted in pretending not to have adventures, in doing the sort of thing John and Michael had been doing all their lives, sitting on stools flinging balls in the air, pushing each other, going out for walks and coming back without having killed so much as a grizzly. To see Peter doing nothing on a stool was a great sight; he could not help looking solemn at such times, to sit still seemed to him such a comic thing to do. He boasted that he had gone walking for the good of his health. For several suns these were the most novel of all adventures to him; and John and Michael had to pretend to be delighted also; otherwise he would have treated them severely.

He often went out alone, and when he came back you were never absolutely certain whether he had had an adventure or not. He might have forgotten it so completely that he said nothing about it; and then when you went out you found the body; and, on the other hand, he might say a great deal about it, and yet you could not find the body. Sometimes he came home with his head bandaged, and then Wendy cooed over him and bathed it in lukewarm（温暖适度的）water, while he told a dazzling tale. But she was never quite sure, you know. There were, however, many adventures which she knew to be true because she was in them herself, and there were still more that were at least partly true, for the other boys were in them and said they were wholly true. To describe them all would require a book as large as an English-Latin, Latin- English Dictionary, and the most we can do is to give one as a specimen of an average hour on the island. The difficulty is which one to choose. Should we take the brush with the redskins at Slightly Gulch? It was a sanguinary [cheerful] affair, and especially interesting as showing one of Peter's peculiarities, which was that in the middle of a fight he would suddenly change sides. At the Gulch, when victory was still in the balance, sometimes leaning this way and sometimes that, he called out, "I'm redskin to-day; what are you, Tootles?" And Tootles answered, "Redskin; what are you, Nibs?" and Nibs said, "Redskin; what are you Twin?" and so on; and they were all redskins; and of course this would have ended the fight had not the real redskins fascinated by Peter's methods, agreed to be lost boys for that once, and so at it they all went again, more fiercely than ever.

The extraordinary upshot of this adventure was—but we have not decided yet that this is the adventure we are to narrate. Perhaps a better one would be the night attack by the redskins on the house under the ground, when several of them stuck in the hollow trees and had to be pulled out like corks. Or we might tell how Peter saved Tiger Lily's life in the Mermaids' Lagoon, and so made her his ally.

背后的故事

童话剧《彼得·潘》

《彼得·潘》的作者詹姆斯·巴里出生于苏格兰的一个织布工人的家庭，1882年毕业于爱丁堡大学，当过编辑，1885年迁居伦敦，从事新闻主笔工作，并开始创作小说。巴里早年爱好戏剧，1897年，他把他的畅销作品、长篇小说《小牧师》改编成剧本上演获得成功，此后，他的大部分作品都是戏剧。1928年巴里当选为英国作家协会主席，1930年受聘为爱丁堡大学名誉校长。

《彼得·潘》是巴里最著名的一部童话剧。巴里迁居伦敦后，住在肯辛顿公园附近，每天上下班都见一群孩子在草地上玩耍。他们用树枝盖小屋，用泥土做点心，扮演童话中的种种角色。巴里被他们的游戏吸引，也加入到其中。这些孩子一个个都成了这位作家故事中的人物，那个最活跃的男孩彼得，便化作了他童话的主人公。《彼得·潘》1904年12月27日在伦敦公演后，引起巨大轰动。从此，每年这一天都在伦敦上演此剧。后来，巴里把它改写成童话故事，从此，《彼得·潘》被译成多种文字传到国外。以彼得·潘的故事为内容的图画故事、纪念册、版画、邮票风行欧美各国，每年圣诞节，西方许多国家都在电视上播放这个节目，作为献给孩子们的礼物。

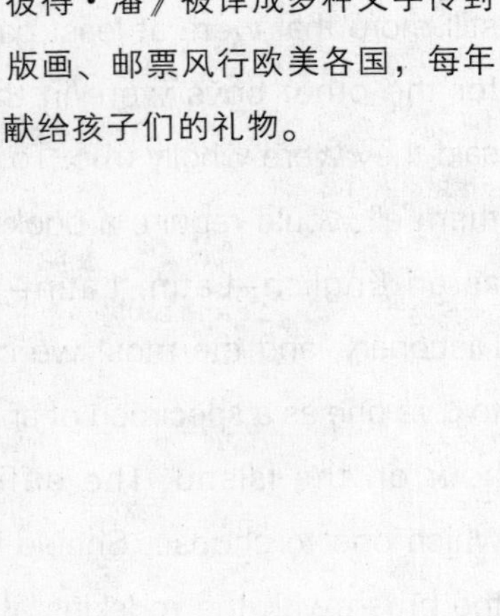

Tale 9

Jack and the Beanstalk

杰克和魔豆

杰克的童年是彩色的，你的童年是什么颜色的？杰克因为有了魔豆，在他身边发生了一连串惊奇的故事，你是否也渴望拥有这样一颗魔豆呢？《杰克和魔豆》这篇童话故事旨在鼓励大家创造机会、把握机会、挑战机会、享受机会，从而也能实现“种豆得豆、开花结果”的梦想。我们每一个人都希望拥有这样一颗种子，并用智慧、青春、能量来作肥料，在“精神”的后花园里，培育出具有神奇魔力的豆田。

慢阅读小语

细细品位字里行间流淌出的语言美和思想美，你就会感受到“Jump and get an apple”的喜悦，不知不觉间自身修养得到了提升……

1 **The stalks had twined and twisted themselves together till they formed quite a ladder.**

豆茎成对的旋转着生长，就像梯子一样。

2 **Jack felt a little tired, and thought for a moment that he would go back again; but he was a very persevering boy, and he knew that the way to succeed in anything is not to give up.**

杰克有些累了，甚至有那么一刻他想爬回去了。但是他是个有恒心的男孩，他知道在通往成功的路上是不能放弃的。

3 **You must get into the castle, and if possible possess yourself of a hen that lays golden eggs, and a harp that talks. Remember, all the giant possesses is really yours.**

你要进入城堡里，如果有可能的话就想办法得到下金蛋的鸡和会说话的竖琴。记住，巨人的所有东西其实都应该是你的。

4 **If you had looked at the gigantic Beanstalk and only stupidly wondered about it, I should have left you where misfortune had placed you, only restoring her cow to your mother. But you showed an inquiring mind, and great courage and enterprise, therefore you deserve to rise; and when you mounted the Beanstalk you climbed the Ladder of Fortune.**

如果当你看到魔茎的时候只是很蠢蠢地表示惊讶的话，我就会让你继续保持着你的不幸，只能和妈妈和奶牛一起生活。不过你表现出了你的探索欲望、勇气和进取心，因此你应该得到好运。当你爬上豆茎的那一刻起，你就爬上了通往财富的梯子。

用奶牛换豌豆

从前，有一个叫做杰克的男孩，他和妈妈生活在一起。杰克的家里十分贫穷，只有一头奶牛与他们相伴。为了不再挨饿，他们只能忍痛卖掉奶牛。妈妈让杰克去集市上卖奶牛，杰克能办好这件妈妈交给他的任务吗？他又从集市带回来了什么神秘的东西呢？

Once upon a time there was a poor widow who lived in a little cottage with her only son Jack.

Jack was a giddy, thoughtless boy, but very kind-hearted and affectionate.

There had been a hard winter, and after it the poor woman had suffered from fever and ague. Jack did no work as yet, and by degrees they grew dreadfully poor. The widow saw that there was no means of keeping Jack and herself from starvation but by selling her cow; so one morning she said to her son, "I am too weak to go myself, Jack, so you must take the cow to market for me, and sell her."

Jack liked going to market to sell the cow very much; but as he was on the way, he met a butcher who had some beautiful beans in his hand.

Jack stopped to look at them, and the butcher told the boy that they were of great value, and persuaded the silly lad to sell the cow for these beans.

When he brought them home to his mother instead of the money she expected for her nice cow, she was very vexed and shed many tears, scolding Jack for his folly. He was very sorry, and mother and son went to bed very sadly that night; their last hope seemed gone.

At daybreak Jack rose and went out into the garden.

"At least," he thought, "I will sow the wonderful beans. Mother says that they are just common scarlet-runners（红花菜豆）, and nothing else; but I may as well sow them."

So he took a piece of stick, and made some holes in the ground, and put in the beans.

That day they had very little dinner, and went sadly to bed, knowing that for the next day there would be none and Jack, unable to sleep from grief and vexation, got up at day-dawn and went out into the garden.

What was his amazement to find that the beans had grown up in the night, and climbed up and up till they covered the high cliff that sheltered the cottage, and disappeared above it! The stalks had twined and twisted themselves together till they formed quite a ladder.

"It would be easy to climb it," thought Jack.

And, having thought of the experiment, he at once resolved to carry it out, for Jack was a good climber. However, after his late mistake about the cow, he thought he had better consult his mother first.

通往天上的梯子

不起眼的豌豆竟然越长越高，一直升到云朵里。杰克和妈妈都被眼前的"豆茎"惊呆了。这使杰克非常好奇，他想爬到天上去一探究竟。于是，杰克真的沿着豆茎向上爬，在天空中有什么惊奇等着他呢？

So Jack called his mother, and they both gazed in silent wonder at the Beanstalk（豆茎）, which was not only of great height, but was thick enough to bear Jack's weight.

"I wonder where it ends," said Jack to his mother; "I think I will climb up and see."

His mother wished him not to venture up this strange ladder, but Jack coaxed（哄）her to give her consent to the attempt, for he was certain there must be something wonderful in the Beanstalk; so at last she yielded to his wishes.

Jack instantly began to climb, and went up and up on the ladder-like bean till everything he had left behind him— the cottage, the village, and even the tall church tower— looked quite little, and still he could not see the top of the Beanstalk.

Jack felt a little tired, and thought for a moment that he would go back again; but he was a very persevering boy, and he knew that the way to succeed in anything is not to give up. So after resting for a moment he went on.

After climbing higher and higher, till he grew afraid to look down for fear he should be giddy（头晕的）, Jack at last reached the top of the Beanstalk, and found himself in a beautiful country, finely wooded, with beautiful meadows covered with sheep. A crystal stream ran through the pastures（牧场）; not far from the place where he had got off the Beanstalk stood a fine, strong castle.

Jack wondered very much that he had never heard of or seen this castle before; but when he reflected on the subject, he saw that it was as much separated from the village by the perpendicular（垂直的）rock on which it stood as if it were in another land.

While Jack was standing looking at the castle, a very strange-looking woman came out of the wood, and advanced towards him.

She wore a pointed cap of quilted red satin turned up with ermine, her hair streamed loose over her shoulders, and she walked with a staff.

Jack took off his cap and made her a bow.

"If you please, ma'am," said he, "is this your house?"

"No," said the old lady. "Listen, and I will tell you the story of that castle."

杰克遇到了一位奇怪的人，她向杰克讲起了一个关于骑士和城堡的故事。骑士一家经历了劫难，骑士被巨人杀死了，城堡和财宝也被巨人抢走了，不过幸运的是骑士的妻子躲过了劫难，还为骑士生下了一个男孩。怪人的故事似乎已经讲完了，其实，一段故事的结束，预示着下一段故事的开始，骑士和城堡的故事已经结束，杰克的故事才刚刚上演。

"Once upon a time there was a noble **knight**, who lived in this castle, which is on the borders of **Fairyland**. He had a fair and beloved wife and several lovely children: and as his

knight 骑士。骑士是指欧洲中世纪时受过正式军事训练的骑兵，后来演变为一种荣誉称号，用于表示一个社会阶层。骑士是战斗、忠诚的象征，每一个骑士都以骑士精神作为守则，是英雄的化身（但实际情况不一定是如此）。Knight有很多习惯用语，常见的有：knight of fortune冒险家、knight of industry骗子、knight of the brush画家、knight of the field流浪汉、knight of the knife小偷。

fairyland 仙境。指神话般的、想象的国土。其实fairyland主要是由单词fairy和land组合而成，而fairy可以和很多词组合，如：fairytale童话式的、fairylike仙女般的，fairy还有一个习惯用语fairy godmother，指（危难时提供及时帮助的）慷慨朋友；救星。

neighbours, the little people, were very friendly towards him, they bestowed on him many excellent and precious gifts. Rumour whispered of these treasures; and a monstrous giant, who lived at no great distance, and who was a very wicked being, resolved to obtain possession of them. So he bribed a false servant to let him inside the castle, when the knight was in bed and asleep, and he killed him as he lay. Then he went to the part of the castle which was the nursery, and also killed all the poor little ones he found there."

"Happily for her, the lady was not to be found. She had gone with her infant son, who was only two or three months old, to visit her old nurse, who lived in the valley; and she had been detained all night there by a storm."

"The next morning, as soon as it was light, one of the servants at the castle, who had managed to escape, came to tell the poor lady of the sad fate of her husband and her pretty babes. She could scarcely believe him at first, and was eager at once to go back and share the fate of her dear ones; but the old nurse, with many tears, besought her to remember that she had still a child, and that it was her duty to preserve her life for the sake of the poor innocent."

"The lady yielded to this reasoning, and consented to remain at her nurse's house as the best place of concealment; for the servant told her that the giant had vowed, if he could find her, he would kill both her and her baby. Years rolled on. The old nurse died, leaving her cottage and the few articles of furniture it contained to her poor lady, who dwelt in it, working as a peasant for her daily bread. Her spinning-wheel（手纺车）and the milk of a cow, which she had purchased with the little money she had with her, sufficed for the scanty subsistence of herself and her little son."

"There was a nice little garden attached to the cottage, in which they cultivated peas, beans, and cabbages, and the lady was not ashamed to go out at harvest time, and glean in the fields to supply her little son's wants."

"Jack, that poor lady is your mother. This castle was once your father's, and must again be yours."

杰克从来不知道自己的身世竟然如此传奇，这让他大吃一惊。他现在该怎么办？他要为父亲报仇吗？他该如何从巨人那里夺回城堡呢？勇敢的杰克能承担如此重任吗？请放心，杰克是不会让任何人失望的。

Jack uttered a cry of surprise.

"My mother! Oh, madam, what ought I to do? My poor father! My dear mother!"

"Your duty requires you to win it back for your mother. But the task is a very difficult one, and full of peril, Jack. Have you courage to undertake it?"

"I fear nothing when I am doing right," said Jack.

"Then," said the lady in the red cap, "you are one of those who slay giants."

You must get into the castle, and if possible possess yourself of a hen that lays golden eggs, and a harp（竖琴）that talks. Remember, all the giant possesses is really yours." As she ceased speaking, the lady of the red hat suddenly disappeared, and of course Jack knew she was a fairy.

Jack determined at once to attempt the adventure; so he advanced, and blew the horn which hung at the castle portal（入口）. The door was opened in a minute or two by a frightful giantess, with one great eye in the middle of her forehead.

As soon as Jack saw her he turned to run away, but she caught him, and dragged him into the castle.

"Ho, ho!" she laughed terribly. "You didn't expect to see me here, that is clear! No, I shan't let you go again. I am weary of my life. I am so overworked, and I don't see why I should not have a page as well as other ladies. And you shall be my boy. You shall clean the knives, and black the boots, and make the fires, and help me generally when the giant is out. When he is at home I must hide you, for he has eaten up all my pages hitherto, and you would be a dainty morsel, my little lad."

While she spoke she dragged Jack right into the castle. The poor boy was very much frightened, as I am sure you and I would have been in his place. But he remembered that fear disgraces a man; so he struggled to be brave and make the best of things.

"I am quite ready to help you, and do all I can to serve you, madam," he said, "only I beg you will be good enough to hide me from your husband, for I should not like to be eaten at all."

"That's a good boy," said the Giantess, nodding her head; "it is lucky for you that you did not scream out when you saw me, as the other boys who have been here did, for if you had done so my husband would have awakened and have eaten you, as he did them, for breakfast. Come here, child; go into my wardrobe: he never ventures to open that; you will be safe there."

And she opened a huge wardrobe which stood in the great hall, and shut him into it. But the keyhole was so large that it ad-mitted plenty of air, and he could see everything that took place through it. By-and-by he heard a heavy tramp on the stairs, like the lumbering along of a great cannon, and then a voice like thunder cried out;

"Fe, fa, fi-fo-fum,

I smell the breath of an Englishman.

Let him be alive or let him be dead,

I'll grind his bones to make my bread."

"Wife," cried the Giant, "there is a man in the castle. Let me have him for breakfast."

"You are grown old and stupid," cried the lady in her loud tones. "It is only a nice fresh steak off an elephant, that I have cooked for you, which you smell. There, sit down and make a good breakfast."

And she placed a huge dish before him of savoury steaming meat, which greatly pleased him, and made him forget his idea of an Englishman being in the castle. When he had breakfasted he went out for a walk; and then the Giantess opened the door, and made Jack come out to help her. He helped her all day. She fed him well, and when evening came put him back in the wardrobe.

杰克的第一件宝贝

杰克趁巨人熟睡的时候，把下金蛋的鸡抱走了。这只鸡本来就应该属于他的，现在只不过是物归原主而已。杰克真是个好孩子，他冒着生命危险把“宝鸡”夺了回来，当他的妈妈看到他的孩子如此懂事的时候，会不会很欣慰呢?

The Giant came in to supper. Jack watched him through the keyhole, and was amazed to see him pick a wolf's bone, and put half a fowl at a time into his capacious mouth.

When the supper was ended he bade his wife bring him his hen that laid the golden eggs.

"It lays as well as it did when it belonged to that paltry (微不足道的) knight," he said; "indeed I think the eggs are heavier than ever."

The Giantess went away, and soon returned with a little brown hen, which she placed on the table before her husband. "And now, my dear," she said, "I am going for a walk, if you don't want me any longer."

"Go," said the Giant; "I shall be glad to have a nap by-and-by."

Then he took up the brown hen and said to her:

"Lay!" And she instantly laid a golden egg.

"Lay!" said the Giant again. And she laid another.

"Lay!" he repeated the third time. And again a golden egg lay on the table.

Now Jack was sure this hen was that of which the fairy had spoken.

By-and-by the Giant put the hen down on the floor, and soon after went fast asleep, snoring so loud that it sounded like thunder.

Directly Jack perceived that the Giant was fast asleep, he pushed open the door of the wardrobe and crept out; very softly he stole across the room, and, picking up the hen, made haste to

quit the apartment. He knew the way to the kitchen, the door of which he found was left ajar; he opened it, shut and locked it after him, and flew back to the Beanstalk, which he descended as fast as his feet would move.

When his mother saw him enter the house she wept for joy, for she had feared that the fairies had carried him away, or that the Giant had found him. But Jack put the brown hen down before her, and told her how he had been in the Giant's castle, and all his adventures. She was very glad to see the hen, which would make them rich once more.

杰克的第二件宝贝

杰克在妈妈去集市的时候又偷偷爬到巨人的城堡里，这次他要从巨人那里夺回什么宝贝呢？真替杰克捏一把汗啊，他会不会被巨人发现呢？巨人的妻子还会帮助他吗？一切都是未知的，但是相信聪明的你一定能猜出结果，快来验证一下你的猜测吧。

Jack made another journey up the Beanstalk to the Giant's castle one day while his mother had gone to market; but first he dyed his hair and disguised himself. The old woman did not know him again, and dragged him in as she had done before, to help her to do the work; but she heard her husband coming, and hid him in the wardrobe, not thinking that it was the same boy who had stolen the hen. She bade him stay quite still there, or the Giant would eat him.

Then the Giant came in saying:

"Fe, fa, fi-fo-fum,

I smell the breath of an Englishman.

Let him be alive or let him be dead,

I'll grind his bones to make my bread."

"Nonsense!" said the wife, "it is only a roasted bullock that I thought would be a tit-bit for your supper; sit down and I will bring it up at once." The Giant sat down, and soon his wife brought up a roasted bullock on a large dish, and they began their supper. Jack was amazed to see them pick the bones of the bullock as if it had been a lark. As soon as they had finished their meal, the Giantess rose and said:

"Now, my dear, with your leave I am going up to my room to finish the story I am reading. If you want me call for me."

"First," answered the Giant, "bring me my money bags, that I may count my golden pieces before I sleep." The Giantess obeyed. She went and soon returned with two large bags over her shoulders, which she put down by her husband.

"There," she said; "that is all that is left of the knight's money. When you have spent it you must go and take another baron's castle."

"That he shan't, if I can help it," thought Jack.

The Giant, when his wife was gone, took out heaps and heaps of golden pieces, and counted them, and put them in piles, till he was tired of the amusement. Then he swept them all back into their bags, and leaning back in his chair fell fast asleep, snoring so loud that no other sound was audible.

Jack stole softly out of the wardrobe, and taking up the bags of money (which were his very own, because the Giant had stolen them from his father), he ran off, and with great difficulty descending the Beanstalk, laid the bags of gold on his mother's table. She had just returned from town, and was crying at not finding Jack.

"There, mother, I have brought you the gold that my father lost."

"Oh, Jack! You are a very good boy, but I wish you would not risk your precious life in the Giant's castle. Tell me how you came to go there again."

And Jack told her all about it.

Jack's mother was very glad to get the money, but she did not like him to run any risk for her.

But after a time Jack made up his mind to go again to the Giant's castle.

会说话的竖琴

巨人那个健忘的妻子有时候也是可爱的，因为她又一次帮助了杰克。不过杰克这次的行动很不成功，是什么打乱了他的计划？就是那只竖琴，当杰克拿起它时，它喊醒了他的主人。那个忠于主人的竖琴没有错，错的是它选错了主人。

So he climbed the Beanstalk once more, and blew the horn at the Giant's gate. The Giantess soon opened the door; she was very stupid, and did not know him again, but she stopped a minute

before she took him in.

She feared another robbery; but Jack's fresh face looked so innocent that she could not resist him, and so she bade him come in, and again hid him away in the wardrobe.

By-and-by the Giant came home, and as soon as he had crossed the threshold he roared out:

"Fe, fa, fi-fo-fum,

I smell the breath of an Englishman.

Let him be alive or let him be dead,

I'll grind his bones to make my bread."

"You stupid old Giant," said his wife, "you only smell a nice sheep, which I have grilled for your dinner."

And the Giant sat down, and his wife brought up a whole sheep for his dinner. When he had eaten it all up, he said:

"Now bring me my harp, and I will have a little music while you take your walk."

The Giantess obeyed, and returned with a beautiful harp. The framework was all sparkling with diamonds and rubies, and the strings were all of gold.

"This is one of the nicest things I took from the knight," said the Giant.

"I am very fond of music, and my harp is a faithful servant."

So he drew the harp towards him, and said:

"Play!"

And the harp played a very soft, sad air.

"Play something merrier!" said the Giant.

And the harp played a merry tune.

"Now play me a **lullaby**（摇篮曲）," roared the Giant; and the harp

lullaby 摇篮曲。摇篮曲旋律轻柔甜美，原是母亲抚慰小儿入睡的歌曲，通常都很简短。许多大作曲家如莫扎特、舒伯特、勃拉姆斯都写有这种歌曲。对于音乐种类，常见的有：小夜曲（serenade）、交响乐（symphony）、钢琴曲（piano music）、协奏曲（concerto）、小提琴曲（violin music）、四重奏（quartet）、爵士乐（Jazz）、嘻哈音乐（Hip-hop）、摇滚乐（Rock and Roll）。

played a sweet lullaby, to the sound of which its master fell asleep.

Then Jack stole softly out of the wardrobe, and went into the huge kitchen to see if the Giantess had gone out; he found no one there, so he went to the door and opened it softly, for he thought he could not do so with the harp in his hand.

Then he entered the Giant's room and seized the harp and ran away with it; but as he jumped over the threshold the harp called out:

"Master! Master!"

And the Giant woke up.

With a tremendous roar he sprang from his seat, and in two strides had reached the door.

But Jack was very nimble. He fled like lightning with the harp, talking to it as he went (for he saw it was a fairy), and telling it he was the son of its old master, the knight.

Still the Giant came on so fast that he was quite close to poor Jack, and had stretched out his great hand to catch him. But, luckily, just at that moment he stepped upon a loose stone, stumbled, and fell flat on the ground, where he lay at his full length.

This accident gave Jack time to get on the Beanstalk and hasten down it; but just as he reached their own garden he beheld the Giant descending after him.

"Mother I mother!" cried Jack, "make haste and give me the axe."

His mother ran to him with a hatchet in her hand, and Jack with one tremendous blow cut through all the Beanstalks except one.

"Now, mother, stand out of the way!" said he.

杰克胜利了

杰克凭借自己的勇敢和智慧，终于战胜了巨人。一个人是需要勇气的，勇气是动力的加速器，他会推着你完成不可能完成的任务。一个人不可能不遇到困难，其实困难不可怕，可怕的是你不敢面对困难的心。当你选择了勇敢去面对，你会发现，原来它没有想象中那么难。

Jack's mother shrank back, and it was well she did so, for just as the Giant took hold of the last branch of the Beanstalk, Jack cut the stem quite through and darted from the spot.

Down came the Giant with a

terrible crash, and as he fell on his head, he broke his neck, and lay dead at the feet of the woman he had so much injured.

Before Jack and his mother had recovered from their alarm and agitation, a beautiful lady stood before them.

"Jack," said she, "you have acted like a brave knight's son, and deserve to have your inheritance restored to you. Dig a grave and bury the Giant, and then go and kill the Giantess."

"But," said Jack, "I could not kill anyone unless I were fighting with him; and I could not draw my sword upon a woman. Moreover, the Giantess was very kind to me."

The Fairy smiled on Jack.

"I am very much pleased with your generous feeling," she said.

"Nevertheless, return to the castle, and act as you will find needful."

Jack asked the Fairy if she would show him the way to the castle, as the Beanstalk was now down. She told him that she would drive him there in her chariot, which was drawn by two peacocks. Jack thanked her, and sat down in the chariot with her.

The Fairy drove him a long distance round, till they reached a village which lay at the bottom of the hill. Here they found a number of miserable-looking men assembled. The Fairy stopped her carriage and addressed them:

"My friends," said she, "the cruel giant who oppressed you and ate up all your flocks and herds is dead, and this young gentleman was the means of your being delivered from him, and is the son of your kind old master, the knight."

The men gave a loud cheer at these words, and pressed forward to say that they would serve Jack as faithfully as they had served his father.

The Fairy bade them follow her to the castle, and they marched thither in a body, and Jack blew the horn and demanded admittance.

The old Giantess saw them coming from the turret loop-hole. She was very much frightened, for she guessed that something had happened to her husband; and as she came downstairs very fast she caught her foot in her dress, and fell from the top to the bottom and broke her neck.

When the people outside found that the door was not opened to them, they took crowbars and forced the portal. Nobody was to be seen, but on leaving the hall they found the body of the Giantess at the foot of the stairs.

Thus Jack took possession of the castle. The Fairy went and brought his mother to him, with the hen and the harp. He had the Giantess buried, and endeavoured as much as lay in his power to do right to those whom the Giant had robbed.

Before her departure for fairyland, the Fairy explained to Jack that she had sent the butcher to meet him with the beans, in order to try what sort of lad he was.

"If you had looked at the gigantic Beanstalk and only stupidly wondered about it," she said, "I should have left you where misfortune had placed you, only restoring her cow to your mother. But you showed an inquiring mind, and great courage and enterprise, therefore you deserve to rise; and when you mounted the Beanstalk you climbed the Ladder of Fortune."

She then took her leave of Jack and his mother.

背后的故事

新时代的《杰克和魔豆》

《杰克和魔豆》一问世就风靡全球，故事写得神奇而又引人入胜，书中塑造了一个聪明、机智、果敢的少年英雄的形象。

2001年，《杰克和魔豆》被搬上银幕，成为一部穿梭天地人神间的魔幻大片，片中的特技之逼真，令人为之惊叹。但在情节的设置上对传统的故事又进行了一些颠覆，把传说中的恶巨人变成好巨人，把勇斗恶巨人的杰克变成偷窃犯和谋杀犯，值得一提的是，片中的超特技效果，让人应接不暇，感觉耳目一新。

最近这个传诵世界的童话故事将被搬上网游，时下最热门竞速网游《超级跑跑》中将会增开全新地图“杰克和魔豆”。该地图场景以同名童话中爬树部分为主题，在弯曲的树枝上奔驰，于树叶之间跳跃，配以多角度的视点切换效果，让人有如置身《杰克和魔豆》的童话世界中，在清新的画面中体会紧张和曲折的故事情节。

Tale 10

The River Bank

河岸

—An Episode from The Wind in the Willows

——节选自《柳林风声》

明白事理的鼹鼠、聪明机灵的老鼠、睿智持重的獾，还有一个放浪不羁的蟾蜍，他们是《柳林风声》中一群快乐的小伙伴，这些个性鲜明的动物形象，其实都是现实世界中孩子们的缩影。作者细致地描写了季节的流转、大自然的变化以及动物们生活中发生的点点滴滴。而且作者还用诗一样的语言将故事娓娓道来，每一位读者都会被紧紧地扣住心弦。《柳林风声》不同于一般的童话，它蕴含了人情世故的幽默诙谐和纯真善良的童趣。细细揣摩，定会别有一番韵味。

慢阅读小语

细细品位字里行间流淌出的语言美和思想美，你就会感受到“Jump and get an apple”的喜悦，不知不觉间自身修养得到了提升……

1 **The sunshine struck hot on his fur, soft breezes caressed his heated brow, and after the seclusion of the cellarage he had lived in so long the carol of happy birds fell on his dulled hearing almost like a shout.**

太阳晒在他的毛皮上，暖烘烘的，微风轻抚着他发热的额头，在洞穴里蛰居了那么久，听觉都变得迟钝了，连小鸟儿欢快的鸣唱，听起来都跟大声喊叫一样。

2 **By the side of the river he trotted as one trots, when very small, by the side of a man who holds one spell-bound by exciting stories.**

他沿着河边，迈着小碎步跑，像个小娃娃紧跟在大人身边，听他讲惊险故事，听得入了迷似的。

3 **Absorbed in the new life he was entering upon, intoxicated with the sparkle, the ripple, the scents and the sounds and the sunlight, he trailed a paw in the water and dreamed long waking dreams.**

他正深深地沉湎在这种新颖生活里，陶醉在波光、涟漪、芳香、水声、阳光之中。他把一只脚爪伸进水里，做着长长的白日梦。

4 **Packing the basket was not quite such pleasant work as unpacking the basket. It never is.**

收拾篮子这种活儿，不像打开篮子那样叫人高兴，向来如此。

春天来了

整个上午，鼹鼠都在勤奋地干活，为他小小的家屋做春季大扫除。春天的气息，在他头上的天空里吹拂，在他脚下的泥土里游动，在他四周围飘荡。春天那奇妙的追求、渴望的精神，钻进了他的小屋。

The Mole had been working very hard all the morning, **spring-cleaning** his little home. First with brooms, then with dusters; then on ladders and steps and chairs, with a brush and a pail of whitewash; till he had dust in his throat and eyes, and splashes of whitewash all over his black fur, and an aching back and weary arms. Spring was moving in the air above and in the earth below and around him, penetrating even his dark and lowly little house with its spirit of divine discontent and longing. It was small wonder, then, that he suddenly flung down his brush on the floor, said "Bother!" and "O blow!" and also "Hang spring-cleaning!" and bolted out of the house without even waiting to put on his coat. Something up above was calling him imperiously, and he made for the steep little tunnel which answered in his case to the gravelled carriage-drive owned by animals whose residences are nearer to the sun and air. So he scraped and scratched and scrabbled and scrooged and then he scrooged again and scrabbled and scratched and scraped, working busily with his little paws and muttering to himself, "Up we go! Up we go!" till at last, pop! his snout came out into the sunlight, and he found himself rolling in the warm grass of a great meadow.

"This is fine!" he said to himself. "This is better than whitewashing!"

The sunshine struck hot on his

spring-cleaning 春季大扫除。一年之计在于春，经过寒冬的考验，春天是一个生机勃勃的季节。为了迎接新的一年，很多人选择了大扫除来代表对新一年的期望，除故纳新。大扫除也是为了卫生，世界上还有一个“世界卫生日”World Health Day，是每年的4月7日。而世界卫生组织的缩写为WHO，全称是World Health Organization。

fur, soft breezes caressed his heated brow, and after the seclusion of the cellarage he had lived in so long the carol of happy birds fell on his dulled hearing almost like a shout. Jumping off all his four legs at once, in the joy of living and the delight of spring without its cleaning, he pursued his way across the meadow till he reached the hedge on the further side.

"Hold up!" said an elderly rabbit at the gap. "Six **pence** for the privilege of passing by the private road!" He was bowled over in an instant by the impatient and contemptuous Mole, who trotted（小跑）along the side of the hedge chaffing the other rabbits as they peeped hurriedly from their holes to see what the row was about. "Onion-sauce! Onion-sauce!" he remarked jeeringly, and was gone before they could think of a thoroughly satisfactory reply. Then they all started grumbling at each other. "How STUPID you are! Why didn't you tell him..." "Well, why didn't YOU say..." "You might have reminded him..." and so on, in the usual way; but, of course, it was then much too late, as is always the case.

第一次坐船

一切都那么美好，好得简直不像是真的。他跑过一片又一片的草坪，沿着矮树篱，穿过灌木丛，匆匆地游逛。处处都看到鸟儿做窝筑巢，花儿含苞待放，叶儿挤挤嚷嚷——万物都显得那么快乐、忙碌、奋进。他漫无目的地闲逛着，忽然来到一条水流丰盈的大河边，他觉得真是快乐绝顶了。

It all seemed too good to be true. Hither and thither through the meadows he rambled busily, along the hedgerows（灌木篱墙）, across the copses（灌木丛）, finding everywhere birds building, flowers budding, leaves thrusting—everything happy, and progressive, and occupied. And instead of having

penny 便士。便士是小额货币，一英镑等于100便士。所有硬币正面皆为英国君主像，背面铸有币值和图案。a penny是很少的钱，但是pretty penny就指很多钱了，意为“一大笔钱”，penny还有一个很实用的谚语：In for a penny, in for a pound.（一不做二不休。）

an uneasy conscience pricking him and whispering "whitewash!" he somehow could only feel how jolly it was to be the only idle dog among all these busy citizens. After all, the best part of a holiday is perhaps not so much to be resting yourself, as to see all the other fellows busy working.

He thought his happiness was complete when, as he meandered aimlessly along, suddenly he stood by the edge of a full-fed river. Never in his life had he seen a river before—this sleek, sinuous, full-bodied animal, chasing and chuckling, gripping things with a gurgle and leaving them with a laugh, to fling itself on fresh playmates that shook themselves free, and were caught and held again. All was a-shake and a-shiver—glints and gleams and sparkles, rustle and swirl, chatter and bubble. The Mole was bewitched, entranced, fascinated. By the side of the river he trotted as one trots, when very small, by the side of a man who holds one spell-bound by exciting stories; and when tired at last, he sat on the bank, while the river still chattered on to him, a babbling procession of the best stories in the world, sent from the heart of the earth to be told at last to the insatiable sea.

As he sat on the grass and looked across the river, a dark hole in the bank opposite, just above the water's edge, caught his eye, and dreamily he fell to considering what a nice snug（温暖舒适的）dwelling-place it would make for an animal with few wants and fond of a bijou（小巧美观的）riverside residence, above flood level and remote from noise and dust. As he gazed, something bright and small seemed to twinkle down in the heart of it, vanished, then twinkled once more like a tiny star. But it could hardly be a star in such an unlikely situation; and it was too glittering and small for a glow-worm. Then, as he looked, it winked at him, and so declared itself to be an eye; and a small face began gradually to grow up round it, like a frame round a picture.

A brown little face, with whiskers.

A grave round face, with the same twinkle in its eye that had first attracted his notice.

Small neat ears and thick silky hair.

It was the Water Rat!

Then the two animals stood and regarded each other cautiously.

"Hullo, Mole!" said the Water Rat.

"Hullo, Rat!" said the Mole.

"Would you like to come over?" enquired the Rat presently.

"Oh, its all very well to TALK," said the Mole, rather pettishly, he being new to a river and riverside life and its ways.

The Rat said nothing, but stooped and unfastened a rope and hauled on it; then lightly stepped into a little boat which the Mole had not observed. It was painted blue outside and white within, and was just the size for two animals; and the Mole's whole heart went out to it at once, even though he did not yet fully understand its uses.

The Rat sculled smartly across and made fast. Then he held up his forepaw as the Mole stepped gingerly (小心翼翼地) down. "Lean on that!" he said. "Now then, step lively!" and the Mole to his surprise and rapture found himself actually seated in the stern of a real boat.

鼹鼠又惊又喜地发现，自己真的坐上了一只真正的小船！这可是他第一次坐船呢。河鼠对鼹鼠以前从没坐过船特别惊讶，坐船是一件多么美好的事啊。听听河鼠是如何评论坐船这项悠哉游哉的消遣吧。

"This has been a wonderful day!" said he, as the Rat shoved off and took to the sculls again. "Do you know, I've never been in a boat before in all my life."

"What?" cried the Rat, open-mouthed: "Never been in a—you never—well I—what have you been doing, then?"

"Is it so nice as all that?" asked the Mole shyly, though he was quite prepared to believe it as he leant back in his seat and surveyed the cushions, the oars, the rowlocks, and all the fascinating fittings, and felt the boat sway lightly under him.

"Nice? It's the ONLY thing," said the Water Rat solemnly, as he leant forward for his stroke. "Believe me, my young friend, there is NOTHING—absolute nothing—half so much worth doing as simply messing about in boats. Simply messing," he went on dreamily: "messing—about—in—boats; messing—"

"Look ahead, Rat!" cried the Mole

suddenly.

It was too late. The boat struck the bank full tilt. The dreamer, the joyous oarsman, lay on his back at the bottom of the boat, his heels in the air.

"about in boats—or WITH boats," the Rat went on composedly, picking himself up with a pleasant laugh. "In or out of 'em, it doesn't matter. Nothing seems really to matter, that's the charm of it. Whether you get away, or whether you don't; whether you arrive at your destination or whether you reach somewhere else, or whether you never get anywhere at all, you're always busy, and you never do anything in particular; and when you've done it there's always something else to do, and you can do it if you like, but you'd much better not. Look here! If you've really nothing else on hand this morning, supposing we drop down the river together, and have a long day of it?"

The Mole waggled his toes from sheer happiness, spread his chest with a sigh of full contentment, and leaned back blissfully into the soft cushions.

划着小船出游

这么美好的春光，不出去好好玩一下就太可惜了。说干就干，河鼠可是个出游的能手，瞧他的装备就知道了。可鼹鼠是第一次来到河边，对任何东西都很好奇，那就听听河鼠的介绍吧。

"What a day I'm having!" he said. "Let us start at once!"

"Hold hard a minute, then!" said the Rat. He looped the painter through a ring in his landing-stage, climbed up into his hole above, and after a short interval reappeared staggering under a fat, wicker luncheon-basket.

"Shove that under your feet," he observed to the Mole, as he passed it down into the boat. Then he untied the painter and took the sculls again.

"What's inside it?" asked the Mole, wriggling with curiosity.

"There's cold chicken inside it," replied the Rat briefly; "coldtongu ecoldhamcoldbeefpickledgherkinssalad frenchrollscresssandwichespottedmea tgingerbeerlemonadesodawater..."

"O stop, stop," cried the Mole in ecstacies: "This is too much!"

"Do you really think so?" enquired the Rat seriously. "It's only

what I always take on these little excursions; and the other animals are always telling me that I'm a mean beast and cut it VERY fine!"

The Mole never heard a word he was saying. Absorbed in the new life he was entering upon, intoxicated (极其兴奋的) with the sparkle, the ripple, the scents and the sounds and the sunlight, he trailed a paw in the water and dreamed long waking dreams. The Water Rat, like the good little fellow he was, sculled steadily on and forebore to disturb him.

"I like your clothes awfully, old chap," he remarked after some half an hour or so had passed. "I'm going to get a black velvet smoking-suit myself some day, as soon as I can afford it."

"I beg your pardon," said the Mole, pulling himself together with an effort. "You must think me very rude; but all this is so new to me. So—this—is—a—River!"

"THE River," corrected the Rat.

"And you really live by the river? What a jolly life!"

"By it and with it and on it and in it," said the Rat. "It's brother and sister to me, and aunts, and company, and food and drink, and (naturally) washing. It's my world, and I don't want any other. What it hasn't got is not worth having, and what it doesn't know is not worth knowing. Lord! The times we've had together! Whether in winter or summer, spring or autumn, it's always got its fun and its excitements. When the floods are on in February, and my cellars and basement are brimming with drink that's no good to me, and the brown water runs by my best bedroom window; or again when it all drops away and, shows patches of mud that smells like plum-cake, and the rushes and weed clog the channels, and I can potter about dry shod over most of the bed of it and find fresh food to eat, and things careless people have dropped out of boats!"

"But isn't it a bit dull at times?" the Mole ventured to ask. "Just you and the river, and no one else to pass a word with?"

"No one else to—well, I mustn't be hard on you," said the Rat with forbearance. "You're new to it, and of course you don't know. The bank is so crowded nowadays that many people are moving away altogether: O no, it isn't what it used to be, at all. Otters, kingfishers, dabchicks, moorhens, all of them about all day long and always wanting you to DO something—as if a fellow had no business of his own to attend to!"

鼹鼠对河那边草地后面黑幽幽的森林很感兴趣，于是他就向河鼠请教。原来那是野林，里面住着一些不友好的动物。而且很可能在将来会与他们打交道呢。但是鼹鼠知道，老是谈论将来可能发生的麻烦事，哪怕只提一下，都不合乎动物界的礼仪规范，所以，他抛开了这个话题。又问起比野林更远的地方是什么，这似乎是一个比较深刻的问题，因为河鼠的回答已很模糊。

"What lies over THERE? " asked the Mole, waving a paw towards a background of woodland that darkly framed the water-meadows on one side of the river.

"That? O, that's just the Wild Wood," said the Rat shortly. "We don't go there very much, we river-bankers."

"Aren't they—aren't they very NICE people in there?" said the Mole, a trifle nervously.

"W-e-ll," replied the Rat, "let me see. The squirrels are all right. AND the rabbits—some of 'em, but rabbits are a mixed lot. And then there's Badger, of course. He lives right in the heart of it; wouldn't live anywhere else, either, if you paid him to do it. Dear old Badger! Nobody interferes with HIM. They'd better not," he added significantly.

"Why, who SHOULD interfere with him?" asked the Mole.

"Well, of course—there—are others," explained the Rat in a hesitating sort of way.

"Weasels—and stoats—and foxes—and so on. They're all right in a way—I'm very good friends with them—pass the time of day when we meet, and all that—but they break out sometimes, there's no denying it, and then—well, you can't really trust them, and that's the fact."

The Mole knew well that it is quite against animal-etiquette (礼节) to dwell on possible trouble ahead, or even to allude to it; so he dropped the subject.

"And beyond the Wild Wood

again?" he asked: "Where it's all blue and dim, and one sees what may be hills or perhaps they mayn't, and something like the smoke of towns, or is it only cloud-drift?"

"Beyond the Wild Wood comes the Wide World," said the Rat. "And that's something that doesn't matter, either to you or me. I've never been there, and I'm never going, nor you either, if you've got any sense at all. Don't ever refer to it again, please. Now then! Here's our backwater at last, where we're going to lunch."

岸边野餐

午饭时间到了，去哪里吃呢？鼹鼠有了个好主意。以天为篷，以地为席，享受着温暖的阳光，品尝着美味，这是何等的逍遥自在？顺便再听听岸边居民的故事，再结交几个朋友，鼹鼠的一天真是多姿多彩啊！

Leaving the main stream, they now passed into what seemed at first sight like a little land-locked lake. Green turf sloped down to either edge, brown snaky tree-roots gleamed below the surface of the quiet water, while ahead of them the silvery shoulder and foamy tumble of a weir, armin-arm with a restless dripping mill-wheel, that held up in its turn a greygabled mill-house, filled the air with a soothing murmur of sound, dull and smothery, yet with little clear voices speaking up cheerfully out of it at intervals. It was so very beautiful that the Mole could only hold up both forepaws and gasp, "O my! O my! O my!"

The Rat brought the boat alongside the bank, made her fast, helped the still awkward Mole safely ashore, and swung out the luncheon-basket. The Mole begged as a favour to be allowed to unpack it all by himself; and the Rat was very pleased to indulge him, and to sprawl at full length on the grass and rest, while his excited friend shook out the table-cloth and spread it, took out all the mysterious packets one by one and arranged their contents in due order, still gasping, "O my! O my!" at each fresh revelation.

When all was ready, the Rat said, "Now, pitch in, old fellow!" and the Mole was indeed very glad to obey, for he had started his spring-cleaning at a very early hour that morning, as people WILL do, and had not paused for bite or sup; and he had been through a very great deal since that distant time which now seemed so many days ago.

"What are you looking at?" said the Rat presently, when the edge of their hunger was somewhat dulled, and the Mole's eyes were able to wander off the table-cloth a little.

"I am looking," said the Mole, "at a streak of bubbles that I see travelling along the surface of the water. That is a thing that strikes me as funny."

"Bubbles? Oho!" said the Rat, and chirruped cheerily in an inviting sort of way.

A broad glistening muzzle showed itself above the edge of the bank, and the Otter hauled himself out and shook the water from his coat.

"Greedy beggars!" he observed, making for the provender. "Why didn't you invite me, Ratty?"

"This was an impromptu affair," explained the Rat. "By the way—my friend Mr. Mole."

"Proud, I'm sure," said the Otter, and the two animals were friends forthwith.

"Such a rumpus everywhere!" continued the Otter. "All the world seems out on the river to-day. I came up this backwater to try and get a moment's peace, and then stumble upon you fellows!—At least—I beg pardon—I don't exactly mean that, you know."

There was a rustle behind them, proceeding from a hedge wherein last year's leaves still clung thick, and a stripy head, with high shoulders behind it, peered forth on them.

"Come on, old Badger!" shouted the Rat.

The Badger trotted forward a pace or two; then grunted, "H'm! Company," and turned his back and disappeared from view.

"That's JUST the sort of fellow he is!" observed the disappointed Rat. "Simply hates Society! Now we shan't see any more of him to-day. Well, tell us, WHO'S out on the river?"

"Toad's out, for one," replied the Otter. "In his brand-new wager-boat;

new togs, new everything!"

The two animals looked at each other and laughed.

"Once, it was nothing but sailing," said the Rat, "Then he tired of that and took to punting. Nothing would please him but to punt all day and every day, and a nice mess he made of it. Last year it was house-boating, and we all had to go and stay with him in his house-boat, and pretend we liked it. He was going to spend the rest of his life in a house-boat. It's all the same, whatever he takes up; he gets tired of it, and starts on something fresh."

"Such a good fellow, too," remarked the Otter reflectively: "But no stability—especially in a boat!"

河岸居民们口中的蟾蜍到底是个什么样的人物呢？老獾和水獭都出场了，怎么能少了大名鼎鼎的蟾蜍呢？这位大家口中的“疯狂公子”就是与众不同，连出场都这么“引人注目”。河鼠和鼹鼠的野餐就要结束了，他们只能下次再邀请蟾蜍来品尝美味了。

From where they sat they could get a glimpse of the main stream across the island that separated them; and just then a wager-boat flashed into view, the rower—a short, stout figure—splashing badly and rolling a good deal, but working his hardest. The Rat stood up and hailed him, but Toad—for it was he—shook his head and settled sternly to his work.

"He'll be out of the boat in a minute if he rolls like that," said the Rat, sitting down again.

"Of course he will," chuckled（吃吃地笑）the Otter. "Did I ever tell you that good story about Toad and the lock-keeper? It happened this way. Toad..."

An errant May-fly swerved unsteadily athwart the current in the intoxicated fashion affected by young bloods of May-flies seeing life. A swirl of water and a "cloop!" and the May-fly was visible no more.

Neither was the Otter.

The Mole looked down. The voice was still in his ears, but the turf whereon he had sprawled was clearly vacant. Not an Otter to be seen, as far as the distant horizon.

But again there was a streak of bubbles on the surface of the river.

The Rat hummed a tune, and the Mole recollected that animal-etiquette forbade any sort of comment on the sudden disappearance of one's friends at any moment, for any reason or no reason whatever.

"Well, well," said the Rat, "I suppose we ought to be moving. I wonder which of us had better pack the luncheon-basket?" He did not speak as if he was frightfully eager for the treat.

"O, please let me," said the Mole. So, of course, the Rat let him.

Packing the basket was not quite such pleasant work as unpacking the basket. It never is. But the Mole was bent on enjoying everything, and although just when he had got the basket packed and strapped up tightly he saw a plate staring up at him from the grass, and when the job had been done again the Rat pointed out a fork which anybody ought to have seen, and last of all, behold! the mustard pot（芥末瓶）, which he had been sitting on without knowing it—still, somehow, the thing got finished at last, without much loss of temper.

背后的故事

英国乡村生活的再现

《柳林风声》为我们描绘了一幅几乎是囊括英国乡村生活的画卷，书中有4个拟人化的动物，鼹鼠、河鼠、獾还有一个蟾蜍，通过这4个动物间发生的故事，一幅幅乡村生活场景被巧妙地串织在一起。在作者格雷厄姆的描述里，能找到他对于家乡风景的熟捻和喜爱，找到那个年代，对于一个绅士的最起码的道德标准和规范。作者是恪守传统道德的保守的英国绅士代表，或许有某些保守的看法，现在看来有些落伍，但从作品本身所带给人的阅读感受来说，无疑这是一本令人放松、颇为解颐的作品。

Tale 11

The Unique Rose

世上唯一的玫瑰

—An Episode from Little Prince

——节选自《小王子》

《小王子》讲述了一个世界上最伤心的故事；一个生命和生活的寓言；一个经久不衰、充满哲理的童话；一部写给大人看的童话。它是一则关于爱与责任的寓言。这就像花一样，如果你爱上了一朵在星星上的花，那么夜间，你看着星空就会感到甜蜜愉快，所有星星上都好像开着花。飞行员与小王子梦幻般的相遇是甜蜜的伤感，小王子和飞行员间交织着温柔、忧伤和感动。所有的大人都曾是小孩子，虽然，只有少数人记得……

慢阅读小语

细细品位字里行间流淌出的语言美和思想美，你就会感受到“Jump and get an apple”的喜悦，不知不觉间自身修养得到了提升……

1 **To me, you are still nothing more than a little boy who is just like a hundred thousand other little boys. And I have no need of you. And you, on your part, have no need of me. To you, I am nothing more than a fox like a hundred thousand other foxes. But if you tame me, then we shall need each other. To me, you will be unique in all the world. To you, I shall be unique in all the world...**

对我来说，你还只是一个小男孩，就像其他千万个小男孩一样。我不需要你。你也同样用不着我。对你来说，我也不过是一只狐狸，和其他千万只狐狸一样。但是，如果你驯服了我，我们就互相不可缺少了。对我来说，你就是世界上唯一的了；我对你来说，也是世界上唯一的了。

2 **It is only with the heart that one can see rightly; what is essential is invisible to the eye.**

只有用心才能看得清。实质性的东西，用眼睛是看不见的。

3 **It is the time you have wasted for your rose that makes your rose so important.**

正因为你为你的玫瑰花费了时间，这才使得你的玫瑰变得如此重要。

4 **You become responsible, forever, for what you have tamed.**

你现在要对你驯服过的一切负责到底。

5 **“What makes the desert beautiful,” said the little prince, “is that somewhere it hides a well...”**

小王子说：“使沙漠更加美丽的，就是在某个角落里，藏着一口井……”

狐狸的智慧

小王子的狐狸朋友总是能说出富有哲理的话来，他似乎比小王子更有智慧，但是他却请求小王子驯服他，如果小王子驯服了狐狸，对于狐狸来说，小王子就成了世上的唯一，而狐狸也成为了小王子世上的唯一。这富于禅理的话语，只有用心才能体会。

It was then that the fox appeared.

"Good morning," said the fox.

"Good morning," the little prince responded politely, although when he turned around he saw nothing.

"I am right here," the voice said, "under the apple tree."

"Who are you?" asked the little prince, and added, "You are very pretty to look at."

"I am a fox," said the fox.

"Come and play with me," proposed the little prince. "I am so unhappy."

"I cannot play with you," the fox said. "I am not tamed (驯服)."

"Ah! Please excuse me," said the little prince.

But, after some thought, he added:

"What does that mean—'tame'?"

"You do not live here," said the fox. "What is it that you are looking for?"

"I am looking for men," said the little prince. "What does that mean—'tame'?"

"Men," said the fox. "They have guns, and they hunt. It is very disturbing. They also raise chickens. These are their only interests. Are you looking for chickens?"

fox 狐狸。和fox相关的短语有：as cunning as a fox（像狐狸一样狡猾），play the fox（耍滑头，装假），set a fox to keep one's geese（引狼入室），fox in a lamb's skin（披着羊皮的狐狸；伪装友善的敌人）。还有两个谚语：When the fox preaches, take care of your geese.（狐狸来说教，当心鹅被盗。）Old foxes want no tutors.（老狐狸不需要教师。）另外，fox还是娱乐公司与电影公司的名称，以及以色列服饰品牌的名称。

"No," said the little prince. "I am looking for friends. What does that mean— 'tame'?"

"It is an act too often neglected," said the fox. "It means to establish ties."

"'To establish ties'?"

"Just that," said the fox. "To me, you are still nothing more than a little boy who is just like a hundred thousand other little boys. And I have no need of you. And you, on your part, have no need of me. To you, I am nothing more than a fox like a hundred thousand other foxes. But if you tame me, then we shall need each other. To me, you will be unique in all the world. To you, I shall be unique in all the world..."

小王子似乎明白了狐狸的话，在小王子心里确实有一个唯一，那就是那朵玫瑰花。那朵把小王子驯服的玫瑰花。看着陷入沉思的小王子，狐狸又一次请求小王子驯服它，但是小王子说出了自己的难处，"我的时间不多了。我还要去寻找朋友，还有许多事物要了解。"对此答复睿智的狐狸却不赞同，因为"世界上没有购买朋友的商店"，"如果你想要一个朋友"，只能驯服对方。

"I am beginning to understand," said the little prince. "There is a flower... I think that she has tamed me..."

"It is possible," said the fox. "On the Earth one sees all sorts of things."

"Oh, but this is not on the Earth!" said the little prince.

The fox seemed perplexed, and very curious.

"On another planet?"

"Yes."

"Are there hunters on this planet?"

"No."

"Ah, that is interesting! Are there chickens?"

"No."

"Nothing is perfect," sighed the fox.

But he came back to his idea.

"My life is very monotonous (单调的)," the fox said. "I hunt chickens; men hunt me. All the chickens are just alike, and all the men are just alike. And, in consequence, I am a little bored. But if you tame me, it will be as if the sun came to shine on my life. I shall know the sound of a step that will be different from all the others. Other steps send me hurrying back underneath the ground. Yours will call me, like music, out of my burrow. And then look: you see the grain-fields down yonder? I do not eat bread. Wheat is of no use to me. The wheat fields have nothing to say to me. And that is sad. But you have hair that is the colour of gold. Think how wonderful that will be when you have tamed me! The grain, which is also golden, will bring me back the thought of you. And I shall love to listen to the wind in the wheat..."

The fox gazed at the little prince, for a long time.

"Please tame me!" he said.

"I want to, very much," the little prince replied. "But I have not much time. I have friends to discover, and a great many things to understand."

"One only understands the things that one tames," said the fox. "Men

have no more time to understand anything. They buy things all ready made at the shops. But there is no shop anywhere where one can buy friendship, and so men have no friends any more. If you want a friend, tame me..."

"What must I do, to tame you?" asked the little prince.

"You must be very patient," replied the fox. "First you will sit down at a little distance from me—like that—in the grass. I shall look at you out of the corner of my eye, and you will say nothing. Words are the source of misunderstandings. But you will sit a little closer to me, every day..."

请对你的"玫瑰"负责

小王子第二天又来见这位睿智的狐狸，每一次相见，小王子总能从狐狸那里学到不一样的智慧。狐狸让小王子"再去看看那些玫瑰花"，只有这样，小王子才会明白，他的那朵玫瑰是世界上独一无二的玫瑰。并且许诺，在小王子回来和狐狸告别时，狐狸会赠送给小王子一个秘密。

The next day the little prince came back.

"It would have been better to come back at the same hour," said the fox. "If, for example, you come at four o'clock in the afternoon, then at three o'clock I shall begin to be happy. I shall feel happier and happier as the hour advances. At four o'clock, I shall already be worrying and jumping about. I shall show you how happy I am! But if you come at just any time, I shall never know at what hour my heart is to be ready to greet you... One must observe the proper rites..."

"What is a rite?" asked the little prince.

"Those also are actions too often neglected," said the fox. "They are what make one day different from other days, one hour from other hours. There is a rite, for example, among my hunters. Every Thursday they dance with the village girls. So Thursday is a wonderful day for me! I can take a walk as far as the **vineyards**（葡萄园）. But if the hunters danced at just any time, every day would be like every other day, and I should never have any vacation at all."

So the little prince tamed the fox. And when the hour of his departure drew near—

"Ah," said the fox, "I shall cry."

"It is your own fault," said the little prince. "I never wished you any sort of harm; but you wanted me to tame you..."

"Yes, that is so," said the fox.

"But now you are going to cry!" said the little prince.

"Yes, that is so," said the fox.

"Then it has done you no good at all!"

vineyard 葡萄园。法国以葡萄酒著称，所以在法国有很多著名的葡萄园。而且在法国有针对葡萄园而开发的旅游观光。游客可以坐上特定的汽车或四轮摩托车，甚至可以骑马去探寻葡萄园的秘密。如果葡萄种植在山坡上，游客还可以骑越野自行车去参观。在酒的世界中，除了红葡萄酒red wine和白葡萄酒white wine以外，还有很多类型的酒，如：啤酒（beer）、扎啤（draught beer）、雪利酒（sherry）、威士忌（whisky）、香槟酒（champagne）、鸡尾酒（cocktail）、马丁尼鸡尾酒（martini）、白兰地（brandy）、伏特加（vodka）、朗姆酒（rum）等。

"It has done me good," said the fox, "because of the color of the wheat fields." And then he added:

"Go and look again at the roses. You will understand now that yours is unique in all the world. Then come back to say goodbye to me, and I will make you a present of a secret."

小王子与狐狸成为了朋友，他的狐狸朋友向他泄露了一个秘密，这秘密如同一切伟大思想一样，是通俗的："本质用眼睛是看不见的，只有用心才能看清楚。"小王子的狐狸朋友还安慰他说，不管怎么说，小王子的玫瑰是独一无二的，小王子的玫瑰之所以有价值，是因为小王子为他的花付出了时间，这才使小王子的玫瑰变得重要。

The little prince went away, to look again at the roses.

"You are not at all like my rose," he said. "As yet you are nothing. No one has tamed you, and you have tamed no one. You are like my fox when I first knew him. He was only a fox like a hundred thousand other foxes. But I have made him my friend, and now he is unique in all the world."

And the roses were very much embarrassed.

"You are beautiful, but you are empty," he went on. "One could

not die for you. To be sure, an ordinary passerby would think that my rose looked just like you—the rose that belongs to me. But in herself alone she is more important than all the hundreds of you other roses: because it is she that I have watered; because it is she that I have put under the glass globe; because it is she that I have sheltered behind the screen; because it is for her that I have killed the caterpillars（毛虫）(except the two or three that we saved to become butterflies); because it is she that I have listened to, when she grumbled, or boasted, or even sometimes when she said nothing. Because she is my rose.

And he went back to meet the fox.

"Goodbye," he said.

"Goodbye," said the fox. "And now here is my secret, a very simple secret: It is only with the heart that one can see rightly; what is essential is invisible to the eye."

"What is essential is invisible to the eye," the little prince repeated, so that he would be sure to remember.

"It is the time you have wasted for your rose that makes your rose so important."

"It is the time I have wasted for my rose…" said the little prince, so that he would be sure to remember.

"Men have forgotten this truth," said the fox. "But you must not forget it. You become responsible, forever, for what you have tamed. You are responsible for your rose..."

"I am responsible for my rose," the little prince repeated, so that he would be sure to remember.

寻找沙漠里的甘露

飞行员和小王子已经在沙漠里走了8天了，死神在向他们走来。最后一滴水已经饮尽，回忆似乎成为了他们唯一的行囊。寻找水源是他们唯一的希望。面对漫漫黄沙，小王子看到的不是绝望，而是沙漠的美丽，因为在沙漠的某个角落里，会藏着一口井。我们看事物往往只看外表，而使它们美丽的东西是看不到的。

It was now the eighth day since I had had my accident in the desert, and I had listened to the story of the merchant as I was drinking the last drop of my water supply.

"Ah," I said to the little prince, "these memories of yours are very charming; but I have not yet succeeded in repairing my plane; I have nothing more to drink; and I, too, should be very happy if I could walk at my leisure toward a spring of fresh water!"

"My friend the fox—" the little prince said to me.

"My dear little man, this is no longer a matter that has anything to do with the fox!"

"Why not?"

"Because I am about to die of thirst..."

He did not follow my reasoning, and he answered me:

"It is a good thing to have had a friend, even if one is about to die. I, for instance, am very glad to have had a fox as a friend..."

"He has no way of guessing the danger," I said to myself. "He has never been either hungry or thirsty. A little sunshine is all he needs..."

But he looked at me steadily, and replied to my thought:

"I am thirsty, too. Let us look for a well..."

I made a gesture of weariness. It is absurd to look for a well, at random, in the immensity（无垠） of the desert. But nevertheless we started walking.

When we had trudged along for several hours, in silence, the darkness fell, and the stars began to come out. Thirst had made me a little feverish, and I looked at them as if I were in a dream. The little prince's last words came reeling back into my memory:

"Then you are thirsty, too?" I demanded.

But he did not reply to my question. He merely said to me:

"Water may also be good for the heart..."

I did not understand this answer, but I said nothing. I knew very well that it was impossible to cross-examine（反复询问）him.

飞行员和小王子在沙漠里走了好几个小时，但是他们还没有找到水井。绝望在一点点吞噬着飞行员的信心。两个人已经筋疲力尽，小王子也已无法再支撑他那衰弱不堪的身体，他们坐了下来，坐在了漫漫黄沙之中，形成了沙漠中一道凄美的风景。不知不觉间，小王子睡着了，飞行员抱着小王子继续寻找水井，此时飞行员的心境已无法用言语来表达，他看着怀里这个脆弱的宝贝，能做的只有珍惜与感动。

He was tired. He sat down. I sat down beside him. And, after a little silence, he spoke again:

"The stars are beautiful, because of a flower that cannot be seen."

I replied, "Yes, that is so." And, without saying anything more, I looked across the ridges of sand that were stretched out before us in the moonlight.

"The desert is beautiful," the little prince added.

And that was true. I have always loved the desert. One sits down on

a desert sand dune（沙丘）, sees nothing, hears nothing. Yet through the silence something throbs, and gleams...

"What makes the desert beautiful," said the little prince, "is that somewhere it hides a well..."

I was astonished by a sudden understanding of that mysterious radiation of the sands. When I was a little boy I lived in an old house, and legend told us that a treasure was buried there. To be sure, no one had ever known how to find it; perhaps no one had ever even looked for it. But it cast an enchantment over that house. My home was hiding a secret in the depths of its heart...

"Yes," I said to the little prince. "The house, the stars, the desert—what gives them their beauty is something that is invisible!"

"I am glad," he said, "that you agree with my fox."

As the little prince dropped off to sleep, I took him in my arms and set out walking once more. I felt deeply moved, and stirred. It seemed to me that I was carrying a very fragile treasure. It seemed to me, even, that there was nothing more fragile on all Earth. In the moonlight I looked at his pale forehead, his closed eyes, his locks of hair that trembled in the wind, and I said to myself: "What I see here is nothing but a shell. What is most important is invisible..."

As his lips opened slightly with the suspicious of a half-smile, I said to myself, again: "What moves me so deeply, about this little prince who is sleeping here, is his loyalty to a flower— the image of a rose that shines through his whole being like the flame of a lamp, even when he is asleep..." And I felt him to be more fragile still. I felt the need of protecting him, as if he himself were a flame that might be extinguished by a little puff of wind...

And, as I walked on so, I found the well, at daybreak.

背后的故事

《小王子》作者的双重身份

《小王子》的作者是圣·埃克苏佩里，他有两个身份：飞行员与作家。这两个身份对于他而言是相辅相成、相映生辉的。从《南方邮件》到《小王子》的16年间，他仅出版了6部作品，而且都是以飞机为工具，从宇宙的高度来观察世界、探索人生。这些作品篇幅不多，体裁新颖，主题是：人的伟大在于人的精神，精神的建立在于人的行动。人不折不挠的意志可以促成自身的奋发有为。在现代文学史上，圣·埃克苏佩里被认为是最早关注人类状况的作家之一。

圣·埃克苏佩里写《小王子》时，自己为小说画了插图。插画拙扑稚气，梦境迷幻。法语版《小王子》1943年在美国出版。评论界和读者对这本书感到意外。一直写飞机的圣·埃克苏佩里这次写了一篇童话！童话往往是大人讲给孩子听的故事，而《小王子》是把故事讲给大人听。那几句不无幽默的献词是理解这本书的钥匙。这部童话的主人公是来自外星球的小王子。童话以一位飞行员作为故事叙述者，讲述了小王子从自己星球出发前往地球的过程中，所经历的各种历险。圣·埃克苏佩里以小王子孩子式的眼光，透视出成人的空虚、盲目和愚妄，用浅显天真的语言写出了人类的孤独寂寞、没有根基随风流浪的命运。随着岁月的推移，《小王子》的寓意在严酷的现实中愈来愈明显。茫茫宇宙中，目前知道只有一个星球住着人，也只有一个人类文明，人的感情也全部倾注在这个星球上。在这个孤单、桀骜不驯的地球上，人既坚强又脆弱，文明既可长存又易毁灭，这取决于人的智慧。这部充满诗情画意的小小作品又像预言一样，告诉全世界：物质丰富弥补不了精神匮乏，人不能忘记精神实体。几十年后，《小王子》在全世界成为大人、小孩、东方人、西方人都爱读的作品。

Tale 12

Little Karl's Island

小卡尔斯岛

—An Episode from The Wonderful Adventures of Nils

——节选自《尼尔斯骑鹅旅行记》

《尼尔斯骑鹅旅行记》是唯一一部荣获诺贝尔文学奖的儿童文学作品，也是瑞典女作家拉格洛芙最有名的作品，更是一部畅销百年的著作。本书将北欧美丽的自然风光与心灵的陶冶巧妙地熔于一炉，成为了童话史上一部难以逾越的罕世经典。作品讲述了一个小男孩骑鹅周游各地、游览自然风光、学习地理文化、经历风险和苦难，在旅途中小男孩逐渐改正了缺点，懂得了如何学习与进步，最终养成了优秀的品德。被小精灵变小了的尼尔斯，骑着家里的鹅竟神奇地飞上天和大雁们一起旅行。一路上，他在各种动物的帮助下，破坏了狐狸斯密尔的许多诡计；从强盗山逃出来，尼尔斯差点被国王铜像踩扁，幸亏木偶帮助了他；还有打败了灰田鼠兵团，救了小松鼠……

慢阅读小语

细细品位字里行间流淌出的语言美和思想美，你就会感受到“Jump and get an apple”的喜悦，不知不觉间自身修养得到了提升……

1 **He had a high, rolling forehead, intelligent eyes, and a good bearing; as if he were a proud and courageous animal.**

他有着高大而凸起的前额、机灵的眼睛和威严的神态，仿佛他是一只高大英武、勇不可当的野鹿。

2 **...the storm abated. The sky grew clear and the moonlight began to play on the waves.**

……大风暴似乎渐渐减弱了势头。天空开始晴朗起来，月亮的清辉开始在波浪上闪烁起来。

3 **To begin with, the large expanse of sea; which now lay blue and sunlit, and rolled forward in glittering swells; was visible. Only upon one and another point did the foam spray up.**

首先可以看到整个大海，蓝色的大海沐浴在日光底下，烟波滚滚，微浪徐徐，只有在靠近一两个岬角处才拍打得溅起白色飞沫。

4 **It was heart-rending to see how the wild beasts had thrown themselves upon the sheep just for sport; only to hunt them and tear them to death.**

这些残暴的野兽扑向羔羊只是为了取乐，只是为了猎取和杀戮，历历惨象看了叫人心如刀割。

5 **One that is little and spry, can put many things to rights.**

有的人虽小但是心眼灵巧，照样也能干出许多惊天动地的大事情来。

巧遇绵羊群

雁群在厄兰岛北岬角过了一夜，然后朝向内陆飞行。在横越卡尔马海峡的时候南风劲吹，把他们朝北边吹过去。他们仍旧奋力朝向陆地高速飞去。就在他们快要靠近第一群礁石岛的时候，猛然传来了一阵呼啦啦巨响，就像是千百只巨翅大鸟一齐拍打翅膀飞了过来一样，海水顿时变成了黑色。这场大风暴实在可怕，大雁们一次又一次地企图折返回去，然而他们却力不从心。尼尔斯骑在鹅背上往下面大海看去，他看到大雁们笔直地朝着这座峭壁飞去，这岂不是自己甘愿撞个粉身碎骨吗？

Friday, April eighth.

THE boy sat for a moment and looked down into the sea. Suddenly he thought it began to roar louder than ever. He glanced up. Right in front of him; only a couple of metres away; loomed a rugged（崎岖的）and bare mountain-wall. At its base the waves dashed into a foam-like spray. The wild geese flew straight toward the cliff, and the boy did not see how they could avoid being dashed to pieces against it. No sooner had he wondered that Akka hadn't seen the danger in time than they were over by the mountain. Then he also noticed that before them was the arched entrance to a grotto（洞穴）, into which the geese steered. The next moment they were safe.

The first thing the wild geese thought of; before they gave themselves time to rejoice over their safety; was to see if all their comrades were also harboured. Yes, there were Akka, Iksi, Kolmi, Neljauml, Viisi, Kuusi, all the six goslings, the goosey-gander, Dunfin and Thumbietot; but Kaksi from Nuolja, the first left-hand goose, was missing; and none knew anything about her **fate**.

When the wild geese discovered

fate 命运。命运字面上意义是指生命的经历。fate的习惯用语有很多，常用的有as sure as fate（千真万确地）、fix one's fate（决定某人的命运）、have sb.'s fate in one's hand（掌握着某人的命运）。fate还有一个谚语：No flying from the fate.（劫数难逃。）fate、destiny、doom都含有命运的意思，但是它们的用法不同。fate指“宿命”，具有神话或迷信色彩，使人有畏惧和无可奈何之感；destiny 除含有“命运注定”之意外，还暗示“充满美好希望”；doom 指“最终的、常常是毁灭性或灾难性的命运”。

that no one but Kaksi had been separated from the flock, they took the matter lightly. Kaksi was old and wise. She knew all their ways and habits, and she, of course, would know how to find her way back to them.

Now the geese began to look around in the cave. Enough daylight came in through the opening so that they could see the grotto was both deep and wide. They were congratulating themselves on having found such a fine night harbour, when one of the flock caught sight of some shining, green dots, that glittered in a dark corner. "Those are eyes!" cried Akka. "There are big animals in here." They rushed toward the opening, but Thumbietot called to them: "There is nothing to run away from! It's only a few sheep lying alongside the grotto wall."

When the wild geese had accu-stomed themselves to the dim daylight in the cave, they could see the sheep very distinctly. The grown-up sheep might be about as many as there were geese; but beside these there were a few little lambs. An old ram（公羊）, with long, twisted horns, appeared to be the most lordly one of the flock.

The wild geese stepped up to him with much bowing and scraping. "Well met in the wilderness!" they greeted, but the big ram lay still, and did not speak a word of welcome.

绵羊群的秘密

大雁们为了躲避风暴而进入一个山洞，在里面竟然看到一群绵羊，不过绵羊似乎不是很欢迎这群陌生的客人，大雁们很纳闷，只能做些解释。可是绵羊听了大雁的解释后只是做了深深的长叹，难道绵羊们有什么难言之隐？大雁知道，羊的秉性怕羞，脾气也有点古怪，可是这些羊的表现却并不是如此，真是叫人弄不明白。

Then the wild geese thought that the sheep were displeased because they had taken shelter in their grotto. "Our coming here is not agreeable perhaps?" said Akka. "But we cannot help it, for we are wind-driven. We have wandered about in the storm all day, and it would be very good to be allowed to stop here to-night." After that there was

a long pause before any of the sheep answered with words; but, on the other hand, it could be heard distinctly that one or two of them heaved deep sighs. Akka knew, to be sure, that sheep are always shy and peculiar; but these seemed to have no idea as to how they should conduct themselves. Finally an old ewe, who had a long and pathetic face and a doleful voice, said: "There isn't one among us that would refuse to let you stay; but this is a house of mourning (悲恸), and we cannot receive guests, as in former days."

"You needn't let that worry you," said Akka. "If you knew what we have endured this day, you would surely understand that we are satisfied if we only get a safe spot to sleep on."

When Akka said that, the old ewe raised herself. "I believe it would be better for you to fly about in the worst kind of storm than to stop here. But, at least you shall not go from here before we have had the **privilege** of offering you the best hospitality which the house affords."

She conducted them to a hollow in the ground, which was filled with water.

Beside it lay a pile of bait and husks (苎麻壳) and chaff (糠); and she bade them make the most of these. "This year we have had a severe snow-winter on the island," said she. "The peasants who own us came out to us with hay and oaten straw, so we shouldn't starve to death. And this trash is all there is left of the good cheer."

The geese promptly made a rush for the food. They thought they had fared well, and were in their best humour. They must have observed, however, that the sheep were anxious; but they knew how easily scared sheep always are, and didn't believe there was any actual danger on foot. As soon

privilege 特权。特权又称自由权，意味着主体可以针对某一客体采取其想采取的行为；通常指的是政治上、经济上在法律和制度之外的权利。如表达“专有特权”用an exclusive privilege，“享受特权”用enjoy privileges，“赋予某人做某事的特权”要用grant sb. the privilege of doing sth. privilege 除了可以表示“特权”外，还可以表示“特殊的荣幸”。

as they had eaten, they meant to stand up to sleep as usual. But presently the big ram got up and walked over to them. The geese thought they had never seen a sheep with such big and coarse horns. In other respects, also, he was noticeable. He had a high, rolling forehead, intelligent eyes, and a good bearing; as if he were a proud and courageous animal.

领头的公羊不忍心让雁群蒙在鼓里而不明真相，他向雁群讲起了绵羊和这座小岛的故事。原来这座小岛上是没有食肉动物的，但是自从有三只狐狸在岛上定居后，一切都发生了变化。小岛不再安宁，狐狸总是在夜里来偷袭羊群。看来聪明的尼尔斯这次又要大显身手了，他又能为羊群想出什么好主意呢？不过这还得要先征得尼尔斯的同意才行。

"I cannot assume the responsibility of letting you geese remain, without telling you that it is unsafe here," he said. "We cannot receive night guests just now."

At last Akka began to comprehend that this was serious. "We will go away, since you really wish it," said she. "But won't you tell us first, what it is that troubles you? We know nothing about it. We do not even know where we are." "This is Little Karl's Island!" said the ram. "It lies outside of Gottland, and only sheep and sea-birds live here." "Perhaps you are wild sheep?" said Akka. "We're not far removed from it," replied the ram. "We have nothing to do with human beings. It's an old agreement between us and some peasants on a farm in Gottland, that they shall supply us with fodder in case we have snow-winter; and as a recompense (报偿) they are permitted to take away those of us who become superfluous. The island is small, so it cannot feed very many of us. But otherwise we take care of ourselves all the year around, and we do not live in houses with doors and locks, but in grottoes like these."

"Do you stay out here in the winter as well?" asked Akka, surprised. "We do," answered the ram. "We have good fodder up here on the mountain throughout the year." "It sounds as if you were better off than other sheep," said Akka. "But what is the misfortune that has befallen you?" "It was bitter cold last winter. The sea froze, and then three foxes came over the ice, and here they have been ever since. Otherwise, there are no dangerous animals on the island." "Oho! do foxes dare to attack such as you?" "Oh, no! not during the day, when I can protect myself and mine," said the ram, shaking his horns. "But they sneak upon us at night when we sleep in the grottoes. We try to keep awake, but one must sleep some of the time; and then they come upon us. They have already killed every sheep in the other grottoes, and there were herds that were just as large as mine."

"It isn't pleasant to tell that we are so helpless," said the old ewe. "We cannot defend ourselves any better than if we were tame sheep." "Do you think that they will come here to-night?" asked Akka. "There is nothing else in store for us," answered the old ewe. "They were here last night, and stole a lamb from us. They'll be sure to come back, as long as there are any of us alive. That is what they have done in the other places." "But if they are allowed to keep this up, you'll become entirely extinct," said Akka. "Oh! it won't be long before it's all over with the sheep on Little Karl's Island," sighed the ewe.

Akka stood there hesitatingly. It was by no means a pleasant prospect to venture out in the storm again, nor was it well to remain in a house where such guests were expected. When she had pondered a while, she turned to Thumbietot. "I wonder if you will help us, as you have done so many times before," said she. Yes, that he would love to do, he replied. "It is a pity for you not to get any sleep!" said the wild goose, "but I wonder if you are able to keep awake until the foxes come, and then to awaken us, so we may fly away." The boy was not very glad of this; but anything was better than going out in the storm again; so he promised to keep awake.

智斗三只狐狸

勇敢的尼尔斯答应帮助羊群，他首先要做的就是守夜，因为领头的公羊说今晚狐狸会来偷袭。尼尔斯走到洞口，将身子缩到一块石头背后去避避大风，就这样睁眼守卫着。虽然还不见狐狸的踪影，可是有些东西倒叫他一见就心惊胆颤。起初尼尔斯走了神，不过当他听到利爪在石头上抓挠的声响时，他知道一场恶战要开始了。

He went over to the grotto opening, crawled in behind a stone that he might be sheltered from the storm, and sat down to watch.

When the boy had been sitting there a while, the storm abated. The sky grew clear and the moonlight began to play on the waves. The boy stepped to the opening to look out. The grotto was rather high up on the mountain. A narrow and steep path led to it. It was probably here that he must await the foxes.

As yet he saw no foxes; but, on the other hand, there was something which, for the moment, terrified him much more. On the land-strip below the mountain stood some giants, or other stone-trolls; or perhaps they were actual human beings.

He thought at first that he was dreaming, but now he was positive that he had not fallen asleep. He saw the big men so distinctly that it could be no illusion. Some stood on the land-strip, others right on the mountain-wall as if about to climb it. Some had big, thick heads; others had no heads at all. Some were one-armed, and some had humps both before and behind. He had never seen anything so extraordinary.

The boy stood there and worked himself into a state of panic because of those trolls, and he almost forgot to keep his eye peeled for the foxes. But now he heard the scraping of claws saw three foxes coming up the steep. As soon as he knew that he had something real to deal with, he was calm again, and not the least bit scared. It occurred to him that it would be a pity to awaken only the geese, and leave the sheep to their fate. He thought he would like to arrange things some other way.

He ran quickly to the other end of the grotto, shook the big ram's horns until he awoke, and at the same time swung himself upon his back. "Get up, daddy, and we'll try to frighten the foxes a bit!" said the boy.

He had tried to be as quiet as possible, but the foxes must have

heard some noise; for when they came up to the mouth of the grotto they stopped and deliberated. "It was certainly some one in there that moved," said one. "I wonder if they are awake." "Just you go ahead!" said another. "At all events, they can't do anything to us."

When they came farther into the grotto, they stopped and sniffed. "Whom shall we take tonight?" whispered the one in the lead. "Tonight we will take the big ram," said the last. "After that, we'll have easy work with the rest."

The boy sat on the old ram's back and saw how they sneaked along. "Now butt straight ahead!" whispered the boy. The ram butted, and the first fox was thrust; top over tail; back to the opening. "Now butt to the left!" said the boy, turning the big ram's head in that direction. The ram measured a terrific assault that caught the second fox in the side. He rolled over several times before he got to his feet again and made his escape. The boy had wished that the third one, too, might have got a bump, but this one had already skedaddled.

"Now I think that they've had enough for to-night," said the boy. "So do I," agreed the big ram. "Now lie down on my back, and creep into the wool! You deserve to have it warm and comfortable, after all the wind and storm that you have been out in."

地狱洞

尼尔斯和公羊打败了三只狐狸，这回他们可以美美地睡一晚了。第二天大公羊驮着尼尔斯在岛上四处转悠，让他看看岛上的风景。这个岛原来就是一块巨大的岩石礁，四周峭崖壁立，顶部平坦，宛如一幢巨大的房屋。尼尔斯不得不承认，这个岛似乎专门是为羊群生活而存在的。山上都是羊儿喜欢吃的酥油草和气味芳香的青草，山下是蓝色的大海，烟波滚滚，微浪徐徐。这个小岛真是羊儿的天堂。

The next day the big ram went around with the boy on his back, and showed him the island. It consisted of a single massive mountain. It was like a large house with perpendicular walls and a flat roof. First the ram walked up on the mountain roof and showed the boy the good grazing lands there; and he had to admit that the island seemed to be especially created for sheep. There wasn't much else than sheep-sorrel and such little spicy growths as sheep are fond of that grew on the mountain.

But indeed there was something beside sheep fodder to look at, for one who was well up on the cliff. To begin with, the large expanse of sea; which now lay blue and sunlit, and rolled forward in glittering swells; was visible. Only upon one and another point did the foam spray up. To the east lay Gottland, with its even and long-stretched coast; and to the southwest lay Great Karl's Island, which was built on the same plan as the little island. When the ram walked to the very edge of the mountain roof, so the boy could look down the mountain walls, he noticed that they were simply filled with birds' nests; and in the blue sea beneath lay surf-scoters and eider-ducks and kittiwakes and guillemots and razor-bills; so pretty and peaceful; busying themselves with fishing for small herring.

"This is really a favoured land," said the boy. "You live in a pretty place, you sheep." "Oh, yes! it's pretty enough here," said the big ram. It was as if he wished to add something; but he didn't, he only sighed. "If you go about here alone you must watch out for the crevices which run all around the mountain," he cautioned after a pause. And this was a good warning, for there were deep and broad crevices in several places. The largest of them was called Hell's Hole.

That crevice was many fathoms deep and nearly six feet wide. "If one were to fall down there, it would certainly be the last of him," said the big ram. The boy thought it sounded as if he had a special meaning in what he said.

Then he conducted the boy down to the narrow strip of shore. Now he could see those giants that had frightened him the night before, at close range. They were nothing but tall rock-pillars. The big ram called them "boulders." The boy couldn't see enough of them. He thought that if there had ever been any trolls who had turned into stone they ought to look just like that.

尽管海滩上景色也很美丽，但是尼尔斯还是更喜欢山顶。因为在沙滩上有惨不忍睹的景象，遍地可以见到羊的尸骸。公羊在尸骸面前没有停住脚步，而是默默地走了过去。可是尼尔斯不能对这些惨象熟视无睹。羊的尸骸唤起了尼尔斯的正义感，但是他对自己不自信，因为他个头太小了，但是公羊给了尼尔斯信心“有的人虽小但是心眼灵巧，照样也能干出许多惊天动地的大事情来……”

Although it was pretty down on the shore, the boy liked it even better on the mountain height. It was ghastly down here; for everywhere they came across dead sheep. It was here that the foxes held their orgies. He saw skeletons whose flesh had been eaten, and bodies that were half-eaten, and others that they had scarcely tasted. It was heart-rending to see how the wild **beasts** had thrown themselves upon the sheep just for sport; only to hunt them and tear them to death.

The big ram did not pause in front of the dead, but walked by them in silence.

But the boy, meanwhile, could not help seeing all the horror.

Then the big ram started up the mountain again. When he was there he stopped and said: "If some one who is capable and wise could see all the misery which prevails here he surely would not be able to rest until these foxes had been punished."

"The foxes must live, too," said the boy.

"Yes," admitted the big ram, "those who do not tear in pieces more animals than they need for their sustenance, they may as well live. But these are felons."

"The peasants who own the island ought to come here and help you," insisted the boy.

"They have rowed over a number of times," replied the ram, "but the foxes always hid themselves in the grottoes and crevices, so they could not shoot at them."

"You surely cannot mean, daddy, that a poor little creature like me should be able to get at them, when neither you nor the peasants have succeeded

beasts 地狱。地狱被一些人认为是人死后灵魂会到的地方。由此可引出一个习语from hell，意为“十分讨厌、最后”。还有一个常用的习语是like hell，它有两个意思，一个是“非常、极其”，如：She worked like hell for her exams.（她为了考试而拼命复习。）另一个是“绝不”，如：I'm coming with you. Like hell you are(= you certainly are not).（“我要和你一起去。”“你想得真美。”）

in getting the better of them."

"One that is little and spry, can put many things to rights," said the big ram.

They talked no more about this, and the boy went over and sat down among the wild geese, who were feeding on the highland. Although he had not cared to show his feelings before the ram, he was very sad on the sheep's account, and he would have been glad to help them. "I can at least talk with Akka and Morten Goosey-gander about the matter," thought he. "Perhaps they can help me with a good suggestion."

"狐"口脱险

尼尔斯从公羊口中得知在岛上有一个"地狱洞"，这个洞非常深，一旦掉进去就没命了。可是没多久，白雄鹅就驮着尼尔斯越过山顶的平地朝着"地狱洞"那边去了。他们被美景迷昏了头脑，并不知道危险就在前方。三只狐狸想偷袭尼尔斯和白雄鹅，可是尼尔斯和白雄鹅却一点防备都没有，真让读者为他们捏一把汗。尼尔斯这次能脱险吗?

A little later the white goosey-gander took the boy on his back and crossed the mountain plain, in the direction of Hell's Hole at that!

He wandered, carefree, on the broad mountain roof; apparently unconscious of how large and white he was. He didn't seek protection behind tufts（丛生植物）, or any other protuberances（隆起）, but went straight ahead. It was singular that he was not more careful, for it was obvious that he had fared badly in yesterday's storm. He limped on his right leg, and his left wing hung and dragged as if it were broken.

He acted as if there were no danger, pecked at a grass-blade here and another there, and did not look about him in any direction. The boy lay stretched out full length on the goose-back, and looked up toward the blue sky. He was so accustomed to riding now that he could both stand and lie down on the goose-back.

While the goosey-gander and the boy were so carefree, they did not observe, of course, that the three foxes had come up on the mountain plain.

And the foxes, who knew that

it was well-nigh impossible to take the life of a goose on an open plain, thought at first that they wouldn't chase after the goosey-gander. But since they had nothing else to do, they finally sneaked down into one of the long cracks, and tried to steal up to him. They went about it so cautiously that the goosey-gander couldn't see a shadow of them.

They were not far off when the goose-gander made an attempt to raise himself into the air. He spread his wings, but he did not manage to lift himself. When the foxes seemed to grasp the fact that he couldn't fly, they hurried forward with greater eagerness than before. They no longer concealed themselves in the cleft, but came out on the highland. They hurried as fast as they could, behind tufts and hollows, coming nearer and nearer to the goosey-gander; without his seeming to notice that he was being hunted. At last the foxes were so near that they could make the final leap. Simultaneously, all three threw themselves with one long jump at the goosey-gander.

But yet at the last moment he must have noticed something, for he ran out of the way, and the foxes missed him. This, at any rate, didn't mean very much, for the goosey-gander only had a couple of metres headway, and, in the bargain, he limped. Anyhow, the poor thing ran ahead as fast as he could.

The boy sat upon the goose-back; backward; and shrieked and called to the foxes. "You have eaten yourselves too fat on mutton, foxes. You can't catch up with a goose even." He teased them so that they became crazed with rage and thought only of rushing forward.

The white one ran right straight to the big cleft. When he was there, he made one stroke with his wings, and was over. Just then the foxes were almost upon him.

The goosey-gander hurried on with the same haste as before, even after he had got across Hell's Hole. But he had hardly run two metres when the boy patted him on the neck, and said: "Now you can stop, goosey-gander."

At that instant they heard wild howls behind them, and a scraping of claws, and heavy falls. But of the foxes they saw nothing more.

The next morning the keeper of the lighthouse on Great Karl's Island found a bit of bark poked under the entrance-door, and on it was carved in slanting, angular letters: "The foxes on the little island have fallen down into Hell's Hole. Take care of them!"

And this the keeper of the lighthouse did, too.

背后的故事

一本关于瑞典的书

《尼尔斯骑鹅旅行记》的作者拉格洛芙（1858～1940年）是瑞典的优秀女作家，1909年获得了诺贝尔文学奖奖金。拉格洛芙生于瑞典西部的一个陆军中尉家中。她从小喜欢听祖母讲故事，喜欢读书，立志要当一名作家。长大后，她在一座小城当了10年中学地理教师。在任教期间，她开始了文学创作，写出了许多优秀的短篇小说。

《尼尔斯骑鹅旅行记》是她唯一为儿童而写的长篇童话，它是根据瑞典教育部的要求，作为一部学校地理教育读物而写的。1902年，塞尔玛·拉格洛夫受瑞典国家教师联盟委托为孩子们编写一部以故事的形式来介绍地理学、生物学和民俗学等知识的教科书，对此她欣然同意。1904年夏她开始跋山涉水到瑞典各地考察，为写“一本关于瑞典的，适合孩子们在学校阅读的书”、“一本富有教益，严肃认真和没有一句假话的书”做准备。1906年至1907年间这本书问世，它成了一部世界名著，成为了世界文学艺术的珍品。因为拉格洛芙的巨大成就，1914年她被选为瑞典皇家学会会员。在瑞典，现在有一项最重要的儿童文学奖，就是用尼尔斯这个名字命名的。由于其文学贡献，从1991年开始，她的肖像出现在瑞典货币20克朗钞票上。

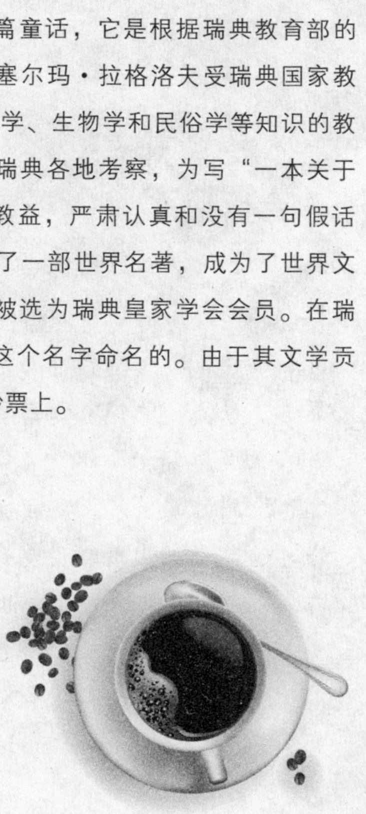

Tale 13

The Winged Monkeys

飞猴

—An Episode from The Wonderful Wizard of Oz

——节选自《绿野仙踪》

《绿野仙踪》讲述了美丽善良的小姑娘多萝茜的奇遇。多萝茜被一场龙卷风刮到了一个陌生而神奇的国度——奥兹国，并迷失了回家的路。在那里，她结识了没有脑子的稻草人、没有心脏的铁皮人和十分胆小的狮子，他们为了实现各自的心愿，互相帮助，携手协作，历尽艰险，遇到许多稀奇古怪的事情。最终，他们凭借自己非凡的智能和顽强的毅力，都如愿以偿地完成自己的心愿。这和中国的名著《西游记》颇有几分相似之处。这部童话用清新灵动的语言向读者表达着一个亘古不变的道理：朋友是最珍贵的。

慢阅读小语

细细品位字里行间流淌出的语言美和思想美，你就会感受到“Jump and get an apple”的喜悦，不知不觉间自身修养得到了提升……

1 They knew, of course, they must go straight east, toward the rising sun; and they started off in the right way. But at noon, when the sun was over their heads, they did not know which was east and which was west, and that was the reason they were lost in the great fields.

当然，他们知道的，必须朝着升起来的太阳，笔直地向东方走，他们就用这个方法动身了。但是在中午，当太阳照在他们头顶上时，他们就不能够分辨哪里是东方，哪里是西方，因此，他们便迷失在广阔的田野里了。

2 If we walk far enough, I am sure we shall sometime come to some place.

假使我们走得够远了，我相信，我们将要在某一个时候，走到了那个地方。

3 But we were careless and happy and full of fun, and enjoyed every minute of the day.

但是我们的生活是无忧无虑的、快活的，并且充满着游戏精神，我们享受着生活中的每一天、每一分钟。

4 Everyone loved her, but her greatest sorrow was that she could find no one to love in return, since all the men were much too stupid and ugly to mate with one so beautiful and wise.

谁都敬爱她，但是她最大的忧愁是找不出一个人，可以用爱情来报答她，因为她认为所有的人都太愚笨了，也太丑陋了，以至于不合适来做她的配偶，因为她自己太漂亮，也太聪明了。

迷路的四位小伙伴

在恶女巫的城堡和翡翠城中间，是没有路的，即使一条小路也没有。当多萝茜和稻草人、铁皮人、小狮子去找寻恶女巫时，不幸的是，恶女巫竟然望见他们了，所以恶女巫就差遣飞猴去把多萝茜他们带到女巫那里。这次的旅行似乎没有以前顺利，他们必须要向着东方行走。可是到中午时，他们分不清哪里是东方，所以他们就迷失在广阔的田野里了。日子一天天过去，他们也没有停止脚步，可是仍旧看不到去翡翠城的路。

You will remember there was no road—not even a pathway—between the castle of the Wicked **Witch** and the Emerald City. When the four travelers went in search of the Witch she had seen them coming, and so sent the Winged Monkeys to bring them to her. It was much harder to find their way back through the big fields of buttercups（毛茛）and yellow daisies（雏菊）than it was being carried. They knew, of course, they must go straight east, toward the rising sun; and they started off in the right way. But at noon, when the sun was over their heads, they did not know which was east and which was west, and that was the reason they were lost in the great fields. They kept on walking, however, and at night the moon came out and shone brightly. So they lay down among the sweet smelling yellow flowers and slept soundly until morning—all but the Scarecrow（稻草人）and the Tin Woodman.

The next morning the sun was behind a cloud, but they started on, as if they were quite sure which way they were going.

"If we walk far enough," said Dorothy, "I am sure we shall sometime come to some place."

Witch 女巫。女巫指会使用魔法，运用魔杖的女性巫师，又称魔女。在民间，占天气、祈丰年、行医的人多是女性，她们被称为"智慧之女"，所以"witch"就是由意思为"智慧之女"的"wicca"变来的。在现在英语中，"witch"一般是指女巫，男巫是"wizard"，但"witch"曾经有男女巫师的意思，只因为巫师中女巫占多数，才把男女巫师分开来，用两个词表示。

But day by day passed away, and they still saw nothing before them but the scarlet fields. The Scarecrow began to grumble a bit.

"We have surely lost our way," he said, "and unless we find it again in time to reach the Emerald City, I shall never get my brains."

"Nor I my heart," declared the Tin Woodman. "It seems to me I can scarcely wait till I get to **Oz**, and you must admit this is a very long journey."

"You see," said the Cowardly Lion, with a whimper, "I haven't the courage to keep tramping forever, without getting anywhere at all."

Then Dorothy lost heart. She sat down on the grass and looked at her companions, and they sat down and looked at her, and Toto found that for the first time in his life he was too tired to chase a butterfly that flew past his head. So he put out his tongue and panted and looked at Dorothy as if to ask what they should do next.

有魔力的金冠

迷路似乎把多萝茜的自信也吞噬了，她垂头丧气地坐在草地上，绞尽脑汁想办法。突然，她想到一个好主意，找田鼠来帮忙！于是她吹起了田鼠皇后送给她的小口笛。听到笛声，许多灰色的小田鼠都跑到多萝茜这里来了，可是田鼠皇后并没有告诉多萝茜去翡翠城的路，不过田鼠皇后告诉她一个大秘密，原来多萝茜戴的金冠是有魔力的。这顶金冠到底有怎样的魔力呢？

"Suppose we call the field mice," she suggested. "They could probably tell us the way to the Emerald City."

"To be sure they could," cried the Scarecrow. "Why didn't we think of that before?"

Dorothy blew the little whistle she had always carried about her neck since the Queen of the Mice had given

Oz 奥兹。Oz是《绿野仙踪》这个童话里一座城堡的名字，在童话中，如果能到达这座城堡，就能实现自己的心愿，所以多萝茜和稻草人、铁皮人、小狮子为了实现各自的愿望而结伴去Oz国。一路上他们经历了很多有趣的事情。OZ还是意大利汽车零部件的生产厂商。另外，oz也是英制计量单位“盎司”的缩写，1盎司=28.350克。

it to her. In a few minutes they heard the pattering of tiny feet, and many of the small gray mice came running up to her. Among them was the Queen herself, who asked, in her squeaky little voice:

"What can I do for my friends?"

"We have lost our way," said Dorothy. "Can you tell us where the Emerald City is?"

"Certainly," answered the Queen; "but it is a great way off, for you have had it at your backs all this time." Then she noticed Dorothy's Golden Cap, and said, "Why don't you use the charm (魔力) of the Cap, and call the Winged Monkeys to you? They will carry you to the City of Oz in less than an hour."

"I didn't know there was a charm," answered Dorothy, in surprise. "What is it?"

"It is written inside the Golden Cap," replied the Queen of the Mice. "But if you are going to call the Winged Monkeys we must run away, for they are full of mischief (恶作剧) and think it great fun to plague (使烦恼) us."

"Won't they hurt me?" asked the girl anxiously.

"Oh, no. They must obey the wearer of the Cap. Good-bye!" And she scampered out of sight, with all the mice hurrying after her.

Dorothy looked inside the Golden Cap and saw some words written upon the lining. These, she thought, must be the charm, so she read the directions carefully and put the Cap upon her head.

"Ep-pe, pep-pe, kak-ke!" she said, standing on her left foot.

"What did you say?" asked the Scarecrow, who did not know what she was doing.

"Hil-lo, hol-lo, hel-lo!" Dorothy went on, standing this time on her right foot.

"Hello!" replied the Tin Woodman calmly.

"Ziz-zy, zuz-zy, zik!" said Dorothy, who was now standing on both feet.

This ended the saying of the charm, and they heard a great chattering and flapping of wings, as the band of Winged Monkeys flew up to them.

The King bowed low before Dorothy, and asked, "What is your command?"

"We wish to go to the Emerald City," said the child, "and we have lost our way."

"We will carry you," replied the King, and no sooner had he spoken than two of the Monkeys caught Dorothy in their arms and flew away with her. Others took the Scarecrow and the Woodman and the Lion, and one little Monkey seized Toto and flew after them, although the dog tried hard to bite him.

The Scarecrow and the Tin Woodman were rather frightened at first, for they remembered how badly the Winged Monkeys had treated them before; but they saw that no harm was intended, so they rode through the air quite cheerfully, and had a fine time looking at the pretty gardens and woods far below them.

Dorothy found herself riding easily between two of the biggest Monkeys, one of them the King himself. They had made a chair of their hands and were careful not to hurt her.

飞猴的故事

多萝茜很好奇，为什么这么神奇的飞猴要听从金冠的命令呢？反正还有很长的路才能到翡翠城，如果在路上听听故事作为消遣，也是不错的选择。于是多萝茜就哀求猴王来讲述金冠与飞猴的故事。猴王没有让多萝茜失望，讲起了飞猴家族的故事。原来最开始时，飞猴家族是一个自由的家族，不过飞猴特别顽皮，非常喜欢做恶作剧。他们一直这样无拘无束的在森林里快乐地生活，直到有一天，来了一位美丽的公主，飞猴为自己的恶作剧付出了代价。这位公主是一位有本领的魔法家，她怎么可能忍受飞猴来捉弄自己的新郎呢？

"Why do you have to obey the charm of the Golden Cap?" she asked.

"That is a long story," answered the King, with a Winged laugh; "but as we have a long journey before us, I will pass the time by telling you about it, if you wish."

"I shall be glad to hear it," she replied.

"Once," began the leader, "we were a free people, living happily in the great forest, flying from tree to tree, eating nuts and fruit, and doing just as we pleased without calling anybody master. Perhaps some of us were rather too full of mischief at times, flying down to pull the tails of the animals that had no wings, chasing birds, and throwing nuts at the people who walked in the forest. But we were careless and happy and full of fun, and enjoyed every minute of the day. This was many years ago, long before Oz came out of the clouds to rule over this land.

"There lived here then, away at the North, a beautiful princess, who was also a powerful sorceress (女魔法师). All her magic was used to help the people, and she was never known to hurt anyone who was good. Her name was Gayelette, and she lived in a handsome palace built from great blocks of ruby. Everyone loved her, but her greatest sorrow was that she could find no one to love in return, since all the men were much too stupid and ugly to mate with one so beautiful and wise. At last, however, she found a boy who was handsome and manly and wise beyond his years. Gayelette made up her mind that when he grew to be a man she would make him her husband, so she took him to her ruby palace and used all her magic powers to make him as strong and good and lovely as any woman could wish. When he grew to manhood, Quelala, as he was called, was said to be the best and wisest man in all the land, while his manly beauty was so great that Gayelette loved him dearly, and hastened to make everything ready for the wedding.

"My grandfather was at that time the King of the Winged Monkeys which lived in the forest near Gayelette's palace, and the old fellow loved a joke better than a good dinner. One day, just before the wedding, my grandfather was flying out with his band when he saw Quelala walking beside the river. He was dressed in a rich costume of pink silk and purple velvet, and my grandfather thought he would see what he could do. At his word the band flew down and seized Quelala, carried him in their arms until they were over the middle of the river, and then dropped him into the water.

" 'Swim out, my fine fellow,' cried my grandfather, "and see if the water has spotted your clothes.' Quelala was much too wise not to swim, and he was not in the least spoiled by all his good fortune. He laughed, when he came to the top of the water, and swam in to shore. But when

Gayelette came running out to him she found his silks and velvet all ruined by the river.

"The princess was angry, and she knew, of course, who did it. She had all the Winged Monkeys brought before her, and she said at first that their wings should be tied and they should be treated as they had treated Quelala, and dropped in the river. But my grandfather pleaded hard, for he knew the Monkeys would drown in the river with their wings tied, and Quelala said a kind word for them also; so that Gayelette finally spared them, on condition that the Winged Monkeys should ever after do three times the bidding of the owner of the Golden Cap. This Cap had been made for a wedding present to Quelala, and it is said to have cost the princess half her kingdom. Of course my grandfather and all the other Monkeys at once agreed to the condition, and that is how it happens that we are three times the slaves（奴隶）of the owner of the Golden Cap, whosoever he may be."

飞猴圆满完成任务

多萝茜对飞猴的故事产生了极大的兴趣，她一定要追问下去。这个飞猴与金冠的故事越来越有意思了。原来飞猴付出的代价就是听从金冠主人的3个命令。现在多萝茜得到了这顶金冠，对多萝茜来说真是天大的好事。现在她和伙伴们有了一条解决困难的捷径了，就是找飞猴帮忙。有飞猴陪伴的旅行真是一次非常舒服的旅行。飞猴的故事讲完了，多萝茜他们也来到了翡翠城。该是告别的时候了，未来的路还是要多萝茜他们自己去探寻了。

"And what became of them?" asked Dorothy, who had been greatly interested in the story.

"Quelala being the first owner of the Golden Cap," replied the Monkey, "he was the first to lay his

wishes upon us. As his bride could not bear the sight of us, he called us all to him in the forest after he had married her and ordered us always to keep where she could never again set eyes on a Winged Monkey, which we were glad to do, for we were all afraid of her.

"This was all we ever had to do until the Golden Cap fell into the hands of the Wicked Witch of the West, who made us enslave the Winkies, and afterward drive Oz himself out of the Land of the West.

Now the Golden Cap is yours, and three times you have the right to lay your wishes upon us."

As the Monkey King finished his story Dorothy looked down and saw the green, shining walls of the Emerald City before them. She wondered at the rapid flight of the Monkeys, but was glad the journey was over.

The strange creatures set the travelers down carefully before the gate of the City, the King bowed low to Dorothy, and then flew swiftly away, followed by all his band.

"That was a good ride," said the little girl.

"Yes, and a quick way out of our troubles," replied the Lion. "How lucky it was you brought away that wonderful Cap!"

背后的故事

中外的《绿野仙踪》

《绿野仙踪全集》又名《OZ国经典童话》，是美国作家弗兰克·鲍姆(Frank Baum)在1900¯1920年期间陆续创作发表的奇幻冒险童话故事集，共14本，有“美国的《西游记》”之称。弗兰克·鲍姆的《绿野仙踪》系列是美国最著名的童话故事，是美国儿童文学协会(CLA)评选的“十部美国最伟大的儿童文学作品”之一，也是美国全国教育协会(NEA)推荐的“最佳童书之一”。问世百年以来被翻译成20多种语言出版，根据《绿野仙踪》故事改编的动画片、电影、舞台剧等更是不计其数，给喜爱OZ国故事的读者献上了丰盛的大餐。

在中国也有一部小说叫做《绿野仙踪》，它是清乾隆年间喜欢谈鬼说怪的李百川写的一部神魔小说，融神魔小说、世情小说、历史小说为一体，在文学上取得了卓越的成就。小说的人物描写十分精彩，尤其是那些活跃于人间凡世的小人物。小说中写达官之子温如玉贪恋烟花，倾家荡产的一段，最是精彩。李百川的朋友陶家鹤也叹赏这部小说为“说部中之极大山水也”，郑振铎先生对这本书的评价更高，他把《绿野仙踪》和《红楼梦》、《儒林外史》并列为清中叶三大小说。

Tale 14

The Queen's Croquet Ground

王后的槌球场

—An Episode from Alice's Adventures in Wonderland

——节选自《爱丽丝漫游奇境记》

《爱丽丝漫游奇境记》以其神奇的幻想、风趣的幽默、昂然的诗情，已经成为童话界的经典。每次品读这部童话，都会从中获得惊奇和喜悦。这个故事讲述的是一个叫爱丽丝的小女孩和姐姐在河边看书时睡着了，梦中她追逐一只穿着背心的兔子而掉进了兔子洞，从而来到一个奇妙的世界。在这个世界里她时而变大时而变小，以至于有一次竟掉进了由自己的眼泪汇成的池塘里；她还遇到了爱说教的公爵夫人、神秘莫测的柴郡猫、神话中的格里芬和假海龟、总是叫喊着要砍别人头的扑克牌女王和一群扑克士兵，参加了一个疯狂茶会、一场古怪的槌球赛和一场审判，直到最后与女王发生冲突时才醒来，发现自己依然躺在河边，姐姐正温柔地拂去落在她脸上的几片树叶，原来在梦里她把那几片树叶当成了扑克牌。

慢阅读小语

细细品位字里行间流淌出的语言美和思想美，你就会感受到“Jump and get an apple”的喜悦，不知不觉间自身修养得到了提升……

1 **A large rose-tree stood near the entrance of the garden: the roses growing on it were white, but there were three gardeners at it, busily painting them red.**

靠近花园门口有一棵大玫瑰树，花是白色的，三个园丁正忙着把白花染红。

2 **Alice was rather doubtful whether she ought not to lie down on her face like the three gardeners, but she could not remember ever having heard of such a rule at processions; “and besides, what would be the use of a procession,” thought she, “if people had all to lie down upon their faces, so that they couldn't see it?” So she stood where she was, and waited.**

爱丽丝不知道该不该像那三个园丁那样，脸朝地趴下，她根本不记得王室行列经过时，还有这么一个规矩。“人们都脸朝下趴着，谁来看呢？这样，这个行列有什么用呢？”她这样想着，仍站在那里，等着瞧。

3 **The chief difficulty Alice found at first was in managing her flamingo: she succeeded in getting its body tucked away, comfortably enough, under her arm, with its legs hanging down, but generally, just as she had got its neck nicely straightened out, and was going to give the hedgehog a blow with its head, it would twist itself round and look up in her face, with such a puzzled expression that she could not help bursting out laughing;…**

起初，爱丽丝很难摆弄红鹤，后来总算很成功地把红鹤的身子舒服地夹在胳膊底下，红鹤的腿垂在下面。可是，当她好不容易把红鹤的脖子弄直，准备用它的头去打那个刺猬时，红鹤却把脖子扭上来，用奇怪的表情看着爱丽丝的脸，惹得爱丽丝大声笑了起来……

4 **They're dreadfully fond of beheading people here: the great wonder is, that there's any one left alive!**

这儿的人太喜欢砍头了！可是很奇怪，现在还有人活着。

5 **...and you've no idea how confusing it is all the things being alive: for instance, there's the arch I've got to go through next walking about at the other end of the ground—and I should have croqueted the Queen's hedgehog just now, only it ran away when it saw mine coming!**

……还有，你简直想象不到，所有的东西都是活的。真讨厌。譬如说，我马上就要把球打进球门，而那个球门却散步去了；再比如我正要用自己的球碰王后的刺猬球，哼，它一见我的球来撒腿就跑掉啦！

花园里的巧遇

爱丽丝参加完那次疯狂的茶会，又一次来到那个很长的大厅里。她拿起了那个小金钥匙，打开了花园的门，然后轻轻地咬了一口蘑菇（她还留了一小块在口袋里呢），直到缩成大约一英尺高，她就走过了那条小过道。终于进入了美丽的花园，到达了漂亮的花坛和清凉的喷泉中间了。靠近花园门口有一棵大玫瑰树，花是白色的，三个园丁正忙着把白花染红。爱丽丝觉得很奇怪，走过去想看个究竟。

A large rose-tree stood near the entrance of the garden: the roses growing on it were white, but there were three gardeners at it, busily painting them red. Alice thought this a very curious thing, and she went nearer to watch them, and, just as she came up to them, she heard one of them say "Look out now, Five! Don't go splashing paint over me like that!"

"I couldn't help it," said Five, in a sulky（生气的）tone. "Seven jogged my elbow."

On which Seven looked up and said "That's right, Five! Always lay the blame on others!"

"You'd better not talk!" said Five. "I heard the Queen say only yesterday you deserved to be beheaded."

"What for?" said the one who had spoken first.

"That's none of your business, Two!" said Seven.

"Yes, it is his business!" said Five. "And I'll tell him—it was for bringing the cook tulip-roots instead of onions."

Seven flung down his brush, and had just begun "Well, of all the unjust things—" when his eye chanced to fall upon Alice, as she stood watching them, and he checked himself suddenly: the others looked round also, and all of them bowed low.

"Would you tell me, please," said Alice, a little timidly, "why you are painting those roses?"

Five and Seven said nothing, but looked at Two. Two began, in a low voice, "Why, the fact is, you see,

Miss, this here ought to have been a red rose-tree, and we put a white one in by mistake; and if the Queen was to find it out, we should all have our heads cut off, you know. So you see, Miss, we're doing our best, afore she comes, to—" At this moment, Five, who had been anxiously looking across the garden, called out "The Queen! The Queen!", and the three gardeners instantly threw themselves flat upon their faces. There was a sound of many footsteps, and Alice looked round, eager to see the Queen.

王后驾到

听了老二的介绍，更加勾起了爱丽丝的好奇心，王后是个什么样的人呢？为什么动不动就要砍别人的脑袋呢？先来看看王后出场的气势吧，真是宏大啊。首先，来了10个手拿狼牙棒的士兵，他们的样子全都和3个园丁一样，都是长方形的平板，手和脚长在板的四角上。接着来了10名侍臣，这些人全都用钻石装饰着，像那些士兵一样，两个两个并排着走。侍臣的后面是王室的孩子们，这些可爱的小家伙，一对对手拉着手愉快地跳着跑来了，他们全都用红心装饰着。后面是宾客，大多数宾客也是国王和王后。接着，是个红心武士，双手托着放在紫红色垫子上的王冠。这庞大的队伍之后，才是红心国王和王后。

First came ten soldiers carrying clubs: these were all shaped like the three gardeners, oblong（长方形）and flat, with their hands and feet at the corners: next the ten courtiers: these were ornamented all over with diamonds, and walked two and two, as the soldiers did. After these came the royal children: there were ten of them, and the little dears came jumping merrily along, hand in hand, in couples: they were all ornamented with hearts. Next came the guests, mostly Kings and Queens, and among them Alice recognised the White Rabbit: it was talking in a hurried nervous manner, smiling at everything that was said, and went by without noticing her. Then followed the Knave（男仆）of Hearts, carrying the King's crown on a crimson velvet cushion; and, last of all this grand procession, came THE KING AND THE QUEEN OF HEARTS.

Alice was rather doubtful whether

she ought not to lie down on her face like the three gardeners, but she could not remember ever having heard of such a rule at processions; "and besides, what would be the use of a procession," thought she, "if people had all to lie down upon their faces, so that they couldn't see it?" So she stood where she was, and waited.

When the procession came opposite to Alice, they all stopped and looked at her, and the Queen said, severely, "Who is this?" She said it to the Knave of Hearts, who only bowed and smiled in reply.

"Idiot!" said the Queen, tossing her head impatiently; and, turning to Alice, she went on: "What's your name, child?"

"My name is Alice, so please **your Majesty**," said Alice very politely; but she added, to herself, "Why, they're only a pack of cards, after all. I needn't be afraid of them!"

"And who are these?" said the Queen, pointing to the three gardeners who were lying round the rose-tree; for, you see, as they were lying on their faces, and the pattern on their backs was the same as the rest of the pack, she could not tell whether they were gardeners, or soldiers, or courtiers, or three of her own children.

"How should I know?" said Alice, surprised at her own courage. "It's no business of mine."

The Queen turned crimson with fury, and, after glaring at her for a moment like a wild beast, began screaming "Off with her head! Off with——"

"Nonsense!" said Alice, very loudly and decidedly, and the Queen was silent.

The King laid his hand upon her arm, and timidly said "Consider, my dear: she is only a child!"

The Queen turned angrily away from him, and said to the Knave "Turn them over!"

The Knave did so, very carefully, with one foot.

"Get up!" said the Queen in a shrill, loud voice, and the three

your Majesty 陛下。Majesty是英语国家对君主的敬称，最初的语源来自拉丁语的Māiestās，演变成古法语的Majesté，再演变成中古英语的Maieste和Mageste，最后演变成Majesty。原先涵义是指“伟大”、“宏大”的意思。your Majesty 加强语气，强调身份，表达说话者的敬意。

the unfortunate gardeners, who ran to Alice for protection.

"You sha'n't be beheaded!" said Alice, and she put them into a large flower-pot that stood near. The three soldiers wandered about for a minute or two, looking for them, and then quietly marched off after the others.

gardeners instantly jumped up, and began bowing to the King, the Queen, the royal children, and everybody else.

"Leave off that!" screamed the Queen. "You make me giddy." And then, turning to the rose-tree, she went on "What have you been doing here?"

"May it please your Majesty," said Two, in a very humble tone, going down on one knee as he spoke, "we were trying—"

"I see!" said the Queen, who had meanwhile been examining the roses.

"Off with their heads!" and the procession moved on, three of the soldiers remaining behind to execute

爱丽丝救了3个园丁后，又糊里糊涂地参加了王后的槌球比赛。爱丽丝的心里也在盘算着接下来会发生什么稀奇古怪的事呢？幸运的是爱丽丝遇到了那只穿背心的小兔子，从小兔子的口中爱丽丝得知了公爵夫人的下落，原来她要被王后处死了，因为公爵夫人打了王后一个耳光！爱丽丝觉得很好玩，高高在上的王后竟然会被打耳光！想想那个场面，爱丽丝就觉得好笑。

"Are their heads off?" shouted the Queen.

"Their heads are gone, if it please your Majesty!" the soldiers shouted in reply.

"That's right!" shouted the Queen. "Can you play **croquet**（槌球游戏）?"

croquet 槌球游戏。起源于法国。在13世纪英国有人玩这种游戏，17世纪又传到苏格兰和意大利。1861年，英国E.劳特利吉第1次编印槌球规则后，这项游戏在英国才得以普遍开展。后来槌球传到美国，在美国有"全英槌球俱乐部"和"全美槌球协会"。20世纪30～40年代，槌球游戏才传到中国。槌球是在平地或草坪上用木槌击球穿过铁环门的一种室外球类游戏。

The soldiers were silent, and looked at Alice, as the question was evidently meant for her.

"Yes!" shouted Alice.

"Come on, then!" roared the Queen, and Alice joined the procession, wondering very much what would happen next.

"It's—it's a very fine day!" said a timid voice at her side. She was walking by the White Rabbit, who was peeping anxiously into her face.

"Very," said Alice. "Where's the **Duchess**?"

"Hush! Hush!" said the Rabbit in a low hurried tone. He looked anxiously over his shoulder as he spoke, and then raised himself upon tiptoe, put his mouth close to her ear, and whispered "She's under sentence of execution."

"What for?" said Alice.

"Did you say "What a pity!" ?" the Rabbit asked.

"No, I didn't," said Alice. "I don't think it's at all a pity. I said "What for?" "

"She boxed the Queen's ears—" the Rabbit began. Alice gave a little scream of laughter. "Oh, hush!" the Rabbit whispered in a frightened tone. "The Queen will hear you! You see she came rather late, and the Queen said—"

奇怪的槌球游戏

"各就各位！"王后雷鸣般地喊了一声，人们就朝各个方向跑开了，撞来撞去的，一两分钟后总算都站好了自己的位置。于是游戏开始了。爱丽丝可还从来没见过这样奇怪的槌球游戏：球场到处都是坎坷不平的，槌球是活刺猬，槌球棒是活红鹤，士兵们手脚着地当球门。爱丽丝能驾驭那只红鹤做的槌球棒吗？似乎槌球和槌球棒都很不配合她，这可让她大伤脑筋。

"Get to your places!" shouted the Queen in a voice of thunder,

Duchess 公爵夫人。顾名思义，就是公爵的夫人。早在古罗马帝国时期，欧洲大陆的公爵称号通常授予守疆拓土、军功卓著的高级指挥官，以后因重大政治变化而中断。几百年后，德国又出现公爵这个爵位。在英国，公爵是仅次于国王或亲王的最高级贵族。派拉蒙优势Paramount Vantage公司曾出品过一部电影，名字就叫做《公爵夫人》。

and people began running about in all directions, tumbling up against each other: however, they got settled down in a minute or two, and the game began.

Alice thought she had never seen such a curious croquet-ground in her life: it was all ridges and furrows: the croquet balls were live hedgehogs（刺猬）, and the mallets（槌棒）live flamingoes（火烈鸟）, and the soldiers had to double themselves up and stand on their hands and feet, to make the arches（拱门）.

The chief difficulty Alice found at first was in managing her flamingo: she succeeded in getting its body tucked away, comfortably enough, under her arm, with its legs hanging down, but generally, just as she had got its neck nicely straightened out, and was going to give the hedgehog a blow with its head, it would twist itself round and look up in her face, with such a puzzled expression that she could not help bursting out laughing; and when she had got its head down, and was going to begin again, it was very provoking to find that the hedgehog had unrolled itself, and was in the act of crawling away: besides all this, there was generally a ridge or furrow in the way wherever she wanted to send the hedgehog to, and, as the doubled-up soldiers were always getting up and walking off to other parts of the ground, Alice soon came to the conclusion that it was a very difficult game indeed.

The players all played at once, without waiting for turns, quarreling all the while, and fighting for the hedgehogs; and in a very short time the Queen was in a furious passion, and went stamping about, and shouting "Off with his head!" or "Off with her head!" about once in a minute.

Alice began to feel very uneasy: to be sure, she had not as yet had any dispute with the Queen, but she knew that it might happen any minute, "and then," thought she, "what would become of me? They're dreadfully fond of beheading people here: the great wonder is, that there's any one left alive!"

遇到柴郡猫

爱丽丝感到非常不安，说真的她还没有同王后发生争吵，可是这是每分钟都可能发生的呀！于是爱丽丝悄悄地逃走，又不慎被人发现了。这时，她注意到天空出现了一个怪东西。起初她惊奇极了，看了一两分钟后，她判断出这是一个笑容，这回爱丽丝高兴了，因为这是柴郡猫，这回爱丽丝可有人说话了。可是柴郡猫惹恼了国王，国王又找来王后帮忙，而王后解决问题的唯一方式就是“砍掉它的头！”。这真让爱丽丝哭笑不得。

She was looking about for some way of escape, and wondering whether she could get away without being seen, when she noticed a curious appearance in the air: it puzzled her very much at first, but after watching it a minute or two she made it out to be a grin, and she said to herself "It's the Cheshire-Cat: now I shall have somebody to talk to."

"How are you getting on?" said the Cat, as soon as there was mouth enough for it to speak with.

Alice waited till the eyes appeared, and then nodded. "It's no use speaking to it," she thought, "till its ears have come, or at least one of them." In another minute the whole head appeared, and then Alice put down her flamingo, and began an account of the game, feeling very glad she had someone to listen to her. The Cat seemed to think that there was enough of it now in sight, and no more of it appeared.

"I don't think they play at all fairly," Alice began, in rather a complaining tone, "and they all quarrel so dreadfully one ca'n't hear oneself speak—and they don't seem to have any rules in particular: at least, if there are, nobody attends to them—and you've no idea how confusing it is all the things being alive: for instance, there's the arch I've got to go through next walking about at the other end of the ground—and I should have croqueted the Queen's hedgehog just now, only it ran away when it saw mine coming!"

"How do you like the Queen?" said the Cat in a low voice.

"Not at all," said Alice: "she's so extremely—" Just then she noticed that the Queen was close behind her, listening: so she went on "—likely to win, that it's hardly worth while finishing the game."

The Queen smiled and passed on.

"Who are you talking to?" said the King, going up to Alice, and looking at the Cat's head with great curiosity.

"It's a friend of mine—a Cheshire-Cat," said Alice: "allow me to introduce it."

"I don't like the look of it at all,"

said the King: "however, it may kiss my hand, if it likes."

"I'd rather not," the Cat remarked.

"Don't be impertinent," said the King, "and don't look at me like that!" He got behind Alice as he spoke.

"A cat may look at a king," said Alice. "I've read that in some book, but I don't remember where."

"Well, it must be removed," said the King very decidedly; and he called the Queen, who was passing at the moment, "My dear! I wish you would have this cat removed!"

The Queen had only one way of settling all difficulties, great or small. "Off with his head!" she said without even looking round.

"I'll fetch the executioner（刽子手）myself," said the King eagerly, and he hurried off.

又回槌球场

离开球场那么久，爱丽丝想起该去看看游戏进行得怎样了。她来到球场，整个场面都是乱糟糟的，弄得她根本不知道什么时候轮到，什么时候不轮到。因此她就走了，找她的刺猬去了。而来抓柴郡猫的士兵又找不到柴郡猫了。一切都混乱不堪，不过，当你真正融入到这个混乱的场面里，真正以一个孩子的视角去看这个场面的时候，你看到的就不是混乱，而是一场妙趣横生的比赛。

Alice thought she might as well go back and see how the game was going on, as she heard the Queen's voice in the distance, screaming with passion. She had already heard her sentence three of the players to be executed for having missed their turns, and she did not like the look of things at all, as the game was in such confusion that she never knew whether it was her turn or not. So she went off in search of her hedgehog.

The hedgehog was engaged in a fight with another hedgehog, which seemed to Alice an excellent opportunity for croqueting one of them with the other: the only difficulty was that her flamingo was gone across the other side of the garden, where Alice could see it trying in a helpless sort of way to fly up into a tree.

By the time she had caught the

flamingo and brought it back, the fight was over, and both the hedgehogs were out of sight: "but it doesn't matter much," thought Alice, "as all the arches are gone from this side of the ground." So she tucked it away under her arm, that it might not escape again, and went back for a little more conversation with her friend.

When she got back to the Cheshire-Cat, she was surprised to find quite a large crowd collected round it: there was a dispute going on between the executioner, the King, and the Queen, who were all talking at once, while all the rest were quite silent, and looked very uncomfortable.

The moment Alice appeared, she was appealed to by all three to settle the question, and they repeated their arguments to her, though, as they all spoke at once, she found it very hard to make out exactly what they said.

The executioner's argument was, that you couldn't cut off a head unless there was a body to cut it off from: that he had never had to do such a thing before, and he wasn't going to begin at his time of life.

The King's argument was that anything that had a head could be beheaded, and that you weren't to talk nonsense.

The Queen's argument was that, if something wasn't done about it in less than no time, she'd have everybody executed, all round. (It was this last remark that had made the whole party look so grave and anxious.)

Alice could think of nothing else to say but "It belongs to the Duchess: you'd better ask her about it."

"She's in prison," the Queen said to the executioner: "fetch her here."

And the executioner went off like an arrow.

The Cat's head began fading away the moment he was gone, and, by the time he had come back with the Duchess, it had entirely disappeared: so the King and the executioner ran wildly up and down, looking for it, while the rest of the party went back to the game.

背后的故事

第一版《爱丽丝漫游奇境记》

《爱丽丝漫游奇境记》的第一版出版于1865年7月4日，距卡罗尔和友人罗宾逊及三个小女儿一起在泰姆士河上泛舟之时，刚好经过了三年。这本童话的最初构思起源于闲暇时卡罗尔给罗宾逊的三个小女儿讲的故事。罗宾逊的二女儿，也就是10岁的爱丽丝很喜欢这个故事，她要卡罗尔把故事写下来给她看，于是1864年11月，卡罗尔写了一份故事的手稿交给爱丽丝，当时的书名叫《爱丽丝地下奇遇记》（Alice's Adventures Under Ground）。很多人都认为这个活泼的金发小女孩就是书中小主角的原型。

这部童话中充满了有趣的文字游戏、双关语、谜语和巧智，因此有时是难以翻译的，比如第二章章名里的“Tale（故事）”因为被爱丽丝听成同音的“Tail（尾巴）”而闹出了笑话。由于这部童话最开始只是一部给朋友的孩子讲的自娱之作，所以故事里的很多角色名都影射了作者身边的人，如第三章里的渡渡鸟（dodo）是作者自己（因为他有口吃的毛病，听起来像dodo这个词）、鸭子（duck）是朋友Duckworth、鹦鹉（Lory）是爱丽丝的姐姐Lorina，小鹰（Eaglet）是爱丽丝的妹妹Edith。

其实早在1863年春天，卡罗尔把未完成的手稿给一个朋友乔治·麦克唐那看时，乔治就建议卡罗尔把这本书付诸出版。1865年，这个童话终于以《爱丽丝漫游奇境记》的名字出版，并使用了刘易斯·卡罗尔这个笔名。书一经出版就大获成功，不仅孩子们喜欢读，很多大人也喜欢，其中包括著名作家奥斯卡·王尔德和当时在位的维多利亚女王。目前这本书已经被翻译成至少125种语言，在全世界风行不衰。

Tale 15

Hansel and Gretel

糖果屋历险记

在人的一生中，童年总是显得太短暂。读童话已经成为成人向纯真的儿童时代回归的一种表现。童话的美感不仅是一条涤荡心灵的小溪或是指引道路的明灯，而且它代替我们说出了已经感到却又不善于用言语表达出来的情感。《糖果屋历险记》就是这样一篇让人回忆起童年的童话，童话中的两兄妹犹如我们身边的伙伴，是那样鲜活，他们以机智战胜了老巫婆，恢复了大森林的平静。他们用勇气与爱心战胜了困难，在贫困中如劲草般顽强成长。这是一篇感人的励志童话，其实在每一个人心中都有自己的“糖果屋”，不同的只是你如何来看待这个“糖果屋”。

慢阅读小语

细细品位字里行间流淌出的语言美和思想美，你就会感受到“Jump and get an apple”的喜悦，不知不觉间自身修养得到了提升……

1 **I will not do that; how can I bear to leave my children alone in the forest?—the wild animals would soon come and tear them to pieces.**

我不能那样做，我怎能忍心把我的孩子们单独丢在林子里呢？野兽很快会来把他们撕成碎片的。

2 **...do not distress yourself, I will soon find a way to help us.**

……不要难过，我自有办法。

3 **He who says A must say B, likewise, and as he had yielded the first time, he had to do so a second time also.**

说了A接下来就应该说B，正如，如果第一次做了让步，第二次就不得不继续让步了。

4 **Hansel reached up above, and broke off a little of the roof to try how it tasted, and Gretel leant against the window and nibbled at the panes.**

亨塞尔便举手掰下一小块屋顶来，尝味道如何。格莱特则站在窗框边，一点一点地咬着那糖玻璃。

恶毒的继母

在一座大森林里，有一对兄妹，他们和爸爸妈妈一起快乐生活。本来是幸福的四口之家，可是不幸的是妈妈去世了，他们的继母是一个狠心肠的女人。他们已经够可怜了，可是祸不单行，又赶上了饥荒，于是恶毒的继母就逼着爸爸抛弃这对兄妹。幸好两个孩子因为挨饿睡不着而听到继母和父亲的谈话，妹妹听到继母的话特别害怕，不过聪明的哥哥想出了一个好办法……

In a great forest dwelt a poor wood-cutter with his wife and his two children. The boy was called Hansel and the girl Gretel. He had little to bite and to break, and once when great dearth fell on the land, he could no longer procure（取得）even daily bread. Now when he thought over this by night in his bed, and tossed about in his anxiety, he groaned and said to his wife: "What is to become of us? How are we to feed our poor children, when we no longer have anything even for ourselves?" "I'll tell you what, husband," answered the woman, "early tomorrow morning we will take the children out into the forest to where it is the thickest; there we will light a fire for them, and give each of them one more piece of bread, and then we will go to our work and leave them alone. They will not find the way home again, and we shall be rid of them." "No, wife," said the man, "I will not do that; how can I bear to leave my children alone in the forest?—the wild animals would soon come and tear them to pieces." "O, you fool!" said she, "then we must all four die of hunger, you may as well plane the planks for our coffins," and she left him no peace until he consented. "But I feel very sorry for the poor children, all the same," said the man.

The two children had also not been able to sleep for hunger, and had heard

what their **stepmother** had said to their father. Gretel wept bitter tears, and said to Hansel: "Now all is over with us." "Be quiet, Gretel," said Hansel, "do not distress yourself, I will soon find a way to help us." And when the old folks had fallen asleep, he got up, put on his little coat, opened the door below, and crept outside. The moon shone brightly, and the white pebbles (小圆石) which lay in front of the house glittered like real silver pennies. Hansel stooped and stuffed the little pocket of his coat with as many as he could get in. Then he went back and said to Gretel: "Be comforted, dear little sister, and sleep in peace, God will not forsake us," and he lay down again in his bed.

寻找回家的路

继母并不知道亨塞尔已经有所准备，所以，天刚蒙蒙亮时她就把兄妹叫醒了，让他们去森林里捡柴。其实，这是继母的阴谋，她想把兄妹骗到森林里后抛弃他们。真是可怜的孩子啊！不过聪明的亨塞尔是不会让我们失望的，他会想出办法找到回家的路的。还记得前一天晚上亨塞尔捡的小石子吗？这就是亨塞尔的秘密武器，他在一路上都扔下了石子，这些石子会在月光下闪闪发光，兄妹就会循着石子指示的路线找回家了。

When day dawned, but before the sun had risen, the woman came and awoke the two children, saying: "Get up, you sluggards! we are going into the forest to fetch wood." She gave each a little piece of bread, and said: "There is something for your dinner, but do not eat it up before then, for you will get nothing else." Gretel took the

stepmother 继母。在文学作品和影视作品中，继母一般都是恶毒的形象，比如《白雪公主》中的继母，简直就是恶毒的代名词。继母用stepmother，由此类推，继父是stepfather。对于家庭成员，除了大家熟知的，还有“婆婆、岳母”mother-in-law，相对应的“公公、岳父”是father-in-law，“女婿”是son-in-law，“儿媳”是daughter-in-law。我们可以发现一个规律，只要不是有血缘关系的家人，而是因为婚姻而走到一起的两家人，在称呼上只要加上“-in-law”就可以了。

bread under her apron, as Hansel had the pebbles in his pocket. Then they all set out together on the way to the forest. When they had walked a short time, Hansel stood still and peeped back at the house, and did so again and again. His father said: "Hansel, what are you looking at there and staying behind for? Pay attention, and do not forget how to use your legs."

"Ah, father," said Hansel, "I am looking at my little white cat, which is sitting up on the roof, and wants to say goodbye to me." The wife said: "Fool, that is not your little cat, that is the morning sun which is shining on the chimneys." Hansel, however, had not been looking back at the cat, but had been constantly throwing one of the white pebble-stones out of his pocket on the road.

When they had reached the middle of the forest, the father said: "Now, children, pile up some wood, and I will light a fire that you may not be cold." Hansel and Gretel gathered brushwood together, as high as a little hill. The brushwood was lighted, and when the flames were burning very high, the woman said: "Now, children, lay yourselves down by the fire and rest, we will go into the forest and cut some wood. When we have done, we will come back and fetch you away."

Hansel and Gretel sat by the fire, and when noon came, each ate a little piece of bread, and as they heard the strokes of the wood-axe they believed that their father was near. It was not the axe, however, but a branch which he had fastened to a withered tree which the wind was blowing backwards and forwards. And as they had been sitting such a long time, their eyes closed with fatigue, and they fell fast asleep. When at last they awoke, it was already dark night. Gretel began to cry and said: "How are we to get out of the forest now?" But Hansel comforted her and said: "Just wait a little, until the moon has risen, and then we will soon find the way." And when the full moon had risen, Hansel took his little sister by the hand, and followed the pebbles which shone like newly-coined silver pieces, and showed them the way.

They walked the whole night long, and by break of day came once more to their father's house. They knocked at the door, and when the woman opened it and saw that it was Hansel and Gretel, she said: "You naughty children, why have you slept so long in the forest?—we thought you were never coming back at all!" The father, however, rejoiced, for it had cut him to the heart to leave them behind alone.

继母的又一次阴谋

继母的第一次阴谋没有成功，她怎么能甘心呢？不巧的是没过多久，全国又发生了饥荒。一天夜里，兄妹听到继母又在怂恿爸爸抛弃他们，善良的爸爸是舍不得抛弃孩子的，但是继母咄咄逼人，让爸爸不得不又一次违背了自己的良心。这次继母把亨塞尔和格莱特带到了森林的更深处。不过，兄妹这次可没有上次幸运了，他们找不到回家的路了，因为亨塞尔沿途扔下面包屑作为记号，不幸的是面包屑都被鸟儿吃光了。这次，兄妹是真正遇到麻烦了。

Not long afterwards, there was once more great dearth throughout the land, and the children heard their mother saying at night to their father: "Everything is eaten again, we have one half loaf left, and that is the end. The children must go, we will take them farther into the wood, so that they will not find their way out again; there is no other means of saving ourselves!" The man's heart was heavy, and he thought: "It would be better for you to share the last mouthful with your children." The woman, however, would listen to nothing that he had to say, but scolded and reproached（责备）him. He who says A must say B, likewise, and as he had yielded the first time, he had to do so a second time also.

The children, however, were still awake and had heard the conversation. When the old folks were asleep, Hansel again got up, and wanted to go out and pick up pebbles as he had done before, but the woman had locked the door, and Hansel could not get out. Nevertheless he comforted his little sister, and said: "Do not cry, Gretel, go to sleep quietly, the good God will help us."

Early in the morning came the woman, and took the children out of their beds. Their piece of bread was given to them, but it was still smaller than the time before. On the way into the forest Hansel crumbled his in his pocket, and often stood still and threw a morsel on the ground. "Hansel, why

do you stop and look round?" said the father, "go on." "I am looking back at my little pigeon which is sitting on the roof, and wants to say goodbye to me," answered Hansel. "Fool!" said the woman, "that is not your little pigeon, that is the morning sun that is shining on the chimney." Hansel, however little by little, threw all the crumbs（面包屑）on the path.

The woman led the children still deeper into the forest, where they had never in their lives been before. Then a great fire was again made, and the mother said: "Just sit there, you children, and when you are tired you may sleep a little; we are going into the forest to cut wood, and in the evening when we are done, we will come and fetch you away." When it was noon, Gretel shared her piece of bread with Hansel, who had scattered his by the way. Then they fell asleep and evening passed, but no one came to the poor children. They did not awake until it was dark night, and Hansel comforted his little sister and said: "Just wait, Gretel, until the moon rises, and then we shall see the crumbs of bread which I have strewn about, they will show us our way home again." When the moon came they set out, but they found no crumbs, for the many thousands of birds which fly about in the woods and fields had picked them all up. Hansel said to Gretel: "We shall soon find the way," but they did not find it. They walked the whole night and all the next day too from morning till evening, but they did not get out of the forest, and were very hungry, for they had nothing to eat but two or three berries, which grew on the ground. And as they were so weary（疲倦的）that their legs would carry them no longer, they lay down beneath a tree and fell asleep.

遇到糖果屋

兄妹离开家已经三天了，他们在森林里不停地走，寻找着回家的路，却不知道其实他们越走越深，已经陷入了森林深处。就在他们快绝望的时候，眼前出现了一只雪白的小鸟，他们跟随小鸟来到一所漂亮的小屋前。这座小屋太神奇了！竟然是一座可以吃的屋子，墙壁是面包做的，屋顶是蛋糕，窗户是明亮的糖块。兄妹迫不及待地吃起了小屋，就在他们吃得津津有味的时候，从屋里传来了声音，兄妹的另一段奇遇就从这里开始了……

It was now three mornings since they had left their father's house. They began to walk again, but they always came deeper into the forest, and if help did not come soon, they must die of hunger and weariness. When it was mid-day, they saw a beautiful snow-white bird sitting on a bough, which sang so delightfully that they stood still and listened to it. And when its song was over, it spread its wings and flew away before them, and they followed it until they reached a little house, on the roof of which it alighted; and when they approached the little house they saw that it was built of bread and covered with cakes, but that the windows were of clear sugar. "We will set to work on that," said Hansel, "and have a good meal. I will eat a bit of the roof, and you Gretel, can eat some of the window, it will taste sweet." Hansel reached up above, and broke off a little of the roof to try how it tasted, and Gretel leant against the window and nibbled at the panes（窗格玻璃）. Then a soft voice cried from the parlor:

"Nibble, nibble, gnaw,

Who is nibbling at my little house?"

The children answered:

"The wind, the wind,

The heaven-born wind," and went on eating without disturbing themselves. Hansel, who liked the taste of the roof, tore down a great piece of it, and Gretel pushed out the whole of one round window-pane, sat down, and enjoyed herself with it. Suddenly the door opened, and a woman as old as the hills, who supported herself on crutches（拐杖）, came creeping out（偷偷溜出）. Hansel and Gretel were so terribly frightened that they let fall what they had in their hands. The old woman, however, nodded her head, and said: "Oh, you dear children, who has brought you here? Do come in, and stay with me. No harm shall happen to you." She took them both by the hand, and led them into her little house. Then good food was set before them, milk and pancakes, with sugar, apples, and nuts. Afterwards two pretty little beds were covered with clean white linen, and Hansel and Gretel lay down in them, and thought they were in heaven.

糖果屋里的巫婆

兄妹并不知道这位给他们食物的婆婆是一个恶妖婆，所以兄妹开始还以为他们到了天堂呢。其实这位婆婆建这座面包小屋就是为了吸引小孩子，只要小孩子落入她的手中，她就会把他们煮了吃掉。当兄妹发现恶婆婆的阴谋时，已经晚了。恶婆婆把哥哥关了起来，又让妹妹为哥哥做好吃的，因为恶婆婆要把小孩养得胖胖的才吃。

The old woman had only pretended to be so kind; she was in reality a wicked witch, who lay in wait for children, and had only built the little house of bread in order to entice them there. When a child fell into her power, she killed it, cooked and ate it, and that was a feast day with her. Witches have red eyes, and cannot see far, but they have a keen（敏锐的）scent like the beasts, and are aware when human beings draw near. When Hansel and Gretel came into her neighbourhood, she laughed with malice（恶意）, and said mockingly（取笑地）: "I have them, they shall not escape me again!" Early in the morning before the children were awake, she was already up, and when she saw both of them sleeping and looking so pretty, with their plump and rosy cheeks she muttered to herself: "That will be a dainty mouthful!" Then she seized Hansel with her shriveled（起皱纹的）hand, carried him into a little **stable**,

stable 厩。又指马棚，也可以泛指牲口棚。在中国《说文》这部书中对厩的解释是这样的："厩，马舍也。"在西方，马是最早的交通工具，所以与stable相关的有一个习语：Lock the stable-door after the horse is stolen.（亡羊补牢。）stable除了作名词外，还可以作形容词，意思为"稳定的"，作不同词性时意思不同，要注意区分。

and locked him in behind a grated door. Scream as he might, it would not help him. Then she went to Gretel, shook her till she awoke, and cried: "Get up, lazy thing, fetch some water, and cook something good for your brother, he is in the stable outside, and is to be made fat. When he is fat, I will eat him." Gretel began to weep bitterly, but it was all in vain, for she was forced to do what the wicked witch commanded.

And now the best food was cooked for poor Hansel, but Gretel got nothing but crab-shells. Every morning the woman crept to the little stable, and cried: "Hansel, stretch out your finger that I may feel if you will soon be fat." Hansel, however, stretched out a little bone to her, and the old woman, who had dim eyes, could not see it, and thought it was Hansel's finger, and was astonished that there was no way of fattening him. When four weeks had gone by, and Hansel still remained thin, she was seized with impatience and would not wait any longer. "Now, then, Gretel," she cried to the girl, "stir yourself, and bring some water. Let Hansel be fat or lean, tomorrow I will kill him, and cook him." Ah, how the poor little sister did lament when she had to fetch the water, and how her tears did flow down her cheeks! "Dear God, do help us," she cried. "If the wild beasts in the forest had but devoured us, we should at any rate have died together." "Just keep your noise to yourself," said the old woman, "it won't help you at all."

完美的结局

妖婆不仅凶恶，而且还很愚蠢，这可是致命的弱点。聪明的格莱特竟把恶妖婆骗入了火炉里，恶婆婆被烧成了灰烬。聪明、勇敢的格莱特救出了哥哥。让他们没有想到的是，他们还得到了恶妖婆的财宝，这真是一个让人欣慰的结局，不过，还有更美好的事情等着他们呢。善良的鸭子帮助兄妹回到了家里，他们和爸爸终于团圆了。他们的恶继母也死了，于是，这个故事的结局就是"一家三口过上了幸福快乐的生活"。

Early in the morning, Gretel had to go out and hang up the cauldron with the water, and light the fire. "We will bake first," said the old woman, "I have already heated the oven, and kneaded the dough."

She pushed poor Gretel out to the oven, from which flames of fire were already darting. "Creep in," said the witch, "and see if it is properly heated, so that we can put the bread in." And once Gretel was inside, she intended to shut the oven and let her bake in it, and then she would eat her, too. But Gretel saw what she had in mind, and said: "I do not know how I am to do it; how do I get in?" "Silly goose," said the old woman. "The door is big enough; just look, I can get in myself!" and she crept up and thrust her head into the oven. Then Gretel gave her a push that drove her far into it, and shut the iron door, and fastened the bolt. Oh! Then she began to howl quite horribly, but Gretel ran away and the godless witch was miserably burnt to death.

Gretel, however, ran like lightning to Hansel, opened his little stable, and cried: "Hansel, we are saved! The old witch is dead!" Then Hansel sprang like a bird from its cage when the door is opened. How they did rejoice and embrace each other, and dance about and kiss each other! And as they had no longer any need to fear her, they went into the witch's house, and in every corner there stood chests full of pearls and **jewels**. "These are far better than pebbles!" said Hansel, and thrust into his pockets whatever could be got in, and Gretel said: "I, too, will take something home with me," and filled her pinafore full. "But now we must be off," said Hansel, "that we may get out of the witch's forest."

When they had walked for two hours, they came to a great stretch of water. "We cannot cross," said Hansel, "I see no foot-plank (脚手板), and no bridge." "And there is also no ferry," answered Gretel, "but a white duck is swimming there: if I ask her, she will help us over." Then she cried:

"Little duck, little duck, dost thou see,

Hansel and Gretel are waiting for thee?

There's never a plank, or bridge in sight,

Take us across on thy back so white."

jewel 珠宝。常见的宝石有：红宝石（ruby）、翡翠（jade）、玛瑙（agate）、蓝宝石（sapphire）、黄水晶（citrine）、珊瑚（coral）、钻石（diamond）、琥珀（amber）、紫水晶（amethyst）、祖母绿（emerald）、珍珠（pearl）。

The duck came to them, and Hansel seated himself on its back, and told his sister to sit by him. "No," replied Gretel, "that will be too heavy for the little duck; she shall take us across, one after the other." The good little duck did so, and when they were once safely across and had walked for a short time, the forest seemed to be more and more familiar to them, and at length they saw from afar their father's house. Then they began to run, rushed into the parlor, and threw themselves round their father's neck. The man had not known one happy hour since he had left the children in the forest; the woman, however, was dead. Gretel emptied her pinafore until pearls and precious stones ran about the room, and Hansel threw one handful after another out of his pocket to add to them. Then all anxiety was at an end, and they lived together in perfect happiness. My tale is done, there runs a mouse; whosoever catches it, may make himself a big fur cap out of it.

背后的故事

3D版《糖果屋》的盛宴

《糖果屋》这部经典的童话早就被搬上银屏，而且和它同名的奇幻剧也有很多。但是随着电影技术的发达，如果高科技能运用到这部童话中，对“糖果屋”的爱好者来说，将是一次视听的盛宴。不负众望，迈克尔·贝（Michael Bay）的The Institue公司将根据这部童话筹划制作一部3D版的《亨塞尔和格莱特》（Hansel and Gretel，又译：《糖果屋》），讲述的是亨塞尔和格莱特兄妹被继母扔在大森林中，迷路的他们来到了女巫的糖果屋，被抓并差点被吃掉，但凭借机智与勇气，两人最终脱离魔掌。这部电影将汇集《格林童话》中许多传奇生物，这些生物都将由Joseph C. Pepe负责设计，他是电影《阿凡达》（Avatar）的首席设计师。期待这部电影的问世吧，预计这部电影将于2011年春在德国开机。

Tale 16

Tom Thumb

大拇指

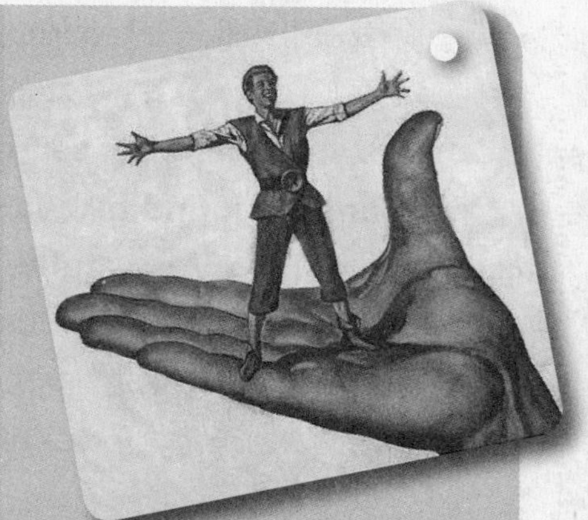

童话故事是风，把蒲公英一样的思绪吹向蓝天；童话故事是帆，带领我们驶向梦的宫殿。在《格林童话》中有一篇《大拇指》，这篇短小的故事每次读来都会让人回味无穷，每次凝神深思，都会有不同的感悟。小小的大拇指在历险中，用自己的智慧、勇气和诚实为父母换来财富，并且战胜了凶恶的强盗。“人不可貌相，海水不可斗量。”有志不在身高，有大智慧的人不一定要显露于表。这位“小不点”背后的故事，还要读者慢慢体会，细细品酌。

慢阅读小语

细细品位字里行间流淌出的语言美和思想美，你就会感受到“Jump and get an apple”的喜悦，不知不觉间自身修养得到了提升……

1 **Still, his eyes were sharp and sparkling, and he soon showed himself to be a clever little fellow, who always knew well what he was about.**

他的眼睛敏锐有神，不久就表现出他是一个聪明伶俐的人。他非常清楚自己该做些什么。

2 **I won't sell him at all; my own flesh and blood is dearer to me than all the silver and gold in the world.**

我决不卖他，他是我的心肝，把世界上所有的金子银子给我，我都不卖。

3 **...so he laid himself down, meaning to sleep till daylight, and then find his way home to his father and mother. But alas! How woefully he was undone! What crosses and sorrows happen to us all in this world!**

……他要躺下来好好休息一下，直到白天来临。然后回家，回到父母身边去。但是，天哪！他还得经受其他的折磨！这个世界还有那么多忧伤和苦难！

4 **But he soon found out where he really was; and was forced to have all his wits about him, that he might not get between the cow's teeth, and so be crushed to death.**

但是不久他就知道自己身处哪里了。为了不让自己被卷到奶牛的牙齿中间给咬碎，他必须要让自己高度警惕起来。

大拇指来到世间

从前，有一位贫穷的樵夫非常想要一个孩子，于是樵夫的妻子就许下一个心愿"要是有一个孩子该多幸福啊！哪怕孩子只有我的大拇指一样大小，我也会心满意足的。"老天似乎总喜欢和人开玩笑，这位善良的女人竟然实现了她的心愿，她不久真的生了一个男孩，这个男孩既健康又强壮，只是男孩真的只有拇指一般大！大拇指的到来，为这个贫穷的家增添了不少快乐。

A poor woodman sat in his cottage one night, smoking his **pipe** by the fireside, while his wife sat by his side spinning（纺纱）. "How lonely it is, wife," said he, as he puffed out a long curl of smoke, "for you and me to sit here by ourselves, without any children to play about and amuse us while other people seem so happy and merry with their children!" "What you say is very true," said the wife, sighing, and turning round her wheel; "how happy should I be if I had but one child! If it were ever so small—nay, if it were no bigger than my thumb—I should be very happy, and love it dearly." Now—odd as you may think it—it came to pass that this good woman's wish was fulfilled, just in the very way she had wished it; for, not long afterwards, she had a little boy, who was quite healthy and strong, but was not much bigger than my thumb. So they said, "Well, we cannot say we have not got what we wished for, and, little as he is, we will love him dearly." And they called

pipe 烟斗。烟草出现时，最初的抽烟方式就是用烟斗，可以说，烟斗是发现烟草的工具。烟斗的历史源远流长，最初古人用石头做烟斗，或者用一个小的圆锥体在地上挖两个连在一起的洞，一个洞里放入具有芬芳香味和麻醉作用的植物树叶，吸烟者躺在另一个洞边吸着烟，或者索性将这些植物直接撒在火中，坐在边上吸入燃烧出的烟。在口语中，会用"Put that in your pipe and smoke it."表示"你仔细想想吧。"这句一般是在劝告某人时所说的。在西方还有一句含pipe的谚语：No longer pipe, no longer dance.（时运不济，万事不利。）需要注意的是，这句谚语里的pipe可不是"烟斗"，而是"笛子"。

him Thomas Thumb.

They gave him plenty of food, yet for all they could do he never grew bigger, but kept just the same size as he had been when he was born. Still, his eyes were sharp and sparkling, and he soon showed himself to be a clever little fellow, who always knew well what he was about.

One day, as the woodman was getting ready to go into the wood to cut fuel, he said, "I wish I had someone to bring the cart after me, for I want to make haste." "Oh, father," cried Tom, "I will take care of that; the cart shall be in the wood by the time you want it." Then the woodman laughed, and said, "How can that be? You cannot reach up to the horse's bridle（缰绳）." "Never mind that, father," said Tom; "if my mother will only harness the horse, I will get into his ear and tell him which way to go." "Well," said the father, "we will try for once."

When the time came the mother harnessed the horse to the cart, and put Tom into his ear; and as he sat there the little man told the beast how to go, crying out, "Go on!" and "Stop!" as he wanted: and thus the horse went on just as well as if the woodman had driven it himself into the wood. It happened that as the horse was going a little too fast, and Tom was calling out, "Gently! gently!" two strangers came up. "What an odd thing that is!" said one: "there is a cart going along, and I hear a carter talking to the horse, but yet I can see no one." "That is queer, indeed," said the other; "let us follow the cart, and see where it goes." So they went on into the wood, till at last they came to the place where the woodman was. Then Tom Thumb, seeing his father, cried out, "See, father, here am with the cart, all right and safe! now take me down!" So his father took hold of the horse with one hand, and with the other took his son out of the horse's ear, and put him down upon a straw, where he sat as merry as you please.

智斗陌生人

两位陌生人看到大拇指能够顺利地驾驶马车，于是心怀鬼胎，他们要买下大拇指。没有父母会卖儿女的，大拇指的父母自然不同意。但是大拇指却偷偷地告诉父亲，让父亲答应陌生人的请求。樵夫虽然也很疑惑，但是看到大拇指非常有信心的样子，于是就很不舍地把大拇指卖给了陌生人。虽然陌生人出的价钱很高，但是冷冰冰的金钱怎么能抵上自己的孩子呢？任何一个孩子在父母的眼中都是无价之宝啊。就这样，大拇指开始了自己的冒险旅途。

The two strangers were all this time looking on, and did not know what to say for wonder. At last one took the other aside, and said, "That little urchin（顽童）will make our fortune, if we can get him, and carry him about from town to town as a show; we must buy him." So they went up to the woodman, and asked him what he would take for the little man. "He will be better off," said they, "with us than with you." "I won't sell him at all," said the father; "my own flesh and blood is dearer to me than all the silver and gold in the world." But Tom, hearing of the bargain they wanted to make, crept up his father's coat to his shoulder and whispered in his ear, "Take the money, father, and let them have me; I'll soon come back to you."

So the woodman at last said he would sell Tom to the strangers for a large piece of gold, and they paid the price. "Where would you like to sit?" said one of them. "Oh, put me on the rim of your hat; that will be a nice gallery for me; I can walk about there and see the country as we go along." So they did as he wished; and when Tom had taken leave of his father they took him away with them.

They journeyed on till it began to be dusky, and then the little man said, "Let me get down, I'm tired." So the man took off his hat, and put him down on a clod（土块）of earth, in a ploughed field by the side of the road. But Tom ran about amongst the furrows, and at last slipped into an old mouse-hole. "Good night, my masters!" said he, "I'm off! mind and look sharp after me the next time." Then they ran at once to the place, and poked the ends of their sticks into the mouse-hole, but all in vain; Tom only crawled farther and farther in; and at last it became quite dark, so that they were forced to go their way without their prize, as sulky (生气的) as could be.

两个愚蠢的小偷

大拇指等到陌生人离开后才重新爬起来，刚才还真是惊险呢。大拇指现在安全了，他接下来要做什么呢？在耕地上摸黑走路可不是什么好主意，因为他太小了，很可能会跌倒丧命的。幸运的是，大拇指遇到一只蜗牛的空壳，这个正好做大拇指的“临时客栈”。就在大拇指要睡觉的时候，他听到两个小偷在窃窃私语，小偷竟然要去偷牧师家的金子。正义的大拇指会袖手旁观吗？大拇指要如何帮助牧师避免这次灾难呢？

When Tom found they were gone, he came out of his hiding-place. “What dangerous walking it is,” said he, “in this ploughed field! If I were to fall from one of these great clods, I should undoubtedly break my neck.” At last, by good luck, he found a large empty snail-shell. “This is lucky,” said he, “I can sleep here very well”; and in he crept.

Just as he was falling asleep, he heard two men passing by, chatting together; and one said to the other, “How can we rob that rich **parson**'s house of his silver and gold?” “I'll tell you!” cried Tom. “What noise was that?” said the thief, frightened; “I'm sure I heard someone speak.” They stood still listening, and Tom said, “Take me with you, and I'll soon show you how to get the parson's money.” “But where are you?” said they. “Look about on the ground,” answered he, “and listen where the sound comes from.” At last the

parson 牧师。一种职业，是在一般基督新教的教会中专职负责带领及照顾其他基督徒的人，在圣经中的意思是“牧羊人”。牧师是基督新教的圣品人，与天主教中神父不同，牧师是可以结婚的，而且女性也可以成为牧师。在三级圣品制里，牧师的上一级是主教，低一级是会吏。不同的牧师英文也不同，如：parson指“教区牧师”，a curate指“助理牧师”，chaplain指“驻机关牧师”，minister指“传道牧师”，missionary则指“传教士”。

thieves found him out, and lifted him up in their hands. "You little urchin!" they said, "what can you do for us?"

"Why, I can get between the iron window-bars of the parson's house, and throw you out whatever you want." "That's a good thought," said the thieves; "come along, we shall see what you can do."

When they came to the parson's house, Tom slipped through the window-bars into the room, and then called out as loud as he could bawl, "Will you have all that is here?" At this the thieves were frightened, and said, "Softly, softly! Speak low, that you may not awaken anybody." But Tom seemed as if he did not understand them, and bawled out again, "How much will you have? Shall I throw it all out?" Now the cook lay in the next room; and hearing a noise she raised herself up in her bed and listened. Meantime the thieves were frightened, and ran off a little way; but at last they plucked up（振作）their hearts, and said, "The little urchin is only trying to make fools of us." So they came back and whispered softly to him, saying, "Now let us have no more of your roguish jokes; but throw us out some of the money." Then Tom called out as loud as he could, "Very well! Hold your hands! Here it comes."

The cook heard this quite plain, so she sprang out of bed, and ran to open the door. The thieves ran off as if a wolf was at their tails: and the maid, having groped（摸索）about and found nothing, went away for a light. By the time she came back, Tom had slipped off into the barn; and when she had looked about and searched every hole and corner, and found nobody, she went to bed, thinking she must have been dreaming with her eyes open.

艰难的回家之路

大拇指又一次胜利了，他用智慧打败了两个愚蠢的小偷。经历了这么多费脑筋的事，大拇指也要好好地睡一觉。更重要的一点是，他想爸爸妈妈了。他离开父母已经太久了，他恨不得赶快回到父母的身边。但是事事难料，回家的路似乎也不是很顺利，大拇指接下来会遇到什么呢？他能顺利回家吗？

The little man crawled about in the hay-loft, and at last found a snug place to finish his night's rest in; so he laid himself down, meaning to sleep till daylight, and then find his way home to his father and mother. But alas! How woefully he was undone! What crosses and sorrows happen to us all in this world! The cook got up early, before daybreak, to feed the cows; and going straight to the hay-loft, carried away a large bundle of hay, with the little man in the middle of it, fast asleep. He still, however, slept on, and did not awake till he found himself in the mouth of the cow; for the cook had put the hay into the cow's rick, and the cow had taken Tom up in a mouthful of it. "Good lack-a-day!" said he, "how came I to tumble into the mill?" But he soon found out where he really was; and was forced to have all his wits about him, that he might not get between the cow's teeth, and so be crushed to death. At last down he went into her stomach. "It is rather dark," said he; "they forgot to build windows in this room to let the sun in; a candle would be no bad thing."

Though he made the best of his bad luck, he did not like his quarters at all; and the worst of it was, that more and more hay was always coming down, and the space left for him became smaller and smaller. At last he cried out as loud as he could, "Don't bring me any more hay! Don't bring me any more hay!"

The maid happened to be just then milking the cow; and hearing someone speak, but seeing nobody, and yet being quite sure it was the same voice that she had heard in the night, she was so frightened that she fell off her stool, and overset the milk-pail. As soon as she could pick herself up out of the dirt, she ran off as fast as she could to her master the parson, and said, "Sir, sir, the cow is talking!" But the parson said, "Woman, thou art surely mad!" However, he went with her into the cowhouse, to try and see what was the matter.

Scarcely had they set foot on the threshold, when Tom called out, "Don't bring me any more hay!" Then the parson himself was frightened; and thinking the cow was surely bewitched, told his man to kill her on the spot. So the cow was killed, and cut up; and the stomach, in which

Tom lay, was thrown out upon a dunghill.

大拇指还真是多灾多难呢，刚从牛胃里逃出来，又落入"狼口"。不过大拇指没有失去勇气，他甚至乐观地想：也许在途中狼还想聊聊天呢。于是他又为饥饿的狼出起了主意，让狼可以饱餐一顿。你可千万不要以为大拇指在帮助狼呢，这可是大拇指大逃亡计划中的一部分。来看看大拇指有什么妙计吧。

Tom soon set himself to work to get out, which was not a very easy task; but at last, just as he had made room to get his head out, fresh ill luck befell him. A hungry wolf sprang out, and swallowed up the whole stomach, with Tom in it, at one gulp, and ran away.

Tom, however, was still not disheartened; and thinking the wolf would not dislike having some chat with him as he was going along, he called out, "My good friend, I can show you a famous treat." "Where's that?" said the wolf. "In such and such a house," said Tom, describing his own father's house. "You can crawl through the drain into the kitchen and then into the pantry, and there you will find cakes, ham, beef, cold chicken, roast pig, apple-dumplings（苹果布丁）, and everything that your heart can wish."

The wolf did not want to be asked twice; so that very night he went to the house and crawled through the drain into the kitchen, and then into the pantry, and ate and drank there to his heart's content. As soon as he had had enough he wanted to get away; but he had eaten so much that he could not go out by the same way he came in.

This was just what Tom had reckoned upon; and now he began to set up a great shout, making all the noise he could. "Will you be easy?" said the wolf; "you'll awaken everybody in the house if you make such a clatter." "What's that to me?" said the little man; "you have had your frolic（快乐）, now I've a mind to be merry myself"; and he

began, singing and shouting as loud as he could.

The woodman and his wife, being awakened by the noise, peeped through a crack in the door; but when they saw a wolf was there, you may well suppose that they were sadly frightened; and the woodman ran for his axe, and gave his wife a scythe（镰刀）. "Do you stay behind," said the woodman, "and when I have knocked him on the head you must rip him up with the scythe." Tom heard all this, and cried out, "Father, father! I am here, the wolf has swallowed me." And his father said, "Heaven be praised! we have found our dear child again"; and he told his wife not to use the scythe for fear she should hurt him. Then he aimed a great blow, and struck the wolf on the head, and killed him on the spot! and when he was dead they cut open his body, and set Tommy free. "Ah!" said the father, "what fears we have had for you!" "Yes, father," answered he; "I have travelled all over the world, I think, in one way or other, since we parted; and now I am very glad to come home and get fresh air again." "Why, where have you been?" said his father. "I have been in a mousehole— and in a snail-shell—and down a cow's throat—and in the wolf's belly; and yet here I am again, safe and sound."

"Well," said they, "you are come back, and we will not sell you again for all the riches in the world."

Then they hugged and kissed their dear little son, and gave him plenty to eat and drink, for he was very hungry; and then they fetched new clothes for him, for his old ones had been quite spoiled on his journey. So Master Thumb stayed at home with his father and mother, in peace; for though he had been so great a traveller, and had done and seen so many fine things, and was fond enough of telling the whole story, he always agreed that, after all, there's no place like HOME!

背后的故事

与《格林童话》相伴

《格林童话》不是创作的童话，是德国的格林兄弟收集的童话集。他们收集整理民间的童话、神话、传记，并且很忠实地把收集到的东西整理成为文字，然后还很严谨地考证这些童话的出处。《格林童话》这本书里充满了冒险、神秘、梦幻的故事。美丽的白雪公主、放鹅姑娘；可爱的小红帽、小精灵；充满危险的黑森林，风光绮丽的城堡……这些奇妙美丽的意境、曲折迷离的故事情节，一定会让你沉浸在故事里，久久难以忘怀。除此之外，这本书中还有一些睿智隽永的民间故事，那些聪明机智、勇敢善良的劳动人民让人感觉那么的亲切。他们好像正透过书页告诉我们，如何分清善良和邪恶，如何与坏人斗智斗勇，如何保持一颗快乐的童心。

有人说，只有读过《格林童话》的童年才算是完整的。这话一点儿都不夸张。这本书里的故事情节曲折、但不离奇；叙述朴素、却不单调，一百多年来，一直都受到世界各地人们的喜爱。试问，如今长大和尚未长大的孩子中，有谁不知道青蛙王子、睡美人和灰姑娘呢?

Tale 17

Mrs. Bedonebyasyoudid and Mrs. Doasyouwouldbedoneby

惩恶仙人和福善仙人

—An Episode from The Water-Babies

——节选自《水孩子》

《水孩子》讲述的是一个扫烟囱的孩子汤姆如何变成水孩子，并在仙女的感化、教育和引导下，闯荡大千世界，经历各种奇遇，克服性格缺陷，最后长大成人的美丽故事。作品中充满了各种讽喻，亦不乏劝诫，但它们在作者幽默诙谐的笔调和生动奇特的想象之下，读来丝毫不觉冰冷生硬，而是妙趣横生，令人忍俊不禁。故事中寄托了作者对自己的孩子和所有孩子的希望：爱清洁，行善事，勇敢正直，健康成长，成为博闻广识、心胸开阔的人。汤姆听到的声音是："下海去！下海去！"他得到的教导是：世界是如此的精彩，如果他想成为一个男子汉的话，就必须到外面的世界闯一闯。他必须像每一个降生到这个世界上的人一样，完全靠自己在外面闯。用自己的眼睛看，用自己的鼻子闻，用自己耳朵听……

慢阅读小语

细细品位字里行间流淌出的语言美和思想美，你就会感受到“Jump and get an apple”的喜悦，不知不觉间自身修养得到了提升……

1 **...if you don't know that fire burns, that is no reason that it should not burn you; and if you don't know that dirt breeds fever, that is no reason why the fevers should not kill you. The lobster did not know that there was any harm in getting into the lobster-pot; but it caught him all the same.**

……不能因为你不知道火可以烫伤你，火就不烫伤你。同样。不能因为你不知道污秽会滋生疾病，就不会生病，或者生病不死。那只龙虾并不知道钻进虾笼里去有什么危险，可是它照样陷进虾笼里去了。

2 **...if you do not know that things are wrong that is no reason why you should not be punished for them;…**

……并不能因为你无心做错事，就不能责罚你。……

3 **I am the ugliest fairy in the world; and I shall be, till people behave themselves as they ought to do. And then I shall grow as handsome as my sister, who is the loveliest fairy in the world; and her name is Mrs. Doasyouwouldbedoneby. So she begins where I end, and I begin where she ends; and those who will not listen to her must listen to me, as you will see.**

我是世界上最丑的仙人。在人类没有全部改过自新之前，我还要一直丑下去。等人类全部改了过来，我就会变得跟我妹妹一样美丽。我的妹妹叫福善仙人，是世界上最美的仙人。所以我们做的工作是各占一半：我做不到的她做，她做不到的我做。那些不听她说的人就得听我说，你看好了。

4 **And as for the pretty lady, I cannot tell you what the colour of her hair was, or, of her eyes: no more could Tom; for, when any one looks at her, all they can think of is, that she has the sweetest, kindest, tenderest, funniest, merriest face they ever saw, or want to see.**

这位美丽的仙人，她的头发和眼睛那种色泽我没法子告诉你。连汤姆也说不出，因为人看见她的时候，他们能想到的只是，这是他们所看见过的，或者想看见的最美、最善良、最温柔、最有趣、最快乐的一张脸了。

5 **...for babies are the best company, and the pleasantest playfellows, in the world; at least, so all the wise people in the world think.**

……孩子们是世界上最好的伴侣，也是最有趣的伴侣。至少，世界上最聪明的人都是这样想的。

6 **...how good little boys ought to be who have kind pussy mammas to cuddle them and tell them stories; and how afraid they ought to be of growing naughty, and bringing tears into their mammas' pretty eyes!**

……那些有慈爱的妈妈抚爱他们，给他们讲故事的小孩子是不是应当学好呢！他们应当多么担心自己变得顽皮，使妈妈美丽的眼睛含了眼泪啊！

白来登的仙人岛

水孩子的家在哪里呢？原来他们就在白来登的仙人岛。你听说过善良的白来登吗？传说他在荒野的开莱海边，和5位隐士向爱尔兰人进行善意的劝导，可是，那些爱尔兰人不肯听他们说，白兰登和他的朋友看见他们一点不听他们说，全都灰心了。一天白来登跑到山上去，眺望着那片怒吼的海水，再从那边眺望着大洋，这时他在天边离落日不远的地方望见一片蔚蓝的仙水，和许多金色的岛屿，这个岛屿后来被白来登誉为仙人岛。

And where is the home of the water-babies? In St. Brandan's fairy isle.

Did you never hear of the blessed St. Brandan, how he preached to the wild Irish on the wild, wild Kerry coast, he and five other **hermits**, till they were weary and longed to rest? For the wild Irish would not listen to them, or come to confession and to mass, but liked better to brew potheen（私酿的威士忌）, and dance the pater o'pee, and knock each other over the head with shillelaghs（橡木棒）, and shoot each other from behind turf-dykes, and steal each other's cattle, and burn each other's homes; till St. Brandan and his friends were weary of them, for they would not learn to be peaceable Christians at all.

So St. Brandan went out to the point of Old Dunmore, and looked over the tide-way roaring round the Blasquets, at the end of all the world, and away into the ocean, and sighed—

hermit 隐士。隐士对繁华尘世都很厌倦，不喜欢过社交过于频繁、打理杂事的生活；此外，隐士都热爱山水、热爱自然。西方当代的隐士们则不拒绝名声，他们往往有很高的社会声誉，并利用这些声誉去做影响社会的公益性事业。比如，爱默生、巴勒斯、利奥波德等等。与hermit相近的词有两个，一个是shut-in，指"A person confined indoors by illness or disability.（因病弱或天气不好而被关在屋内的人）"；另一个是recluse，指"A person who withdraws from the world to live in seclusion and often in solitude.（逃遁离开这个世界而居住于偏僻之地、且常常是独处的人。）"。

"Ah that I had wings as a dove!" And far away, before the setting sun, he saw a blue fairy sea, and golden fairy islands, and he said, "Those are the islands of the blest." Then he and his friends got into a hooker, and sailed away and away to the westward, and were never heard of more. But the people who would not hear him were changed into gorillas, and gorillas they are until this day.

And when St. Brandan and the hermits came to that fairy isle they found it overgrown with cedars and full of beautiful birds; and he sat down under the cedars and preached to all the birds in the air. And they liked his sermons so well that they told the fishes in the sea; and they came, and St. Brandan preached to them; and the fishes told the water babies, who live in the caves under the isle; and they came up by hundreds every Sunday, and St. Brandan got quite a neat little Sunday school. And there he taught the water-babies for a great many hundred years, till his eyes grew too dim to see, and his beard grew so long that he dared not walk for fear of treading on it, and then he might have tumbled down. And at last he and the five hermits fell fast asleep under the cedar-shades, and there they sleep unto this day. But the fairies took to the water-babies, and taught them their lessons themselves.

And some say that St. Brandan will awake and begin to teach the babies once more: but some think that he will sleep on, for better for worse, till the coming of the Cocqcigrues. But, on still clear summer evenings, when the sun sinks down into the sea, among golden cloud-capes and cloud-islands, and locks and friths of azure sky, the sailors fancy that they see, away to westward, St. Brandan's fairy isle.

But whether men can see it or not, St. Brandan's Isle once actually stood there; a great land out in the ocean, which has sunk and sunk beneath the waves. Old Plato called it Atlantis, and told strange tales of the wise men who lived therein, and of the wars they fought in the old times. And from off that island came strange flowers, which linger still about this land:- the Cornish heath, and Cornish moneywort, and the delicate Venus's hair, and the London-pride which covers the Kerry mountains, and the little pink butterwort of Devon, and the great blue butterwort of Ireland, and the Connemara heath, and the bristle-fern of the Turk waterfall, and many a strange plant more; all fairy tokens left for wise men and good children from off St. Brandan's Isle.

登上仙人岛

汤姆来到仙人岛，发现这座岛原来耸立在许多的圆柱子上面。在仙人岛上他发现了仙人和水孩子们。那些仙人要体贴得多，公正得多。仙人给海葵、珊瑚、石蚕全穿上颜色和花纹最最美丽的衣裳，使人望去就像一大片鲜艳的花田似的。让汤姆惊奇的是，在夜里，岛上并不用巡查的人或者警察来防止盗贼，而是有千百条水蛇守护着。有些水蛇有三百个脑袋，有些尾巴上长了眼睛，有些每一个骨节都长了眼睛，他们都是异常机警的侦探家。

Now when Tom got there, he found that the isle stood all on pillars, and that its roots were full of caves. There were pillars of black basalt（玄武岩）, like Staffa; and pillars of green and crimson serpentine, like Kynance; and pillars ribboned with red and white and yellow sandstone, like Livermead; and there were blue grottoes like Capri, and white grottoes like Adelsberg; all curtained and draped with seaweeds, purple and crimson（深红色的）, green and brown; and strewn with soft white sand, on which the water-babies sleep every night. But, to keep the place clean and sweet, the crabs picked up all the scraps off the floor and ate them like so many monkeys; while the rocks were covered with ten thousand sea anemones（海葵）, and corals and madrepores, who scavenged the water all day long, and kept it nice and pure. But, to make up to them for having to do such nasty work, they were not left black and dirty, as poor chimneysweeps and dustmen are. No; the fairies are more considerate and just than that, and have dressed them all in the most beautiful colours and patterns, till they look like vast flower-beds of gay blossoms. If you think I am talking nonsense, I can only say that it is true; and that an old gentleman named Fourier used to say that we ought to do the same by chimney-sweeps and dustmen, and honour them instead of despising them; and he was a very clever old gentleman: but, unfortunately for him and the world, as mad as a March hare.

And, instead of watchmen and policemen to keep out nasty things at night, there were thousands and thousands of water-snakes, and most wonderful creatures they were. They were all named after the Nereids, the sea-fairies who took care of them, Eunice and Polynoe, Phyllodoce and Psamathe, and all the rest of the pretty darlings who swim round their Queen Amphitrite, and her car of cameo shell. They were dressed in green velvet, and black velvet, and purple velvet; and were all jointed in rings; and some of them had three hundred brains apiece, so that they must have been uncommonly shrewd（精明的）detectives; and some had eyes in their tails; and some had eyes in every joint, so that they kept a very sharp look-out; and when they wanted a baby-snake, they just grew one at the end of their own tails, and when it was able to take care of itself it dropped off; so that they brought up their families very cheaply. But if any nasty thing came by, out they rushed upon it; and then out of each of their hundreds of feet there sprang a whole cutler's（刀匠的）shop of Scythes, Javelins, Billhooks, Lances, Pickaxes, **Halberts**, Forks, Gisarines, Penknives, Poleaxes, Rapiers, Fishhooks, Sabres, Bradawls, Yataghans, Gimblets, Creeses, Corkscrews, Ghoorka swords, Pins, Tucks, Needles, And so forth, which stabbed, shot, poked, pricked,

halberd 戟。是一种在15世纪和16世纪人们使用的武器，是由安装在一长柄末端的斧状刀刃和钢矛组成。实际上戟是戈和矛的合成体，它既有直刃又有横刃，呈“十”字或“卜”字形，因此戟具有钩、啄、刺、割等多种用途，其杀伤能力胜过戈和矛。常见的冷兵器有：剑（sword）、匕首（dagger）、弓（bow）、斧子（axe）、棍子（staff）、长矛（spear）、锤（mace）；热兵器有：手枪（hand gu n）、机关枪（machine gun）、气枪（Air gun）、狙击枪（snipe gun）；弹药有：地雷（mine）、手榴弹（grenade）、炸弹（bomb）、子弹（bullet）。

scratched, ripped, pinked, and crimped those naughty beasts so terribly, that they had to run for their lives, or else be chopped into small pieces and be eaten afterwards. And, if that is not all, every word, true, then there is no faith in microscopes, and all is over with the Linnaean Society.

And there were the water-babies in thousands, more than Tom, or you either, could count.—All the little children whom the good fairies take to, because their cruel mothers and fathers will not; all who are untaught and brought up heathens, and all who come to grief by ill-usage or ignorance or neglect; all the little children who are overlaid, or given gin when they are young, or are let to drink out of hot kettles, or to fall into the fire; all the little children in alleys and courts, and tumble-down cottages, who die by fever, and cholera, and measles, and scarlatina, and nasty complaints which no one has any business to have, and which no one will have some day, when folks have common sense; and all the little children who have been killed by cruel masters and wicked soldiers; they were all there, except, of course, the babes of Bethlehem who were killed by wicked King Herod; for they were taken straight to heaven long ago, as everybody knows, and we call them the Holy Innocents.

惩恶仙人来了

我们真希望汤姆不要再做那些顽皮的勾当了，不要再捉弄别人了。可是事实可不是这样的，汤姆仍旧是个淘气的男孩，他总去找岛上的那些动物捣蛋。他搔石蚕的痒，使它们吓得躲到沙里面去，从沙里用眼梢窥测他。他把石子放进海葵的嘴里，使海葵幻想是晚饭到嘴了。别的水孩子警告汤姆，小心“惩恶仙人要来了”。可是汤姆从不理睬他们，依旧是嘻嘻哈哈，兴高采烈的样子。终于有一天清晨，惩恶仙人果然来了。

But I wish Tom had given up all his naughty tricks, and left off tormenting dumb animals now that he had plenty of playfellows to amuse him. Instead of that, I am sorry to say, he would meddle with the creatures, all but the water-snakes, for they would stand no nonsense. So he tickled the madrepores, to make them shut up; and frightened the crabs, to make them hide in the sand and peep out at him with the tips of their eyes; and put stones into the anemones' mouths, to make them fancy that their dinner was coming.

The other children warned him, and said, "Take care what you are at. Mrs. Bedonebyasyoudid is coming." But Tom never heeded them, being quite riotous with high spirits and good luck, till, one Friday morning early, Mrs. Bedonebyasyoudid came indeed.

A very tremendous lady she was; and when the children saw her they all stood in a row, very upright indeed, and smoothed down their bathing dresses, and put their hands behind them, just as if they were going to be examined by the inspector.

And she had on a black bonnet, and a black shawl, and no crinoline at all; and a pair of large green spectacles, and a great **hooked** nose, hooked so much that the bridge of it stood quite up above her eyebrows; and under her arm she carried a great birch-rod. Indeed, she was so ugly that Tom was tempted to make faces at her: but did not; for he did not admire the look of the birch-rod under her arm.

And she looked at the children one by one, and seemed very much pleased with them, though she never asked them one question about how they were behaving; and then began giving them all sorts of nice sea-things—sea-cakes, sea-apples, sea-oranges, sea-bullseyes, sea-toffee; and to the very best of all she gave sea-ices, made out of sea-cows' cream, which never melt under water.

Now little Tom watched all these sweet things given away, till his mouth watered, and his eyes grew as round as an owl's. For he hoped that his turn would come at last; and so it did. For the lady called him up, and held out her fingers with something in them, and popped it into his mouth; and, lo

hooked 钩状的。这个词是由hook"钩子"演变而来的。与hook相关的习惯用语有：by hook or by crook，是"不择手段"的意思；get the hook，指"被非正式地解雇或中止工作"；hook, line, and sinker，指"无保留地、完全地"，例如：He swallowed the excuse hook, line, and sinker.（他完全相信了这个借口。）还有一个用语是on (one's) own hook，是"凭借自身的努力"的意思。例如：She succeeded on her owe hook.（她凭借自身的努力获得了成功。）

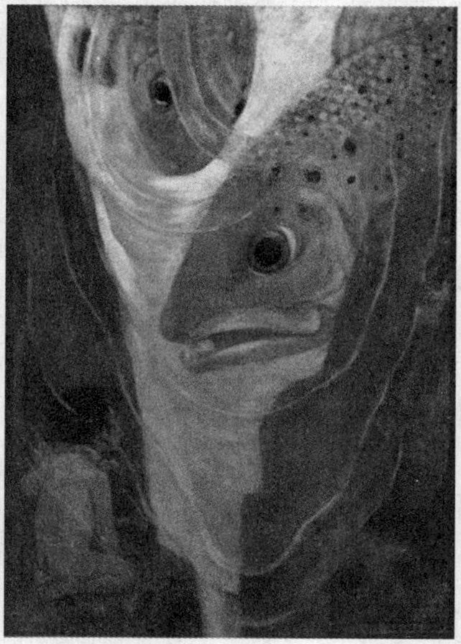

and behold, it was a nasty cold hard pebble.

"You are a very cruel woman," said he, and began to whimper.

"And you are a very cruel boy; who puts pebbles into the seaanemones' mouths, to take them in, and make them fancy that they had caught a good dinner! As you did to them, so I must do to you."

"Who told you that?" said Tom.

"You did yourself, this very minute."

Tom had never opened his lips; so he was very much taken aback indeed.

"Yes; every one tells me exactly what they have done wrong; and that without knowing it themselves. So there is no use trying to hide anything from me. Now go, and be a good boy, and I will put no more pebbles in your mouth, if you put none in other creatures'."

"I did not know there was any harm in it," said Tom.

"Then you know now. People continually say that to me: but I tell them, if you don't know that fire burns, that is no reason that it should not burn you; and if you don't know that dirt breeds fever, that is no reason why the fevers should not kill you. The lobster did not know that there was any harm in getting into the lobster-pot; but it caught him all the same."

"Dear me," thought Tom, "she knows everything!" And so she did, indeed.

"And so, if you do not know that things are wrong that is no reason why you should not be punished for them; though not as much, not as much, my little man" (and the lady looked very kindly, after all), "as if you did know."

惩恶仙人的教诲

汤姆觉得惩恶仙人对自己太严厉了，可惩恶仙人却不这么想，因为惩恶仙人是每一个做错事人的朋友，只要碰到人做错事，惩恶仙人就要责罚他们。惩恶仙人是世界上最丑的仙人。在人类没有全部改过自新之前，惩恶仙人还要一直丑下去。等人类全部改了过来，她才能变得跟她的妹妹福善仙人一样美丽。

"Well, you are a little hard on a poor lad," said Tom.

"Not at all; I am the best friend you ever had in all your life. But I will tell you; I cannot help punishing people when they do wrong. I like it no more than they do; I am often very, very sorry for them, poor things: but I cannot help it. If I tried not to do it, I should do it all the same. For I work by machinery, just like an engine; and am full of wheels and springs inside; and am wound up very carefully, so that I cannot help going."

"Was it long ago since they wound you up?" asked Tom. For he thought, the cunning little fellow, "She will run down some day: or they may forget to wind her up, as old Grimes used to forget to wind up his watch when he came in from the public-house; and then I shall be safe."

"I was wound up once and for all, so long ago, that I forget all about it."

"Dear me," said Tom, "you must have been made a long time!"

"I never was made, my child; and I shall go for ever and ever; for I am as old as Eternity, and yet as young as Time."

And there came over the lady's face a very curious expression—very solemn, and very sad; and yet very, very sweet. And she looked up and away, as if she were gazing through the sea, and through the sky, at something far, far off; and as she did so, there came such a quiet, tender, patient, hopeful smile over her face that Tom thought for the moment that she did not look ugly at all. And no more she did; for she was like a great many people who have not a pretty feature in their faces, and yet are lovely to behold, and draw little children's hearts to them at once because though the house is plain enough, yet from the windows a beautiful and good spirit is looking forth.

And Tom smiled in her face, she looked so pleasant for the moment.

And the strange fairy smiled too, and said:

"Yes. You thought me very ugly just now, did you not?"

Tom hung down his head, and got very red about the ears.

"And I am very ugly. I am the ugliest fairy in the world; and I shall be, till people behave themselves as they ought to do. And then I shall grow as handsome as my sister, who is the loveliest fairy in the world; and her name is Mrs. Doasyouwouldbedoneby. So she begins where I end, and I begin where she ends; and those who will not listen to her must listen to me, as you will see.

汤姆对这位老仙人倒也并不是不喜欢，不过禁不住觉得她太狠毒了一点。可是汤姆想问她一个问题："为什么不把那些坏心的师傅叫了来，也把他们惩罚一下呢？"这个问题让惩恶仙人的脸变得严肃起来，她会给汤姆一个什么样的答复呢?

Tom did not quite dislike the old lady: but he could not help thinking her a little spiteful—and no wonder if she was, poor old soul; for if she has to wait to grow handsome till people do as they would be done by, she will have to wait a very long time.

Poor old Mrs. Bedonebyasyoudid! she has a great deal of hard work before her, and had better have been born a washerwoman, and stood over a tub all day: but, you see, people cannot always choose their own profession.

But Tom longed to ask her one question; and after all, whenever she looked at him, she did not look cross at all; and now and then there was a funny smile in her face, and she chuckled to herself in a way which gave Tom courage, and at last he said:

"Pray, ma'am, may I ask you a question?"

"Certainly, my little dear."

"Why don't you bring all the bad masters here and serve them out too? The butties（监工）that knock about the poor collier-boys; and the nailers that file off their lads' noses and hammer their fingers; and all the master sweeps, like my master Grimes? I saw him fall into the water long ago; so I surely expected he would have been here. I'm sure he was bad enough to me."

Then the old lady looked so very stern that Tom was quite frightened, and sorry that he had been so bold. But she was not angry with him. She only answered, "I look after them all the week round; and they are in a very different place from this, because they knew that they were doing wrong."

She spoke very quietly; but there was something in her voice which made Tom tingle from head to foot, as if he had got into a shoal of sea nettles.

"But these people," she went on, "did not know that they were doing wrong: they were only stupid and impatient; and therefore I only punish them till they become patient, and learn to use their common sense like reasonable beings. But as for chimney-sweeps, and collier-boys, and nailer lads, my sister has set good people to stop all that sort of thing; and very much obliged to her I am; for if she could only stop the cruel masters from ill-using poor children, I should grow handsome at least a thousand years sooner. And now do you be a good boy, and do as you would be done by, which they did not; and then, when my sister, MADAME DOASYOUWOULDBEDONEBY, comes on Sunday, perhaps she will take notice of you, and teach you how to behave. She understands that better than I do." And so she went.

美丽的福善仙人

福善仙人果然来了。所有的孩子看见她来，都拍手跳舞。汤姆也使劲地跟着跳舞。这位美丽的仙人，是他们所看见过的，或者想看见的最美、最善良、最温柔、最有趣、最快乐的一张脸了。汤姆简直不敢相信自己的眼睛了，他愣愣地站着不动。福善仙人像妈妈一样抱着汤姆，让汤姆感受到了母亲般的温暖，以至于汤姆真想永远都不离开福善仙人的怀抱。

Tom was very glad to hear that there was no chance of meeting Grimes again, though he was a little sorry for him, considering that he used sometimes to give him the leavings of the beer: but he determined to be a very good boy all Saturday; and he was; for he never frightened one crab, nor tickled any live corals, nor put stones into the sea anemones' mouths, to make them fancy they had got a dinner; and when Sunday morning came, sure enough, MRS. DOASYOUWOULDBEDONEBY came too. Whereat all the little children began dancing and clapping their hands, and Tom danced too with all his might.

And as for the pretty lady, I cannot tell you what the colour of her hair was, or, of her eyes: no more could Tom; for, when any one looks at her, all they can think of is, that she has the sweetest, kindest, tenderest, funniest, merriest face they ever saw, or want to see. But Tom saw that she was a very tall woman, as tall as her sister: but instead of being gnarly（多瘤的）and horny, and scaly, and prickly, like her, she was the most nice, soft, fat, smooth, pussy, cuddly, delicious creature who ever nursed a baby; and she understood babies thoroughly, for she had plenty of her own, whole rows and regiments（大群）of them, and has to this day. And all her delight was, whenever she had a spare moment, to play with babies, in which she showed herself a woman of sense; for babies are the best company, and the pleasantest playfellows, in the world; at least, so all the wise people in the world think. And therefore when the children saw her, they naturally all caught hold of her, and pulled her till she sat down on a stone, and climbed into her lap, and clung round her neck, and caught hold of her hands; and then they all put their thumbs into their mouths, and began cuddling and purring like so many kittens, as they ought to have done. While those who could get nowhere else sat down on the sand, and cuddled her feet—for no one, you know, wear shoes in the water, except horrid old bathing–women, who are afraid of the water–babies pinching their horny toes. And Tom stood staring at them; for he could not understand what it was all about.

"And who are you, you little darling?" she said.

"Oh, that is the new baby!" they all cried, pulling their thumbs out of their mouths; "and he never had any mother," and they all put their thumbs back again, for they did not wish to lose any time.

"Then I will be his mother, and he shall have the very best place; so get out, all of you, this moment."

And she took up two great armfuls of babies—nine hundred under one arm, and thirteen hundred under the other—and threw them away, right and left, into the water. But they minded it no more than the naughty boys in Struwelpeter minded when St. Nicholas dipped them in his inkstand; and did not even take their thumbs out of their mouths, but came paddling and wriggling back to her like so many tadpoles（蝌蚪）, till you could see nothing of her from head to foot for the swarm of little babies.

But she took Tom in her arms, and laid him in the softest place of all, and kissed him, and patted him, and talked to him, tenderly and low, such things as he had never heard before in his life; and Tom looked up into her eyes, and loved her, and loved, till he fell fast asleep from pure love.

And when he woke she was telling the children a story. And what story did she tell them? One story she told them, which begins every Christmas Eve, and yet never ends at all for ever and ever; and, as she went on, the children took their thumbs out of their mouths and listened quite seriously; but not sadly at all; for she never told them anything sad; and Tom listened too, and never grew tired of listening. And he listened so long that he fell fast asleep again, and, when he woke, the lady was nursing him still.

"Don't go away," said little Tom. "This is so nice. I never had any one to cuddle me before."

"Now," said the fairy to Tom, "will you be a good boy for my sake, and torment no more sea-beasts till I come back?"

"And you will cuddle me again?" said poor little Tom.

"Of course I will, you little duck. I should like to take you with me and cuddle you all the way, only I must not;" and away she went.

So Tom really tried to be a good boy, and tormented no sea-beasts after that as long as he lived; and he is quite alive, I assure you, still.

Oh, how good little boys ought to be who have kind pussy mammas to cuddle them and tell them stories; and how afraid they ought to be of growing naughty, and bringing tears into their mammas' pretty eyes!

背后的故事

《水孩子》的诞生

《水孩子》为英国19世纪作家查尔斯·金斯利所著的一部儿童文学经典名著，亦为其儿童文学创作的代表作。作者始终感觉在为自己的孩子写书，所以口吻总是针对着孩子，而且常带有调笑的口吻，叫人读来更加觉得亲切，便是成人读来，也觉得非常风趣。作品中那些对于现代文明弊病和生硬教育方式的隐晦的抨击，即便是成人读后，也不免掩卷沉思。而作者对于真诚、正义、善良、慷慨、无私、勤劳、勇敢等美好品质的拥护和赞颂，和对于虚伪、邪恶、凶残、贪婪、自私、懒惰、怯懦等丑陋品质的憎恶和谴责，至今具有不朽的意义。

金斯利的女儿露丝叙述了这部书的一段创作经过：“在一个春天的早晨，我们用早餐的时候，有人提醒我父亲，说家里3个大孩子都有他们的书了（指《希腊英雄传》），可是，最小的弟弟，那时还不过4岁，父亲曾经答应过给他写本书，至今还没有写出来。父亲听了并不答话，起身进了书房，把门锁上。经过一小时光景，他从书房里出来，手里拿的就是《水孩子》的第一章。这本书整本写得就是这样迅速而且轻快……”

Tale 18

A Voyage to Lilliput

小人国游记

—An Episode from Gulliver's Travels

——节选自《格列佛游记》

《格列佛游记》是一部奇书，它不是单纯的少儿读物，而是饱寓讽刺和批判的文学杰作，英国著名作家乔治·奥威尔一生中读了不下6次，他说："如果要我开一份书目，列出哪怕其他书都被毁坏时也要保留的6本书，我一定会把《格列佛游记》列入其中。"《格列佛游记》更是被称为"文学的伟大宝库之一"。在这部伟大的作品中，斯威夫特将叙事技巧和讽刺才能发挥到了极致。整部作品都是以外科医生格列佛的冒险经历为线索写成的，格列佛冒险的第一站就是小人国（利立浦特）。格列佛随航不幸途中遇险，但他死里逃生,漂到利立浦特(小人国),被小人捆住，要将他献给国王。一次惊险的奇遇正在远处等着格列佛……

慢阅读小语

细细品位字里行间流淌出的语言美和思想美，你就会感受到“Jump and get an apple”的喜悦，不知不觉间自身修养得到了提升……

1 **I lay down on the grass, which was very short and soft, where I slept sounder than ever I remember to have done in my life.**

我在草地上躺下来，草很短，软绵绵的，一觉睡去，真是从未有过的酣畅香甜。

2 **I attempted to rise, but was not able to stir for, as I happened to he on my back, I found my arms and legs were strongly fastened on each side to the ground; and my hair, which was long and thick, tied down in the same manner. I likewise felt several slender ligatures across my body, from my armpits to my thighs. I could only look upwards; the sun began to grow hot, and the light offended my eyes.**

我想起来，却动弹不得，我仰天躺着，发现自己的胳膊和腿都被紧紧地缚在地上；我的头发又密又长，也被绑在地上；从腋下到大腿，我能觉出身上也横捆着细细的带子。我只能向上看。太阳渐渐热起来，阳光刺痛了我的眼睛。

3 **In my thoughts I could not sufficiently wonder at the intrepidity of these diminutive mortals, who dare venture to mount and walk upon my body, while one of my hands was at liberty, without trembling at the very sight of so prodigious a creature as I must appear to them.**

我又禁不住暗自惊讶。这些小人竟如此大胆，在我一只手自由后，还敢爬到我身上走来走去。在他们眼中我一定是个庞然大物，可是他们一点儿没有害怕的样子。

船只失事

在前往东印度群岛去的途中，格列佛乘坐的船只失事了。因风势太猛，他们的船向礁石直冲过去，船身立刻触礁裂开。6名船员，连格列佛在内，把救生的小船放下海去，拼尽全力离开大船和礁石。但是他们太累了，没有力气来划船了，只好听凭海浪的摆布。不久，海上刮来的一阵北风又将小船打翻了。小船上的同伴已不知去向，至于格列佛自己，只是靠着命运的指引和风浪的推动向前游着。

In our passage from thence to the East Indies, we were driven by a violent storm to the northwest of Van Diemen's Land. By an observation, we found ourselves in the latitude(纬度) of 30 degrees 2 minutes south. Twelve of our crew were dead by immoderate（过度的） labor and ill food, the rest were in a very weak condition. On the fifth of November, which was the beginning of summer in those parts, the weather being very hazy, the seamen spied a rock, within half a cable's length of the ship; but the wind was so strong, that we were driven directly upon it, and immediately split. Six of the crew, of whom I was one, having let down the boat into the sea, made a shift to get clear of the ship, and the rock. We rowed by my computation about three leagues, till we were able to work no longer, being already spent with labor while we were in the ship. We therefore trusted ourselves to the mercy of the waves, and in about half an hour the boat was overset by a sudden flurry from the north. What became of my companions in the boat, as well as of those who escaped on the rock, or were left in the vessel, I cannot tell; but conclude they were all lost. For my own part, I swam as fortune directed me, and was pushed forward by wind and tide. I often let my legs drop, and could feel no bottom.

就在格列佛几乎绝望的时候，他忽然发觉水深已经不能灭顶了，这时风暴也渐渐弱了。格列佛来到了一个岛上。格列佛太疲惫了，加上炎热的天气，还有离开大船时喝的半品脱白兰地，使格列佛昏昏欲睡。他在草地上躺下来，很快就睡着了。可是当他醒来，他觉得自己仿佛置身于另一个世界中。

When I was almost gone, and able to struggle no longer, I found myself within my depth; and by this time the storm was much abated. The declivity（斜坡）was so small, that I walked near a mile before I got to the shore, which I conjectured（推测，猜想）was about eight o'clock in the evening. I then advanced forward near half a mile, but could not discover any sign of houses or inhabitants; at least I was in so weak a condition, that I did not observe them. I was extremely tired, and with that, and the heat of the weather, and about half a pint of **brandy** that I drank as I left the ship, I found myself much inclined to sleep. I lay down on the grass, which was very short and soft, where I slept sounder than ever I remember to have done in my life, and, as I reckoned, above nine hours; for when I awakened, it was just daylight. I attempted to rise, but was not able to stir for, as I happened to he on my back, I found my arms and legs were strongly fastened on each side to the ground; and my hair, which was long and thick, tied down in the same manner. I likewise felt several slender ligatures across my body, from my armpits to my thighs. I could only look upwards; the sun began to grow

brandy 白兰地。它是以水果为原料，经发酵、蒸馏制成的酒。通常所称的白兰地专指以葡萄为原料，通过发酵再蒸馏制成的酒。而以其他水果为原料，通过同样的方法制成的酒，常在白兰地酒前面加上水果原料的名称以区别其种类。比如，以樱桃为原料制成的白兰地称为樱桃白兰地（Cherry Brandy），以苹果为原料制成的白兰地称为苹果白兰地（Apple Brandy）。“白兰地”一词属于术语，相当于中国的“烧酒”。白兰地是烈酒中的一种，烈酒通常被习惯分为6大类：金酒（Gin）、威士忌（Whisky）、白兰地（Brandy）、伏特加（Vodka）、兰姆酒（又叫罗姆酒、蓝姆酒或朗姆酒）（Rum）和龙舌兰酒（Tequila）。

hot, and the light offended my eyes. I heard a confused noise about me, but in the posture I lay, could see nothing except the sky. In a little time I felt something alive moving on my left leg, which advancing gently forward over my breast, came almost up to my chin; when bending my eyes downwards as much as I could, I perceived（察觉）it to be a human creature not six inches high, with a bow and arrow in his hands, and a quiver at his back. In the meantime, I felt at least forty more of the same kind (as I conjectured) following the first.

与小人交战

格列佛醒来后，发现自己被小人包围着，成了他们的俘虏，他非常吃惊。他想努力挣脱，但是，没想到小人竟然也如此厉害。弓箭是小人的主要武器，虽然格列佛个头很大，但是寡不敌众，几番交战下来，饥肠辘辘的格列佛选择了保存实力。

I was in the utmost astonishment, and roared so loud, that they all ran back in a fright; and some of them, as I was afterwards told, were hurt with the falls they got by leaping from my sides upon the ground. However, they soon returned, and one of them, who ventured so far as to get a full sight of my face, lifting up his hands and eyes by way of admiration, cried out in a shrill but distinct voice, Hekinah degul: the others repeated the same words several times, but I then knew not what they meant. I lay all this while, as the reader may believe, in great uneasiness: at length, struggling to get loose, I had the fortune to break the strings, and wrench out the pegs that fastened my left arm to the ground; for, by lifting it up to my face, I discovered the methods they had taken to bind me, and at the same time, with a violent pull, which gave me excessive pain, I a little loosened the strings that tied down my hair on the left side, so that I was just able to turn my head about two inches. But the creatures ran off a second time, before I could seize them; whereupon there was a great shout in a very shrill (刺耳的) accent, and after it ceased, I heard one of them cry aloud, Tolgo phonac; when in an instant I felt above a hundred arrows discharged on my left hand, which pricked me like so many needles; and besides they shot another flight into the air, as we do bombs in Europe, whereof many, I suppose, fell on my body (though I felt them not) and some on my face, which I immediately covered with my left hand. When this shower of arrows was over, I fell a groaning with grief and pain, and then striving again to get loose, they discharged another volley larger than the first, and some of them attempted with spears to stick me in the sides; but, by good luck, I had on me a buff jerkin (男用无袖短上衣), which they could not pierce. I thought it the most prudent (有先见之明的) method to lie still, and my design was to continue so till night, when, my left hand being already loose, I could easily free myself: and as for the inhabitants, I had reason to believe I might be a match for the greatest armies they could bring against me, if they were all of the same size with him that I saw.

小人国的盛情款待

格列佛自己想象得很好，但是命运却另有安排。在格列佛休息的时候，来了一位小人国的大臣，虽然他们语言不通，但是手势是最有效的沟通方式。他们明白了格列佛的意思，为他送来了酒和肉，格列佛美美地吃了一顿。他的食量之大，让小人们惊叹不已。

But fortune disposed otherwise of me. When the people observed I was quiet, they discharged no more arrows; but, by the noise I heard, I knew their numbers increased; and about four yards from me, over against my right ear, I heard a knocking for above an hour, like that of people at work; when turning my head that way, as well as the pegs and strings would permit me, I saw a stage erected, about a foot and a half from the ground, capable of holding four of the inhabitants, with two or three ladders to mount it: from whence one of them, who seemed to be a person of quality, made me a long speech, whereof I understood not one syllable. But I should have mentioned, that before the principal person began his oration, he cried out three times, Langro dehul san (these words and the former were afterwards repeated and explained to me). Whereupon immediately about fifty of the inhabitants came, and cut the strings that fastened the left side of my head, which gave me the liberty of turning it to the right, and of observing the person and gesture of him that was to speak. He appeared to be of a middle age, and taller than any of the other three who attended him, whereof one was a page that held up his train, and seemed to be somewhat longer than my middle finger; the other two stood one on each side to support him. He acted every part of an orator, and I could observe many periods of threatenings, and others of promises, pity, and kindness. I answered in a few words, but in the most submissive manner, lifting up my left hand and both my eyes to the sun, as calling him for a witness; and being almost famished with hunger, having not eaten a morsel for some hours before I left the ship, I found the demands of nature so strong upon me, that I could not forbear showing my impatience (perhaps against the strict rules of decency) by putting my finger frequently on my mouth, to signify that I wanted food. The Hurgo (for so they call a great lord, as I afterwards learned) understood me very well. He descended from the stage, and commanded that several ladders should be applied to my sides, on which above a hundred of the inhabitants mounted, and walked towards my mouth, laden with baskets full of meat, which had been provided, and sent thither（到那边）by the King's orders, upon the first intelligence he received of me. I observed there was the flesh of several animals, but could not distinguish them by the taste. There were shoulders, legs, and loins, shaped like those of mutton, and very well dressed, but smaller than the wings of a lark. I ate them by two or three at a mouthful, and took three loaves at a time, about the bigness of musket bullets. They supplied me as they could, showing a thousand marks of wonder and astonishment at my bulk and appetite. I then made another sign that I wanted drink. They found by my eating that a small quantity would not suffice me, and being a most ingenious people, they slung up with great dexterity one of their largest hogsheads（大桶）, then rolled it toward my hand, and beat out the top; I drank it off at a draught, which I might well do, for it did not hold half a pint, and tasted like a small wine of **Burgundy**, but much more delicious. They brought me a second hogshead, which I drank in the same manner, and made signs for more, but they had none to give me. When I had performed these wonders, they shouted for joy, and danced upon my breast, repeating several times as they did at first, Hekinah degul. They made me a sign that I should throw down the two hogsheads, but first warning the people below to stand out of the way, crying aloud, Borach mivola, and when they saw the vessels in the air, there was a universal shout of Hekinah degul. I confess I was often tempted, while they were passing backwards and forwards on my body, to seize forty or fifty of the first that came in my reach, and dash them against the ground. But the remembrance of what I had felt, which probably might not be the worst they could do, and the promise of honor I made them, for so I interpreted my submissive behavior, soon drove out these imaginations. Besides, I now considered myself as bound by the laws of hospitality to a people who had treated me with so much expense and magnificence. However, in my thoughts I could not sufficiently wonder at the intrepidity of these diminutive mortals, who dare venture to mount and walk upon my body, while one of my hands was at liberty, without trembling at the very sight of so prodigious a creature as I must appear to them.

Burgundy 勃艮第地区。法国中东部原公爵领地，首府第戎，法语名 Bourgogne，该地区以葡萄酒闻名。勃艮第的葡萄酒早在古罗马时代就已享有盛誉，白酒通常为干酒，红酒则甘醇浓郁。其中尚贝尔旦被誉为“酒中之王”，霍马内·泛蒂是“酒中之后”。

吃饱之后

格列佛吃饱之后，又来了一位国王派来的要员，看来格列佛还真是福大命大，国王都要接见他。但是见国王可不是件容易的事，而且也不轻松，格列佛要被像俘虏一样运走。这不觉让格列佛又产生了逃跑的念头。但是国王可不是呆子，不会让格列佛有可乘之机。他竟然在格列佛的酒中放了安眠药。我们可怜的格列佛要沉沉地睡上一阵了。

After some time, when they observed that I made no more demands for meat, there appeared before me a person of high rank from his Imperial Majesty. His Excellency, having mounted on the small of my right leg, advanced forwards up to my face, with about a dozen of his retinue. And producing his credentials under the Signet Royal, which he applied close to my eyes, spoke about ten minutes, without any signs of anger, but with a kind of determinate resolution; often pointing forwards, which, as I afterwards found, was towards the capital city, about half a mile distant, whither it was agreed by his Majesty in council that I must be conveyed. I answered in few words, but to no purpose, and made a sign with my hand that was loose, putting it to the other (but over his Excellency's head, for fear of hurting him or his train) and then to my own head and body, to signify that I desired my liberty. It appeared that he understood me well enough, for he shook his head by way of disapprobation, and held his hand in a posture to show that I must be carried as a prisoner. However, he made other signs to let me understand that I should have meat and drink enough, and very good treatment. Whereupon I once more thought of attempting to break my bonds, but again, when I felt the smart of their arrows upon my face and hands, which were all in blisters, and many of the darts still sticking in them, and observing likewise that the number of my enemies increased, I gave tokens to let them know that they might do with me what they pleased. Upon this the Hurgo and his train withdrew with much civility and cheerful countenances. Soon after I heard a general shout, with frequent repetitions of the words, Peplom selan, and I felt great numbers of the people on my left side relaxing the cords to such a degree, that I was able to turn upon my right, and to ease myself with making water; which I very plentifully did, to the great astonishment of the who conjecturing by my motions what I was going to do, immediately opened to the right and left on that side, to avoid the torrent which fell with such noise and violence from me. But before this, they had daubed my face and both my hands with a sort of ointment（软膏） very pleasant to the smell, which in a few minutes removed all the smart of their arrows. These circumstances, added to the refreshment I had received by their victuals and drink, which were very nourishing, disposed me to sleep. I slept about eight hours, as I was afterwards assured; and it was no wonder, for the physicians, by the Emperor's order, had mingled a sleepy potion in the hogsheads of wine.

背后的故事

讽刺大师斯威夫特

乔纳森·斯威夫特（1667–1745年）是英国启蒙运动中激进民主派的创始人，18世纪英国最杰出的政论家和讽刺小说家。他父亲是定居爱尔兰的英格兰人，早在他出生前7个月就已去世。斯威夫特由叔父抚养长大，就读于著名的都柏林三一学院（以天主教的“三位一体”命名）。他的志趣在于历史及文学。凭着一纸表示不堪深造（其实他后来还是取得了硕士及博士学位）的“特许文凭”，他只好到母亲的远亲邓波尔爵士家去作私人秘书，处境无异于“识字的奴仆”。不久，他便以见解精辟、讽刺犀利的文章显示了才华。斯威夫特晚景凄凉，亲人去世，头晕耳聋，每逢清醒，仍执笔写作，直至78岁逝世。

斯威夫特的传世之作中，以《格列佛游记》（1726）流传最广，也最为各国读者所喜爱。该书通过里梅尔·格列佛船长之口，叙述了周游四国的奇特经历。但仔细体会，却处处揭露着英国社会的黑暗现实，并寄寓着作者的理想。比如在《小人国之旅》这卷中，小人国的两党以鞋跟高矮为区分标志，这里影射的是当年英国的托利党（即保守党的前身）和辉格党（后来发展成自由党）两党政治；而吃鸡蛋时是从大头敲开还是从小头敲开，则指的是天主教与新教（亦称清教，即加尔文教派）之间关于教会仪式的无稽之争。

Tale 19

Cinderella

灰姑娘

没有一个童话故事能像《灰姑娘》那样受到广泛的喜爱。几乎世界上的每一个国家都有一种版本。“Cinderella”已经成为所有女孩幸福的期待和梦想，从这个童话一诞生就承载了许多的祝愿。在美与丑之间、幸福与痛苦之间、善良与邪恶之间、高贵与平凡之间、梦想与现实之间，每个女孩都希望自己成为那个叫做“灰姑娘”的女孩。因为会有仙子帮灰姑娘变出马车、晚礼服、水晶鞋，让她参加舞会。而且，因为美丽的灰姑娘有一颗善良的心，所以她成为了王妃，从此能与王子快乐的生活在一起。这个童话是否也满载了你的梦？可是，你的那双水晶鞋在哪里呢？

慢阅读小语

细细品位字里行间流淌出的语言美和思想美，你就会感受到“Jump and get an apple”的喜悦，不知不觉间自身修养得到了提升……

1 **Always be a good girl, and I will look down from heaven and watch over you.**

你要永远做个善良的孩子，我会在天上看着你的。

2 **And the snow spread a beautiful white covering over the grave; but by the time the sun had melted it away again, her father had married another wife.**

雪像一条美丽的毯子似的盖在墓上，但是当积雪被太阳晒化的时候，她的父亲娶了继母。

3 **There she was forced to do hard work; to rise early before daylight, to bring the water, to make the fire, to cook and to wash. Besides that, the sisters plagued her in all sorts of ways and laughed at her.**

她在那儿必须从早到晚地干重活，天没亮就起身，打水、生火、煮饭、洗衣。除此之外，那两个姐姐还想出种种方式欺侮她、嘲笑她。

4 **In the evening when she was tired she had no bed to lie down on, but was made to lie by the hearth among the ashes; and then, as she was of course always dusty and dirty, they called her Cinderella.**

夜晚，她干活干累了，没有床铺睡觉，只好躺在灶旁边的炭灰里。因此，她总是脏兮兮的，满身灰尘，她们就叫她“灰姑娘”。

5 **Then the mother gave her a knife, and said, “Never mind, cut it off; when you are queen you will not care about toes, you will not want to go on foot.”**

于是她母亲把一把刀递给她，说：“没关系，把它砍掉，如果你当了王后，你就不在乎脚趾了，也用不着走路了。”

灰色的童年

从前，有一位富人的妻子病了，她在弥留之际把自己的独生女儿唤到床前，让女儿永远做一个善良的孩子。妈妈离开了人间，留下了可怜的小女孩。小女孩每天都会去她的墓地上哭泣，而且始终遵守着妈妈的教诲：永远保持忠实、善良的本性。但是当小女孩有了继母之后，她的生活变了，变得让人心碎。

The wife of a rich man fell sick, and when she felt that her end drew nigh, she called her only daughter to her bedside, and said, "Always be a good girl, and I will look down from heaven and watch over you." Soon afterwards she shut her eyes and died, and was buried in the garden; and the little girl went every day to her grave and wept, and was always good and kind to all about her. And the snow spread a beautiful white covering over the grave; but by the time the sun had melted it away again, her father had married another wife. This new wife had two daughters of her own, that she brought home with her: they were fair in face, but foul at heart, and it was now a sorry time for the poor little girl. "What does the good for nothing thing want in the parlor（客厅）?" said they; "they who would eat bread should first earn it, away with the kitchen maid!" Then they took away her fine clothes, and gave her an old grey frock（连衣裙式工作服）to put on, and laughed at her and turned her into the kitchen.

There she was forced to do hard work; to rise early before daylight, to bring the water, to make the fire, to cook and to wash. Besides that, the sisters plagued（折磨）her in all sorts of ways and laughed at her. In the evening when she was tired she had no bed to lie down on, but was made to lie by the hearth among the ashes; and then, as she was of course always dusty and dirty, they called her **Cinderella**.

神奇的小鸟

一天，小女孩的父亲要去集市，他打算给女儿们带些礼物。灰姑娘没有要漂亮衣服，也不要珍珠和宝石，而是一根树枝。父亲并不知道灰姑娘的用意，真的为她带回了树枝。这根树枝似乎有灵性，它会为灰姑娘带来好运的。

It happened once that the father was going to the fair, and asked his wife's daughters what he should bring them. "Fine clothes," said the first; "Pearls and diamonds," cried the second. "Now, child," said he to his own daughter, "what will you have?" "The first sprig, dear father, that rubs against your hat on your way home," said she. Then he bought for the two first the fine clothes and pearls and diamonds they had asked for; and on his way home as he rode through a green copse, a sprig of hazel（榛树）brushed against him, and almost pushed off his hat; so he broke it off and brought it away; and when he got home he gave it to his daughter. Then she took it and went to her mother's grave and planted it there, and cried so much that it was watered with her tears; and there it grew and became a fine tree. Three times every day she went to it and wept;

Cinderella 灰姑娘。cinder就是“灰”的意思，比如“incinerate把……弄成灰烬”里面的ciner就是cinder的变体,ella是女性后缀，比如slanderella是“诽谤姑娘”，就是喜欢诽谤别人的女孩，所以，Cinderella就是“灰姑娘”。童话中的那个女孩受继母及其两个女儿的虐待，被迫烧火做饭，身上头上尽是灰烬，所以，人们叫她灰姑娘！译者将它翻译成灰姑娘是意译，如果音译就是“辛德瑞拉”。

and soon a little bird came and built its nest upon the tree, and talked with her, and watched over her, and brought her whatever she wished for.

继母的刁难

国王宣布举办一个3天的大宴会，目的是为王子选未婚妻。继母和她的两个女儿听到这个消息自然非常高兴。可是灰姑娘却无法参加这个舞会，因为她没有漂亮的鞋子和衣服，但是她很想去参加，所以她苦苦哀求继母，为了能参加舞会，她任凭两位姐姐和继母使唤自己、刁难自己。除了哭泣之外，灰姑娘找来了自己的伙伴们来帮忙。

Now it happened that the king of the land held a feast which was to last three days, and out of those who came to it his son was to choose a bride for himself; and Cinderella's two sisters were asked to come. So they called her up, and said, "Now comb our hair, brush our shoes, and tie our sashes（腰带）for us, for we are going to dance at the king's feast." Then she did as she was told, but when all was done she could not help crying, for she thought to herself, she should have liked to go to the dance too; and at last she begged her mother very hard to let her go. "You! Cinderella?" said she; "you who have nothing to wear, no clothes at all, and who cannot even dance, you want to go to the ball?" And when she kept on begging, to get rid of her, she said at last, "I will throw this basin full of peas into the ash heap, and if you have picked them all out in two hours' time you shall go to the feast too." Then she threw the peas into the ashes; but the little maiden ran out at the back door into the garden, and cried out:

"Hither, hither, through the sky,
Turtle **doves** and linnets, fly!

dove 鸽子。dove被誉为"和平的象征"，出自《圣经》中的诺亚方舟（Noah's ark）这个典故。在《旧约·创世记》中，上帝因看到人类罪孽深重而震怒，于是决定发大洪水惩罚人类。只有义人、完人诺亚在上帝面前蒙恩，按照上帝的吩咐建造了方舟，保全了家人和每种动物雌雄各一只。洪水在地上泛滥了150天后才逐渐消退。诺亚把鸽子放出去，鸽子叼回了一片橄榄叶，由此诺亚知道地上的洪水退了，于是诺亚全家和各种生物才出舟继续繁衍生息。现在英语中经常用"诺亚方舟"来喻指避难所或大灾难中仅存的安全地带。同样根据这个故事，人们把鸽子(dove)和橄榄叶(olive leaf)视为和平与安宁的象征。

Blackbird, thrush, and chaffinch gay,

Hither, hither, haste away !

One and all, come help me quick,

Haste ye, haste ye, – pick, pick, pick!"

Then first came two white doves flying in at the kitchen window; and next came two turtle doves; and after them all the little birds under heaven came chirping and fluttering in, and flew down into the ashes, and the little doves stooped（低头）their heads down and set to work, pick, pick, pick, and picked out all the good grain and put it in a dish, and left the ashes. At the end of one hour the work was done, and all flew out again at the windows. Then she brought the dish to her mother, overjoyed at the thought that now she should go to the wedding. But she said, "No, no! You slut, you have no clothes and cannot dance, you shall not go." And when Cinderella begged very hard to go, she said, "If you can in one hour's time pick two of those dishes of peas out of the ashes, you shall go too." And thus she thought she should at last get rid of her. So she shook two dishes of peas into the ashes; but the little maiden went into the garden at the back of the house, and cried out as before:

"Hither, hither, through the sky,

Turtle doves and linnets, fly!

Blackbird, thrush, and chaffinch gay,

Hither, hither, haste away!

One and all, come help me quick,

Haste ye, haste ye, – pick, pick, pick!"

Then first came two white doves in at the kitchen window; and next came two turtle doves; and after them all the little birds under heaven came chirping and hopping about, and flew down about the ashes; and the little doves put their heads down and set to work, pick, pick, pick; and then the others began pick, pick, pick; and put all the good grain into the dishes, and left all the ashes. Before half an hour's time all was done, and out they flew again. And then Cinderella took the dishes to her mother, rejoicing to that she should now go to the ball. But her mother said, "It is all of no use, you cannot go; you have no clothes, and cannot dance, and you would only put us to shame." And off she went with her two daughters to the feast.

王子的舞会

继母最终也没有同意灰姑娘去参加舞会，无助的灰姑娘坐到榛树下伤心地哭泣起来。这时，奇妙的事情发生了，小鸟为灰姑娘送来了漂亮衣服和华丽舞鞋，灰姑娘顿时变成了一位美丽的公主。她终于可以去参加舞会了，她的王子会和她跳舞吗？

Now when all were gone, and nobody left at home, Cinderella went sorrowfully and sat down under the hazel tree, and cried out:

"Shake, shake, hazel tree,
Gold and silver over me!"

Then her friend the bird flew out of the tree and brought a gold and silver dress for her, and slippers of spangled（缀满亮晶晶的饰片的）silk, and she put them on, and followed her sisters to the feast. But they did not know her, and thought it must be some strange princess, she looked so fine and beautiful in her rich clothes, and they never once thought of Cinderella, but took for granted that she was safe at home in the dirt.

The king's son soon came up to her, and took her by the hand and danced with her and no one else; and he never left her hand; but when any one else came to ask her to dance, he said, "This lady is dancing with me." Thus they danced till a late hour of the night; and then she wanted to go home; and the king's son said, "I shall go and take care of you to your home." for he wanted to see where the beautiful maid lived. But she slipped away from his unawares, and ran off towards home, and the prince followed her; but she jumped up into the pigeon-house and shut the door. Then he waited till her father came home, and told him that the unknown maiden who had been at the feast had hid herself in the pigeon house. But when they had broken open the door they found no one within; and as they came back into the house, Cinderella lay, as she always did, in her dirty frock by the ashes, and her dim little lamp burnt in the chimney; for she had run as quickly as she could through the pigeon house and on to the hazel tree, and had there taken off her beautiful clothes, and laid them beneath the tree, that the bird might carry them away, and had seated herself amid the

ashes again in her little grey frock.

第二天，宴会又开始了，父亲和继母还有两个姐姐都去参加宴会了。灰姑娘又来到榛树下，灰姑娘这次拥有了一套比前一天还华贵的衣服，她是宴会上最漂亮的姑娘，也成为了王子的专属舞伴。

The next day when the feast was again held, and her father, mother, and sisters were gone, Cinderella went to the hazel tree, and said:

"Shake, shake, hazel tree,
Gold and silver over me!"

And the bird came and brought a still finer dress than the one she had worn the day before. And when she came in it to the ball, every one wondered at her beauty; but the king's son, who was waiting for her, took her by the hand, and danced with her; and when any one asked her to dance, he said as before, "This lady is dancing with me." When night came she wanted to go home; and the king's son followed her as before, that he might see into what house she went: but she sprung away from him all at once into the garden behind her father's house. In this garden stood a fine large pear tree full of ripe fruit; and Cinderella not knowing where to hide herself jumped up into it without being seen. Then the king's son could not find out where she was gone, but waited till her father came home, and said to him, "The unknown lady who danced with me has slipt away, and I think she must have sprung into the pear tree." The father thought to himself, "Can it be Cinderella?" So he ordered an axe to be brought; and they cut down the tree, but found no one upon it. And when they came back into the kitchen, there lay Cinderella in the ashes as usual; for she had slipped down on the other side of the tree, and carried her beautiful clothes, back to the bird at the hazel tree, and then put on her little grey frock.

第三天，灰姑娘又像前一天一样，穿着比前两天都漂亮的衣服来参加宴会。但是到了晚上，她不得不回家了。可是王子怎么舍得错过如此漂亮的公主呢？在慌忙中，灰姑娘掉了一只金舞鞋，这是王子得到幸福的唯一希望。

The third day, when her father and mother and sisters were gone, she went again into the garden, and said:

"Shake, shake, hazel tree,
Gold and silver over me!"

Then her kind friend the bird brought a dress still finer than the former one, and slippers which were all of gold; so that when she came to the feast no one knew what to say for wonder at her beauty; and the king's son danced with her alone; and when any one else asked her to dance, he said, "This lady is my partner." Now when night came she wanted to go home; and the king's son would go with her, and said to himself, "I will not lose her this time," but however she managed to slip away from him, though in such a hurry that she dropped her left golden slipper upon the stairs.

寻找真正的新娘

王子带着舞鞋来找灰姑娘的父亲，并且非常认真地说，他会娶舞鞋的主人为妻。贪心的继母竟然为了能让自己的女儿们能穿得上灰姑娘的舞鞋，而不惜砍掉大女儿的脚趾和弄破二女儿的脚后跟，虽然贪心恶毒的人能够暂时欺骗别人，但是事实是无法改变的。神奇的榛树已将真相完完全全地告诉了王子。王子也终于找到了自己的新娘，从此王子与灰姑娘过上了幸福快乐的生活。

So the prince took the shoe, and went the next day to her father, and said, "I will take for my wife the lady that this golden slipper fits." Then both the sisters were overjoyed to hear this; for they had beautiful feet, and had no doubt that they could wear the golden slipper. The oldest went first into the room where the slipper was and wanted to try it on, and the mother stood by. But her great toe could not go into it, and the shoe was altogether much too small for her. Then the mother gave her a knife, and said, "Never mind, cut it off; when you are queen you will not care about toes, you will not want to go on foot." So the silly girl cut her great toe off, and squeezed（挤）the shoe on, and went to the king's son. Then he took her for his bride, and set her beside him on his horse and rode away with her.

But on their way home they had to pass by the hazel tree that Cinderella had planted, and there sat a little dove on the branch singing:

"Back again! Back again! Look to the shoe!

The shoe is too small, and not made for you!

Prince ! Prince ! Look again for thy bride,

For she's not the true one that sits by thy side."

Then the prince got down and looked at her foot, and saw by the blood that streamed from it what a trick she had played him. So he turned his horse round and brought the false bride back to her home, and said, "This is not the right bride; let the other sister try and put on the slipper." Then she went into the room and got her foot into the shoe, all but the heel, which was too large. But her mother squeezed it in till the blood came, and took her to the king's son; and he set her as his bride by his side on his horse, and rode away with her.

But when they came to the hazel tree the little dove sat there still, and sang:

"Back again! Back again! Look to the shoe!

The shoe is too small, and not made for you!

Prince! Prince! Look again for thy bride,

For she's not the true one that sits by thy side."

Then he looked down and saw that the blood streamed so from the shoe that her white stockings were quite red. So he turned his horse and brought her back again also. "This is not the true bride," said he to the father; "have you no other daughters?... No," said he; "there is only a little dirty Cinderella here, the child of my first wife; I am sure she cannot be the bride." However, the prince told him to send her. But the mother said "No, no she is much too dirty, she will not dare to show herself." However, the prince would have her come. And she first washed her face and hands, and then went in and curtsied to him, and he reached her the golden slipper. Then she took her clumsy shoe off her left foot, and put on the golden slipper; and it fitted her as if it had been made for her. And when he drew near and looked at her face he knew her, and said, "This is the right bride." But the mother and both the sisters were frightened and turned pale with anger as he took Cinderella on his horse, and rode away with her. And when they came to the hazel-tree, the white dove sang:

"Home! Home! Look at the shoe!

Princess! The shoe was made for you!

Prince! Prince! Take home thy bride,

For she is the true one that sits by thy side!"

And when the dove had done its song, it came flying and perched (停留，暂栖) upon her right shoulder, and to went home with her.

背后的故事

"灰姑娘"的起源

在世界各地流传的"灰姑娘"式的童话故事不下于1500篇。在中国56个民族及一些已消亡融合的民族里也有不少类似的传说，被记录保存至今的故事就有72篇，数量之多实为惊人。可见千百年来人们对"灰姑娘"的现象都存在难以割舍的情结。

现在大家通常认为童话《灰姑娘》的作者是格林兄弟。其实，我国唐代段成式在其编撰的《酉阳杂俎》续集《支诺皋》里所记录的《叶限》故事是世界上"灰姑娘"型民间故事的最早记载（约为公元9世纪中期）。在这个故事里，帮助女主人公的是鱼骨头，为她带来幸福的是只金履。因为《叶限》的记录年代更确切更久远，以及文本中所暗示的当时民众对此故事常有耳闻的语气，使得"叶限"故事看起来似更接近于此类故事的本来面目，因而有些学者由此认为该类故事起源于中国。

但是，1697年，由巴黎出版的佩罗所编写的《鹅妈妈的故事》，这本故事集在很长一段时间里，使人们一直认为它所收录的"灰姑娘"故事是欧洲此类故事的最早记载。当然，现在，在欧洲已发现了一些记录年代更早的类似故事，但是佩罗的"灰姑娘"故事却是其中影响最大的一个。在这些相似的故事中，只有在佩罗的故事里，才有仙女、南瓜车和水晶鞋这些为人们所熟知的"灰姑娘"元素。